EARLY CHILDHOOD EDUCATION SERIES
Leslie R. Williams, Editor
Millie Almy, Senior Advisor

ADVISORY BOARD: Barbara T. Bowman, Harriet K. Cuffaro, Stephanie Feeney, Doris Pronin Fromberg, Celia Genishi, Dominic F. Gullo, Alice Sterling Honig, Elizabeth Jones, Gwen Morgan, David Weikart

Caring for Other People's Children:
A Complete Guide to Family Day Care
FRANCES KEMPER ALSTON

Family Day Care: Current Research for Informed Public Policy
DONALD L. PETERS & ALAN R. PENCE, Eds.

The Early Childhood Curriculum:
A Review of Current Research, 2nd Ed.
CAROL SEEFELDT, Ed.

Reconceptualizing the Early Childhood Curriculum: Beginning the Dialogue
SHIRLEY A. KESSLER &
BETH BLUE SWADENER, Eds.

Ways of Assessing Children and Curriculum: Stories of Early Childhood Practice
CELIA GENISHI, Ed.

The Play's The Thing:
Teachers' Roles in Children's Play
ELIZABETH JONES
GRETCHEN REYNOLDS

Scenes from Day Care:
How Teachers Teach and What Children Learn
ELIZABETH BALLIETT PLATT

Raised in East Urban:
Child Care Changes
in a Working Class Community
CAROLINE ZINSSER

United We Stand:
Collaboration for Child Care
and Early Education Services
SHARON L. KAGAN

Making Friends in School:
Promoting Peer Relationships
in Early Childhood
PATRICIA G. RAMSEY

Play and the Social Context
of Development in Early Care
and Education
BARBARA SCALES, MILLIE ALMY,
AGELIKI NICOLOPOULOU, &
SUSAN ERVIN-TRIPP, Eds.

The Whole Language Kindergarten
SHIRLEY RAINES
ROBERT CANADY

Good Day/Bad Day:
The Child's Experience of Child Care
LYDA BEARDSLEY

Children's Play and Learning:
Perspectives and Policy Implications
EDGAR KLUGMAN
SARA SMILANSKY

Serious Players in the Primary Classroom:
Empowering Children Through
Active Learning Experiences
SELMA WASSERMANN

Child Advocacy for
Early Childhood Educators
BEATRICE S. FENNIMORE

Managing Quality Child Care Centers:
A Comprehensive Manual for
Administrators
PAMELA BYRNE SCHILLER
PATRICIA M. DYKE

Multiple Worlds of Child Writers:
Friends Learning to Write
ANNE HAAS DYSON

Young Children Continue to Reinvent
Arithmetic—2nd Grade: Implications
of Piaget's Theory
CONSTANCE KAMII

Literacy Learning in the Early Years:
Through Children's Eyes
LINDA GIBSON

The Good Preschool Teacher:
Six Teachers Reflect on Their Lives
WILLIAM AYERS

A Child's Play Life:
An Ethnographic Study
DIANA KELLY-BYRNE

Professionalism and the
Early Childhood Practitioner
BERNARD SPODEK, OLIVIA N. SARACHO,
& DONALD L. PETERS, Eds.

(Continued)

(Early Childhood Education Series titles, continued)

Looking at Children's Play: The Bridge
from Theory to Practice
PATRICIA A. MONIGHAN-NOUROT,
BARBARA SCALES, JUDITH L. VAN HOORN,
& MILLIE ALMY

The War Play Dilemma: Balancing
Needs and Values in the
Early Childhood Classroom
NANCY CARLSSON-PAIGE
DIANE E. LEVIN

The Piaget Handbook
for Teachers and Parents
ROSEMARY PETERSON
VICTORIA FELTON-COLLINS

Teaching and Learning in a Diverse
World: Multicultural Education
for Young Children
PATRICIA G. RAMSEY

The Full-Day Kindergarten
DORIS PRONIN FROMBERG

Promoting Social and Moral
Development in Young Children
CAROLYN POPE EDWARDS

A Teacher at Work:
Professional Development and
the Early Childhood Educator
MARGARET V. YONEMURA

Today's Kindergarten
BERNARD SPODEK, Ed.

Supervision in
Early Childhood Education
JOSEPH J. CARUSO
M. TEMPLE FAWCETT

Visions of Childhood: Influential
Models from Locke to Spock
JOHN CLEVERLEY
D. C. PHILLIPS

Starting School: From Separation
to Independence
NANCY BALABAN

Young Children Reinvent Arithmetic:
Implications of Piaget's Theory
CONSTANCE KAMII

Ideas Influencing Early
Childhood Education
EVELYN WEBER

Diversity in the Classroom:
A Multicultural Approach
FRANCES E. KENDALL

The Joy of Movement
in Early Childhood
SANDRA R. CURTIS

Island of Childhood:
Education in the Special World
of Nursery School
ELINOR FITCH GRIFFIN

CARING FOR OTHER PEOPLE'S CHILDREN

A Complete Guide to Family Day Care

by
Frances Kemper Alston, Ed.M.

Illustrated by
Gail Alison LaCava

Teachers College, Columbia University
New York & London

Published by Teachers College Press, 1234 Amsterdam Avenue
New York, New York

An edition of this book was previously published by University Park Press

Copyright © 1992 by Teachers College, Columbia University

All rights reserved. No part of this publication may be reproduced or transmitted in any form or by any means, electronic or mechanical, including photocopy, or any information storage and retrieval system, without permission from the publisher.

Library of Congress Cataloging-in-Publication Data

Alston, Frances Kemper.
    Caring for other people's children : a complete guide to family
  day care / by Frances Kemper Alston ; illustrated by Gail Alison
  LaCava.
        p.   cm. — (Early childhood education series)
  Originally published: Baltimore : University Park Press, c1984.
  Includes index.
  ISBN 0-8077-3218-4
    1. Family day care—United States.   I. Title. II. Series.
HV854.A7   1992
362.7′12′068—dc20   92-17036

ISBN 0-8077-3218-4 (pbk.)

Printed on acid-free paper
Manufactured in the United States of America

99 98 97 96 95 94 93 92   8 7 6 5 4 3 2 1

Contents

Preface / vii

Acknowledgments / ix

1. The Family Day Care Provider / 1
2. The Business of Providing / 11
3. Beginnings and Endings in Family Day Care / 31
4. Providing Room for Family Day Care / 45
5. Providing and Planning Activities / 57
6. The Provider and the Parents / 77
7. Solving Problems in Family Day Care / 87
8. Providing for Growth and Development / 101
9. Providing for Infants / 111
10. Providing for Toddlers / 137
11. Providing for Language Development / 151
12. Providing for Preschoolers / 167
13. Providing School Readiness / 181
14. Providing for School Children / 195
15. Providing Discipline / 209
16. Providing Care for the Sick Child / 221
17. Providing in an Emergency / 233
18. Providing for Special Children / 253
19. Providing Food for Growth and Strength / 265
20. The Family Day Care Provider—A Summing Up / 279

Index / 291

Preface

In the Preface to the first printing of *Caring for Other People's Children*, I described the major upheavals that were affecting family day care providers at that time. The first was the loss of government subsidy for any child care during the Reagan administration, and the second was the remarkable increase in the number of full-time working parents that occurred in the 1970s and 1980s. Today, almost a decade later, we have some of the same and some additional forces impacting on family day care. In the last year the government has responded to the need for child care services by passing the Child Development and Block Grant, which provides some new money for day care services. It is still not clear how much of that money will actually reach family day care providers, in terms of subsidies, or as additional support services or training. But this is the first time since the Great Depression that Congress and the President have recognized the need for child care in this country, and it is even possible that there will be additional funding for family day care in years to come. One thing is clear: Parents and child care professionals have banded together to create a strong voice for children in this country, and the President and Congress must listen and respond.

At this writing the country is experiencing an economic recession, which is having an impact on child care professionals, along with workers of every kind, from automobile manufacturers to bankers, from computer technologists to government employees. Family day care providers are especially aware of the effects of the recession. There are fewer mothers who can afford to remain at home to care for their children for the first year, and so the demand for family day care for infants and toddlers continues to grow. At the same time, a number of young mothers, who wish to remain at home for at least a year or two, have realized that they can make up for some of their lost salary during this time by caring for one or two other children in their home. These parents are becoming family day care providers for at least a few years.

Then there is an altogether new trend that is affecting family day care providers today. This is the shift in some states from licensing family day care professionals to voluntary registration of family day care homes. This is another result of the current economic recession. States that used to have child care consultants and supervisors who visited and monitored family day care homes can no longer afford the expense, and are therefore making the decision to shift to voluntary registration of family day care homes. This puts the responsibility for quality child care squarely on the family day care provider.

Family day care providers have always been essentially alone in their work. Their days are spent with young children, and even in the states that license family day care, their homes are rarely visited; many do not have family day care organizations to join. The quality of care is determined by the providers' own standards about what is right in caring for children. Since most family day care providers choose the work because they enjoy children, offering high quality care comes naturally.

Today the entire responsibility for learning about child development, understanding individual differences, recognizing the stresses that children of working parents experience, and helping each child grow strong and confident, able to respect others and be respected, often falls on the family day care provider. It is awesome work, and the women who perform it deserve the gratitude and respect of the nation. This book is written to assist and support these child care professionals.

Acknowledgments

Many friends agreed to read, comment on, and criticize chapters of this book. Their willingness and responses are what constitute real friendship. Among the diligent readers, I want to especially thank Susan Bancroft, Elizabeth and Martha White, Alfred Karlson, Rowena Alston, Isabel Sanders, Burton White, Clara and Wallace Kemper, Virginia Tan, Marvin Green, Audrey Glick, and Jimmell Bryant. Each brought a valuable perspective from her or his own point of view and field of expertise.

Ruby Richardson contributed many practical and creative ideas from her considerable knowledge of and experience with family day care. So did Stephen Ruffins.

Vann Spruiell is the epitome of an editor. He has an unerring sense of form and the knowledge to go with it. I join the ranks of the many who are grateful for his inspired editing.

Joyce Black and Marjorie Grosett of the Day Care Council of New York have taught me a great deal, with patience and good humor. They are exceptional co-workers and deserve a special vote of thanks.

All of these people enriched my understanding and supported my efforts. None, however, is responsible for any of the views expressed.

Ann Buckley, Lauren Simon, Stephen Wolfe, and Daniel Freund are the beautiful children on the cover.

Finally, my thanks to Charles Cumming, who found a home for the idea; to Mahmoud Wahba, for place and time; to Burton White, who made looking at infants and children a discipline; and to Harvey Corman, who helped make sense of a great deal.

*For Bill, Rowena, and Kemper,
providers of pride and many laughs*

CARING FOR
OTHER PEOPLE'S CHILDREN

1

The Family Day Care Provider

Somewhere in America in a living room filled with the personal effects of several children's lives a woman sits on a couch, two children seated on one side, one on the other. A baby sits in her lap, resting her head on the woman's chest. The baby is holding one of the woman's hands in her two little hands, carefully bending down the woman's fingers one at a time. The three other children and the woman are playing a game "I remember something that happened when I was very young." As usual, the woman has been persuaded to go first, and, as usual, the children want to know more and more about the story. They are much more interested in the details of her story than in taking turns telling one of their own.

These children do not seem to be related—one has dark skin, one has light skin, one has curly blond hair, one has very black hair, one has blue eyes, two have very brown eyes. Their ages range from the 18-month-old baby to an almost teenager. It is late afternoon and they are all waiting for someone. What kind of family is this? Who is this woman?

This is a day care family, and this woman is a family day care provider—sometimes called a family day care mother. There are thousands of such families all over the country—families of children who spend the day in homes other than their own in the care of women who are professionals in child care. As more women go to work, the need for child care grows. Half of the women working today have children under 6, and each year the number increases. For this reason, more and more women are considering taking in one or two children to care for in their homes. For all of those who are already providing family day care, and for all of the women who are thinking of going into the business, this book is written.

FAMILY DAY CARE: THE CARE OF OTHER PEOPLE'S CHILDREN IN THE HOME

Family day care is the most popular form of day care in the country today, and the women who offer it make up the largest single group of professional child care workers in the country. (These women are often called *providers* not simply *day care mothers* because the care they provide requires many different skills.)

There are more women working now than ever before, but there are not enough day care centers to care for their children. Furthermore, very few group day care centers accept children under 2 years of age. For working mothers with very young children, family day care is often the only care available.

Years ago, many women who worked sometimes took their children with them. On a farm it was not too difficult to take a little child along. In a factory, of course, it was both difficult and dangerous, but some women had no choice. Some women were lucky and had aunts, grandparents, or cousins who were happy to look after the children. Today, fewer families have those luxuries. Almost every American moves three or more times in his or her lifetime, and ends up living far from the rest of the family. For many of today's young parents, family day care is the answer to their child care needs.

GROUP DAY CARE AND FAMILY DAY CARE

Of the two kinds of day care in this country—family and group—family day care is both the oldest and the most common. Group day care centers on a large scale began to appear during the Depression to allow women to go to work as well as to provide jobs for women. During World War II, women began to replace men in the guns and ammunition factories while the men went off to fight. The number of day care centers grew. When the war ended, the men came home and took back the jobs in the factories, and the women returned to the home. More than half of the day care centers in the country closed within a year or two of the war's end.

Family day care, on the other hand, existed before the depression and continues to exist. For many years women with full- or part-time jobs have managed to find a pleasant, capable, and caring neighbor to look after their children while they work. Even when group day care centers are available, many parents prefer family day care. There are three main reasons for this.

The first is that family day care is home-like. Many parents want their children to have personal care in a home, rather than group care in a center. They also want to have a close relationship with the person who cares for their children and to feel that this woman is like a member of the family.

When two women are able to create this kind of relationship, it is reassuring for both of them, and it is very good for the child or children they share. (See Chapter 6 for more on this subject.) When looking for help or advice, the parents have someone to talk to who is familiar and trusted. Likewise, it is helpful for children to have more than one or two adults to turn to.

A second reason that women often prefer family day care is that it suits their individual needs. They can make private agreements with the provider, leaving and picking up the children at the time that is best for their individual work schedules. They can leave an infant in the care of a family day care provider. It is often hard to find a group day care center that takes children younger than 2 or 3 years old. Furthermore, parents can leave two children in a family day care home, even though the children's ages may be very different. Two children of the same family but of different ages are rarely able to be together in a group day care center.

The third reason that family day care is preferred is convenience. The family day care provider usually lives close to the parents. This makes it both easier and faster in the mornings and evenings for parents to transport their children. When the family day care provider is a neighbor and a member of the same community as the children she cares for, there is an added sense of security and closeness for the children and for their parents.

THE JOB OF THE FAMILY DAY CARE PROVIDER

The provider has a very complicated job. She is more than a nurse maid or baby-sitter who takes care of children in their own homes. She has no employer giving her instructions. She is her own boss, and *she* is the expert.

The biggest difference between family day care and nursing, or teaching, or baby-sitting, however, is that family day care is really a small business. The business operates in the provider's home, but the provider must do everything that the head of a small business does. She must start the business, see that it runs well, and make sure that her customers are satisfied and will recommend it to their friends. She must also see that the business brings her a profit. Finally, because her business involves human beings—children— she must do the very best job she possibly can.

To understand what a complicated business family day care is, one must consider the many different jobs the provider does. For example, she is a:

1. **Nurse** As a nurse, the family day care provider takes care of the physical needs of children from tiny infants to high school age children when they are well and when they are not well, when they hurt themselves, or when they come down with an illness.

2. **Teacher** As a teacher, the family day care provider is responsible for the basic education of the children while they are with her. She teaches the little ones to feed themselves, use the toilet, count, and understand how to take care of themselves in the world. She helps the older children with their school work, teaches them how to get along with others, and teaches them the things it takes to be successful human beings. She also teaches them various skills, like cooking, gardening, and sewing, introduces them to art, music, and literature, and helps them develop into interested, interesting people.
3. **Nutritionist** She prepares meals and snacks to keep the children healthy and strong, always on a budget.
4. **Social Worker** She counsels the parents, explaining the children's needs, stages of development, and learning strengths and weaknesses. She helps the parents make good decisions about the children, and even sometimes about their own lives.
5. **Accountant** She keeps books on all of her expenses and income, checking regularly to make sure that her business is doing well.
6. **Paramedic** She knows first aid and the care of the sick so thoroughly that she is able to act instantly in case of accident or sudden illness.
7. **Architect and Interior Decorator** She transforms her living space into a work space during business hours. She knows how to make the most of the space she has and how to make sure it is safe, as well as interesting and comfortable for the children and an easy work space for herself. At the same time she keeps her home comfortable and pleasant for herself and her family.
8. **Psychologist** She is a specialist in human behavior. She knows why children at certain ages or stages do certain things. She knows what to expect of children at every age and how to encourage their best behavior. Most of all, she knows how to plan for children to support their growth and development and to avoid developmental difficulties.
9. **Student of Human Development** As with all specialists in human nature, she is also a student, constantly learning more about why people behave as they do.

Very few jobs require so many different skills or combine so many different professions.

THE JOB OF THE FAMILY DAY CARE PROVIDER

When a woman decides to take care of children in her own home, she is making a serious decision. This is not a job for someone in poor health, or someone with little energy, or someone who just wants an easy life. Life with children keeps people on their feet *and* on their toes. It is a tiring life, a demanding life, but at the same time a very rewarding one.

When a woman decides on family day care as a profession, she should also realize that many people do not appreciate what being a provider demands and that she will have to educate her clients and everyone else she comes into contact with about her work. She can do this by telling the parents something each day about their child's activities, by introducing the children she cares for to the people she knows, and by letting the people she meets (when she takes the children out shopping, to a park, or to a playground) know that she is a family day care provider.

Not only do many people think that taking care of children is easy, but some have the notion that one should not make money doing it. They have the feeling that loving children should be enough and should not be discussed in the same breath with making money. Of course, loving children is a very important part of child care, but the family day care provider needs to make a living and know that she has the security of being able to save for the future. Just like any other job a person chooses, part of deciding on that job is knowing that it will provide a living.

What the family day care provider charges for taking care of children depends on several things. The most important is, of course, the service. The more she offers, the more she can charge. What she offers, furthermore, is not measured by the place she lives in, or the furniture and equipment she has, and not even by the toys or games she provides. It is measured by the product of her work: the children. If the children she cares for are alert and bright, relaxed and contented, healthy and strong, then she is offering a superior service and should not be embarrassed to be paid for it.

THE REQUIREMENTS FOR BEING A FAMILY DAY CARE PROVIDER

These requirements begin with the provider herself but include her family, if she has one living with her, and her home. First, there are those that concern the provider herself.

Feelings about Children

The most important question concerns the provider's feelings about children. Does she find children interesting, or do they get on her nerves? Does she enjoy having them around, or does she wish for peace and quiet? Is she comfortable with a certain disorder, or is she only happy when her home is neat and orderly? Can she tolerate anger, sadness, and excitement around her, or does she believe in a lot of self-control? These are important questions because they involve feelings and attitudes that are part of every adult's personality and are not easy to change, or, in many cases, even *possible* to change. No matter how old and mature people become, they never really forget the feelings left over from their childhood. When adults are faced with the strong emotions of children, those old feelings come back in full force. An adult who is mature enough to help children learn self-control can put up with these outbursts of emotion and remain reasonably calm. This is important because it is impossible for children to learn self-control from adults who easily lose their own.

Health and Energy

Other important questions a woman who wants to care for children should ask herself are: How strong and energetic am I? How good is my health? There are very few jobs that demand more physical strength than caring for children. Lifting, carrying, bending down, getting up, running, reaching, and being on her feet a good part of the day are all part of the job. Besides the physical effort involved, taking care of children exposes the provider to colds, flu, and all of the illnesses that children have. If a woman is physically strong and healthy, she can care for children without catching all their colds and viral infections. Anyone who decides to be a family day care provider needs a checkup every year to make sure she is healthy. Good planning will allow her time to rest and relax a part of each day, but in order to enjoy her work and do a good job, she must be both strong and energetic.

Self-confidence

Someone considering the profession of family day care also needs to ask herself about her own feelings of security and self-confidence. People who are secure do not have to have their own way all the time, they can accept other people's ways. Secure people are less critical of other people and do not need to show that they themselves are superior. When caring for and raising children, the provider should have enough security to allow children to grow and develop in their own individual ways, in their own time, without insisting on having them do things any particular way, and without making judgments about the parents. There will be times when the provider does feel that her way is better, and often she will be right, but she will not need to show these feelings if she is secure. Often the parents' beliefs will not only be different from the provider's but also from each others'. If she believes in herself and tolerates other people well, her example will be a more powerful teacher than anything she can say or do to change other people's views.

Living in Public

Another result of taking children into one's own home is that suddenly one finds oneself living in public. Children in day care naturally talk about what they do all day when they are with their day care family. The more attached they are to the provider, the more they talk about her with their parents. She is very important to them and they want to share her. Most children also sense that their parents are curious about this person with whom they spend so much time. Children in day care need to put together the pieces of their lives—the all-day piece that they spend with the provider and the rest of the day piece that they spend with their own family. The result of this need is that children talk with their parents about their day care family and with their provider about their own family.

Most people are not comfortable about having their home lives made public. Everyone makes mistakes and would prefer to keep the mistakes private; and yet when a woman becomes a provider there is no way to avoid some publicity. What can she do about it? The answer lies in her attitude about herself and her work. If she sees herself as a professional, then whatever she does with and for the children becomes part of her profession. Whatever happens while they are in her care is part of the service she offers—what she does is her *work*, not her private life. Her work can be made public, because it is then the *service* not the *person* that is being discussed. When the provider sees herself as a professional, the parents will see her as one as well and will speak of her with respect.

THE DEMANDS OF FAMILY DAY CARE OUTSIDE OF THOSE MADE ON THE PROVIDER

After looking at how well suited she is for the job, a person considering family day care should look at the other people concerned. Unless she lives alone, there are other people in her family to consider.

Her Own Children

If she has children of her own, what are their ages? If they are still young, they probably require a lot of her time and attention. With children it is never a case of "a couple more won't make any difference." They *will* make a difference, a very big difference. It is more a case of each child doubling the work. A provider with young children may have to deal with her own children's unhappiness about sharing their mother. Every child growing up thinks at one time or another "Mommy is paying more attention to him (or her) than to me." If she has several children to care for, the provider's own children are more apt to have these feelings, and if these feelings are strong enough, they can cause behavior problems and unhappiness.

If the children are older it is often possible to discuss the decision to go into family day care with them. They can understand that this is a business venture, and if the children are made a part of the business, they can be very helpful. Older children can enjoy taking care of babies and toddlers. They can play games and do projects with school-aged children. They make excellent tutors for homework help (they not only enjoy showing what they have already learned, but their own confidence increases). If they are consulted about arranging the rooms for day care, they will probably have good suggestions, and, more importantly, they will not feel that they are being moved out.

Other Family Members

The provider must also consult with the other adults she lives with. Older people can be very helpful with young children, and if the provider's parents or an aunt or uncle live with her, they can make a real contribution to the business. If, however, they themselves need a lot of care, she will have less time to devote to child care. If she feels that she can include the other adults in her work in a positive way, so that they are involved in the activities, then both the business and the children will benefit. A multigeneration family has much to offer children.

Her Home

Once the person considering day care has the cooperation of her own family, she must look at her home. In order to make her own life easier, she will probably have to change some of the rooms around. (The use of space is discussed in Chapter 4.) First, however, she needs to consider how she feels about using her rooms and furnishings to make a home for children—other people's children. Her valuables and breakables have to be put away. The furniture needs to be covered with something washable. In the bedrooms she needs a place for all of the children who nap. What arrangements can she make for her own and her family's privacy? How will she adjust to the disorder and the inevitable breakage and damage? Can she be content to have her home and business in the same place? If she is proud of the work she does, the answer is yes. She will be pleased to have her friends and her family see the evidence of her work in her home. She will enjoy having the pictures and projects the children are working on out where everyone can see them. She will want everyone to know that she provides an interesting, busy learning environment for the children. She will not sacrifice a comfortable living room, she will combine it with work and play space for the children who are growing up in her care. She will speak with pride of the new abilities and interests each child is developing, surrounded by the evidence of his or her progress.

THE PROVIDER AS PROFESSIONAL

Having considered all of the demands on the family day care provider, it would be easy for a person to wonder if anyone could possibly meet all of these requirements. It must be remembered, however, that these are the descriptions of the ideal, not the characteristics of the beginner. Furthermore, a person is not a professional because that person is perfect, but because that person knows the standards of the profession and is determined to live up to them.

Certainly there is no profession more deserving of high standards than that of caring for the next generation. The children of today will create the world of tomorrow out of what they have learned and become in the process of growing up. Everyone who contributes to the development of one child contributes to the world of the future. The professional in child care is not as concerned about what the child is doing today as she is with what that child will need for tomorrow.

Finally, the family day care provider who sees herself as a professional will do a professional job and will be treated accordingly. Everything that she needs to know in order to do this job is contained in this book. With that information, a real love of children, and a reasonably mature personality, she can provide first-class family day care.

2

The Business of Providing

Having decided to offer family day care, the provider is ready to think about the business. In order to make money (and that is the main reason for going into business) it is necessary to find out what the costs will be and what to charge for the service. Most other child care professions are well paid although in many cases the hours are shorter and the job less demanding. For instance, doctors, psychologists, nurses, and teachers can expect to earn a good living. The job of family day care is more varied, more constantly demanding, and often has a greater effect on the child's life than any of these and is, therefore, every bit as worthy of adequate pay.

LICENSING, REGISTRATION, AND APPROVAL

One of the first things the family day care provider needs to consider is the question of licensing. In some states there are several possible choices. A provider can be licensed to care for children who are paid for from public funds, she can be licensed to care for privately paid children, she can be registered as a family day care provider, or she can be "approved." She can also take in children without being licensed, registered, or approved. She may want to list all of the reasons for getting licensed and registered and all of the reasons for operating privately. She can then consider her choices and make the best decision for herself.

BENEFITS OF BEING LICENSED, REGISTERED, OR APPROVED

Many states, counties, and cities have regulations that require those who care for children in their homes to have a license. Although there are probably 10 or more providers without licenses for every one who is licensed, and although a family day care license is not taken as seriously as a driver's license, for instance, it *is* on the books in all but two states. Providers know that they offer an extremely important service and most providers agree that they should receive more appreciation and public support than they do. The first step toward becoming recognized is becoming licensed. As long as she is unlicensed, a provider may feel that she cannot talk about her profession either in her neighborhood, or in letters to the editor of the newspaper, or in requests for donations from storekeepers. With a license, however, she has the freedom to speak out for family day care. Providers who choose to remain unlicensed and unregistered also remain outsiders, and their status and income probably do not improve very much. The new tax laws require parents to name their child care provider and provide her Social Security number in order to take the child care tax credit. This is another reason providers are now considering becoming licensed or registered.

There can be some financial benefits for licensed providers as well. These differ, of course, from state to state and county to county. To find out what is available, it is necessary to get a copy of the guidelines from the local licensing agency. These usually include all licensing and registering regulations as well as whatever support services are available. The best way to begin is by telephoning the city government, or in small towns, the county office. Someone there can usually provide the name and telephone number of the office to contact. It may take from three to five telephone calls to get in touch with the person in charge, but once reached, he or she will usually send all of the information by mail. In addition, many state universities have Extension Services for Family Day Care. If there is a state university near you, or a branch of the university, it is a good source of information and materials.

Regulations, as well as any agency benefits, are in what is called the *public domain*. This means that everyone has a right to look at them. If the local office does not have extra copies of these to send out, it may be necessary to go into the office with a pencil and paper to copy down the information. The agency staff is usually very helpful to anyone who says she is considering offering family day care and needs information about registering and licensing, and will eagerly offer a list of the available benefits. These might include:

> Reimbursement for children's food
> Some equipment and supplies

Referral of children
Receiving fees for children referred
Lending library of toys and books
Training and education programs for the provider
Newsletters and organizations to join
Group medical and liability insurance rates

Reimbursement for Children's Food

In most parts of the country, the United States Department of Agriculture (USDA) Child Care Food Program reimburses the cost of food for children in family day care. If the provider is licensed, registered, or approved, food allowances are usually available, and this can be a very worthwhile benefit. Often training in nutrition comes with the USDA reimbursement, and this is also useful.

Equipment and Supplies

A few licensing agencies provide cribs, strollers, high chairs, carriages, tricycles, or other equipment, and others have allowances for supplies such as toys, art materials, and records. Bookkeeping supplies may also be available. A complete list of the equipment and supplies the agency provides is usually part of the packet of information.

Referral of Children

Some agencies have lists of licensed family day care providers available for parents who need the service. For a working parent, or for someone who has just moved to a new neighborhood and is looking for family day care, the first place she is apt to go is the county, state, or city office that licenses day care. For providers who don't have as many children as they want, being on the list of licensed or registered providers is a good way to get business. Although agencies do not make personal recommendations to parents, most will give out a list of all the licensed providers.

Receiving Fees for Children Eligible for Public Funding

For parents who qualify, some state departments of social services not only place the child but also pay some of the fee for the child's care. Providers should find out how much their agency pays per child and whether there is a long delay in receiving the reimbursement.

Lending Library of Toys and Books

This can be a useful service. Not only do children tire of the same toys after a while, but their interests change with age. Games, puzzles, and books can be borrowed and returned when they are no longer being used. If there is no such service, however, the public library is an excellent resource for books.

Training and Education Programs

Courses in a variety of subjects are offered to family day care providers by some agencies. Courses in subjects such as nutrition, business, child development, first aid, creative arts, human relations, and career development are all useful for the provider. The knowledge gained as well as the credentials earned (whether certificate or college credit) add to the professional standing of the provider. These courses or training programs also put the provider in touch with other women doing the same work. Many state university extension offices offer family day care training courses.

Newsletters and Organizations to Join

Licensed, registered, or approved family day care providers can join organizations and receive newsletters which are very helpful. The organizations meet and discuss family day care issues, problems, and projects, and often publish newsletters. These make the job of family day care less lonely and more interesting for the individual provider, who otherwise may not have anyone she can talk with about her business.

Group Insurance Rates

A few organizations have obtained group insurance rates for family day care providers. This includes liability insurance, and sometimes medical and dental insurance which, if the provider has none, is an important benefit. Being part of a group lowers the cost of insurance and makes it affordable for the individual provider. Any medical or dental insurance plan would have to be compared with any benefits that the provider and her family may already have in order to decide if it is worth buying.

Other Benefits of Being Licensed

Some agencies may provide other services such as substitutes when the provider is ill or on vacation, group activities in the community for the children, assistance in counseling parents, or consultation for the special needs of certain children. If the local agency offers any of these, or any other services not listed here, they are well worth considering.

REGULATIONS FOR LICENSING, REGULATION, OR APPROVAL

Once the provider has the list of requirements for licensing, she can go over them, decide what it will cost to meet them, and consider how many are things she would have done anyway. She also needs to look at ongoing requirements such as the number of inspections her home will receive in a year, the number of children she is permitted to care for (this often includes her own children), and the amount of reporting and paper work the agency requires. Finally, she needs to find out how difficult it is going to be to find children on her own.

Besides the number of children the provider is allowed to care for (in most states it is six, except in the case of infant care), there may be regulations covering the following: 1) a health check on the provider and all members of her family; 2) a report of good character on herself and her family (that is, no criminal records); 3) a check on the safety and cleanliness of her home. Some other requirements usually are window guards, adequate heating, a telephone, smoke detector, fire extinguisher, covered electrical outlets, and no lead paint. Most homes have adequate facilities, whether they are houses, apartments, or trailers, and with a little bit of work can be made suitable. In order to deduct any business expenses, such as the purchase of equipment or repainting a few rooms, from her taxes, the provider will need to be licensed or registered if her state requires it.

Going into Business

Once the provider has made the decision about becoming licensed, she can figure out what it will cost her go to into the business of family day care. She can begin by listing all start-up expenses.

Childproofing the Home

Chapter 4 describes the safety precautions that are necessary and that make it easier to supervise children and keep them safe. These include any safety regulations that the licensing agency is apt to require. The provider needs to make a list of the equipment she will need to purchase (gates for the stairs, plastic plates, glasses and cutlery, locks for cabinets, and so forth) and estimate the cost. She needs to see if any equipment is paid for by local agencies. If so, the cost can be subtracted from the total start-up cost.

Equipment and Supplies

To figure out the equipment needed for a total of six children, for example, including the provider's own, she might begin with the space needed for sleep. Not all of the children need beds if some are too old to nap and others are in school until 3 p.m. If they should feel tired or ill, they can use one of the family's beds; however, cribs are needed for infants and a bed or cot for each preschooler. Infants will need a high chair or other feeding chair and a stroller or carriage to go out in. A table with enough chairs for all of the children and the provider and a comfortable chair or rocker are also necessary. Then there are the smaller expenses such as a low stool for the toilet and washbasin, a potty chair, places for the children's outdoor clothes, and so on.

One important one-time expense is storage equipment. When a home also houses a business, it is necessary to be very well organized. The better the organization, the easier the work. A large closet can be outfitted with shelves (or metal storage shelves can be bought from a discount store) so that the files, supplies, and records can be stored on the top shelf and the equipment for the children on the lower shelves. Included in the cost of equipment for supply storage will be kitchen shelves for extra food storage and for extra unbreakable dishes, napkins, paper towels, cutlery, cleaning equipment, and cookware. In the bathroom, the provider needs a complete first aid kit as well as towels and washcloths for each child. The bedroom will require at least one sheet, blanket, and pillow for each child.

Once the cost of all these items has been determined (check second-hand prices and discount store prices), an estimate of the total start-up costs can be made. Before going out to buy cribs, strollers, high chairs, or a lot of toys, however, the provider should know the ages and number of children she will have in her care.

Other Start-Up Expenses

As mentioned above, group insurance is cheaper than an individual policy, and it might be possible to join an organization or group of providers. (The licensing agency will know if there already is a providers' association or organization.) Several insurance agents should be questioned before deciding which insurance policy is best. The main thing is to have some insurance. This is very important for someone in family day care. The provider should insure against accident or injury to any child in the home as well as on trips. This is called liability insurance. It is also necessary to carry insurance against fire and theft, as well as for the provider's loss of time at work because of illness, fire, or other catastrophe.

There may be other expenses such as advertising (the cost of materials to make signs or the cost of an advertisement in the newspaper), medical checkups for the provider and all her family, and membership in a providers' association. Among the one-time expenses are items such as bookkeeping equipment, filing box, file folders, a ledger for expenses and income, a loose-leaf notebook and fillers, writing paper, and envelopes. A calculator can be very helpful.

Once all of these expenses have been added, the total amount needed to go into business can be figured. If it is more than the provider feels she can lay out, she might consider making it a policy to accept infants only if the heavy equipment, such as cribs, strollers, and high chairs, is provided by the parents. If she decides to do this, it should be included in her list of parent responsibilities (see Chapter 3). This policy could also be applied to other equipment, such as tricycles, wagons, car seats, and so forth. If the provider decides to ask parents to provide some equipment, she must remember that whatever is considered a policy must apply to everyone, unless for some good reason an exception is made.

GETTING CLIENTS

Because there are more women with young children going to work each year, family day care will continue to be in increasing demand. In most places, the demand is greater than the supply. Recruiting children in a city is therefore apt to be easier than in a small town, simply because of the greater number of working women. In small towns, it may be necessary to advertise the service to find enough children. It is best to begin with a low-cost advertisement, such as making signs that announce the provider's name, address, and telephone number (see Figure 1), and placing them in local churches, synagogues, schools, libraries, and shops.

In many parts of the country there are child care resource and referral agencies. Providers are listed with the agency and receive referrals of parents who live in the area and need child care. These agencies are also a good source of information about other family day care organizations and services. They often offer family day care providers training and lending libraries of books and toys. If no one in your area knows who the local agency is, you can call the National Association of Child Care Resource and Referral Agencies in Washington, D.C.

The number of responses to these low-cost efforts will give an idea of the difficulty of finding clients. If the cheaper methods do not produce

Figure 1.

the number of children desired, a newspaper advertisement or listing in the Yellow Pages can be tried. Should that fail and if there is no resource and referral service in the community, the licensing agency is the next place to go. This may mean that the provider who did not intend to be licensed will have to reconsider.

DECIDING HOW MUCH TO CHARGE

Providers who are not receiving referrals from a public agency need to negotiate a private fee with each parent. They also need to decide whether the parents are to provide certain things such as disposable diapers and baby food or formula, certain equipment, and perhaps even certain toys such as roller skates and bicycles for their own children. Some providers ask the parents to send lunch, and some parents prefer to provide their children's food. The hours of service can be adapted to suit both the provider's and the parents' needs. Any extra hours should be considered overtime, whether these are added to the half-day or the whole-day rate. The provider must decide whether or not to charge for days the child is absent due to illness or other reason. On a large sheet of paper the provider should put the expenses she expects to have, the hours she will be working, and some estimate of the wear and tear on her belongings. Then she should figure the number of children she will care for and the fee she plans to charge. With a full group she should make at least the minimum wage after covering all her costs. There are, of course, times when a provider wants to limit her income, such as when she is over 65 years old and is receiving Social Security.

RECORDKEEPING

No business ever succeeded without good recordkeeping. The business of family day care demands well-organized records in order to know what to charge and to apply for reimbursement from the USDA for meals and snacks. There are two kinds of records necessary, daily or weekly and permanent. The first can be kept in a loose-leaf notebook with dividers for the sections used daily, weekly, and monthly (see Figure 2).

Daily Records

Attendance In front of the loose-leaf notebook are the daily records such as attendance. Attendance records are important for financial, legal, and health reasons. A financial problem, for instance, could arise if a particular child is often absent. The parent would need to be told that regular attendance means a regular income for the provider who plans for a full group, and who cannot afford to have less than that too often. Another reason for records is the legal question that could arise over taxes, insurance, or parent fees. Finally, there are reasons of health that require careful records. In the case of any contagious illness, it is helpful to know which children were exposed to the sick child and how long each child was absent with a particular illness.

The attendance record should also show times of arrival and departure. This is required for food reimbursement, and can also be useful when making a list of things to discuss with the parents.

At the beginning of each week, a record of who pays the weekly fee is made by writing "paid" by each child's name in the attendance list.

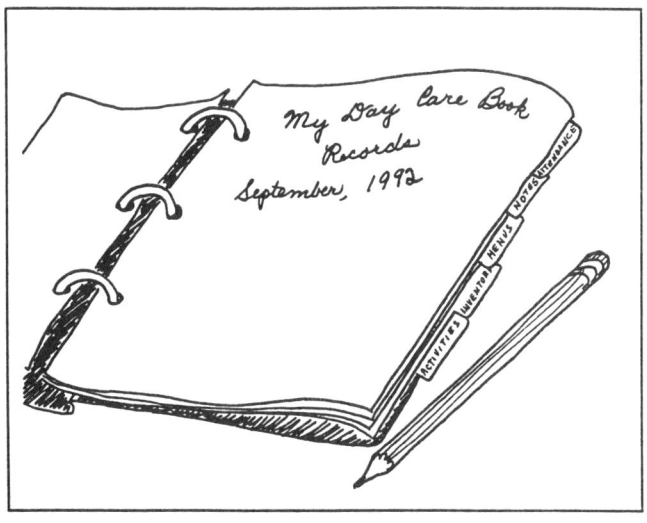

Figure 2.

Notes on the Children The section after attendance in the loose-leaf notebook should contain a page for each child. On these pages the provider can make notes of things she wants to remember and things she wants to mention to the parent. Each page should be dated. For infants, a record of the times and amounts of feedings, and how much time the infant slept is important, and for toddlers, a record of naptimes. Anything unusual such as lack of appetite, tired or cross behavior, a fever, cough, or diarrhea should be noted. Amusing things a child says or does should also be recorded if possible for the parents. School children can put papers they want to take home in the notebook for safekeeping. Special requests for the parent, such as an extra sweater or pair of socks, would also be written in the notebook.

An accident record must be kept on each child. In even the best run home accidents can occur. As soon as the situation has been properly taken care of, the provider must take time to write a short description of what happened and put it into the file. An example of what to write could be: "Katrina was running through the living room at 11 a.m., December 2, 1991, and fell and cut her lower lip. I put ice in a cloth on the lip and called her mother to report. She agreed with me that Katrina should see a doctor. I took Katrina to the clinic at 11:20 a.m. The doctor on duty said to continue putting ice on it, that stitches were not necessary." When the parent picks up the child, the provider can show her the written record. This kind of sharing and keeping notes may protect the provider from the possibility of legal trouble later.

The loose-leaf notebook should be put in a handy place so that the parents can look at it when they come to collect their children.

Weekly Records

Menus and Shopping List Menus and food planning are discussed in Chapter 19 in detail. The week's menus and a list of the food needed are kept in the notebook. When making a shopping list for the week's meals, the provider can refer to the Inventory section and make sure there are no supplies that need to be added, such as toilet paper, crayons, sponges, or soap pads.

Inventory Keeping an inventory of the supplies on hand simplifies planning and shopping. It is a good idea to have some extra food on hand in case of bad weather or illness. Material for activities—paper, glue, crayons, toothpicks, knitting wool, anything needed to carry out projects—should be on hand as well. Housekeeping supplies such as light bulbs, cleaning equipment, and paper towels all go in the inventory (see Figure 3). When something is used up or getting low, a check is put by that

```
                              INVENTORY

Food Supplies          Household Supplies      Activity Supplies

spaghetti _____      paper towels _____    tissue paper _____
macaroni _____       toilet paper _____    construction paper ___
noodles _____        garbage bags _____    tablets _____
crackers _____       paper napkins _____   gift wrap _____
rice _____           paper cups _____      paper doilies _____
coffee _____         paper plates _____    sand paper _____
tea _____            waxed paper _____     chalk _____
sugar _____          foil _____            crayons _____
flour _____          plastic bags _____    paste _____
salt _____           light bulbs _____     felt tip pens _____
cornmeal _____       batteries _____       clay _____
grits _____          toothpaste _____      paint _____
yeast _____          mouthwash _____       scissors _____
dried beans _____    dental floss _____    yarn _____
dried peas _____     bathroom soap _____   fabric scraps _____
cereals _____        disposable diapers ___  buttons _____
chocolate squares ___  powder _____          shells _____
chocolate chips ___    baby oil _____        beads _____
raisins _____        Band-aids _____       string _____
nuts _____           disinfectant _____    toothpicks _____
popcorn _____        Vaseline _____        liquid paste _____
peanut butter _____  cotton balls _____    ribbons _____
jam _____            dishwashing detergent   felt scraps _____
jelly _____          soap pads _____       playing cards _____
jell-O _____         cleansers _____       puzzles _____
puddings _____       bleach _____          flower and vegetable
juices _____         laundry detergent ___     seeds _____
dried milk _____     clothespins _____     potting soil _____
cocoa _____          etc.                    paper clips _____
tuna _____                                   rubber bands _____
cocoanut _____                               glitter _____
canned tomatoes ___                            thumb tacks _____
baking powder ___                              etc.
baking soda _____
vanilla extract _____
etc.
```

Figure 3.

item so that it will get on the shopping list. Once the item is purchased, the check is erased.

Permanent Records

In addition to the daily record a permanent file is also needed. A cardboard carton in which file folders fit standing up will do nicely. The following records are kept in the file.

Clients One folder on each child contains the permanent records, the medical records including immunizations, a copy of the emergency telephone numbers, and the interview forms (see Chapter 3). Pages from the Notes on Children section of the loose-leaf notebook go into this file at the end of the month. In addition, all records and observations on the development of each child (see Chapter 8) are kept in this folder.

Menus The menus are transferred from the notebook into this file at the end of each week. This allows the provider to look them over to get ideas when she cannot come up with something new and the children have no suggestions. The menus also need to be checked against food costs from time to time to be sure that they are well planned for economy as well as nutrition. If the provider finds that she has spent more on food in one month than in another, she can look over menus to see whether it was because of a series of special meals (for birthdays or holidays), or because the cost of food went up, or perhaps because the menus were not planned carefully enough.

Expenses All cashier slips from food and supply shopping and insurance forms are placed in the file each month. This is necessary for figuring income tax. Records of this kind must be kept for 7 years.

Attendance The attendance sheets of previous months are kept in a file folder.

Daily Activities Old plans of activities should be kept as reminders when thinking of new activities. If a wall calendar is used, the pages can be folded and kept in a file. Everyone gets stale on ideas from time to time, and it is helpful to look over old plans to be reminded of which were successes and which were not. Ideas cut out of newspapers, magazines, or newsletters also go into this file.

Forms There are several forms that need to be kept on hand. These can be made up in a batch and put into a folder for future use.

FIELD TRIP FORMS Signed permission forms to take children on trips are needed. One signed form can cover all trips (see Figure 4).

EMERGENCY MEDICAL CARE FORMS This form is similar to the form for trips (see Figure 5). It is the parent's permission for the provider to act on behalf of the child in an emergency. In some states this form has to be notarized. This should be checked with the licensing agency.

INCOME TAX FORMS Old income tax declarations should be kept as a guide and a reference. Occasionally it is necessary to refer to these in dealing with the Internal Revenue Service.

```
                    FIELD TRIP PERMISSION FORM

    I _____ give permission to _____
            (name of parent)                           (name of care provider)

    to take my child _____ on trips outside
                               (name of child)

    the home by public transportation, car, or on foot.


        Signed: _____

        Dated:  _____
```

Figure 4.

```
                    EMERCENCY CARE PERMISSION FORM

    In case of accident or illness, I _____
                                              (name of parent)

    give permission to _____ to take my child
                            (name of care provider)

    _____ to _____
              (name of child)                  (name of doctor or hospital)

    for treatment. I will pay all reasonable expenses for medical care.


        Signed: _____

        Dated:  _____
```

Figure 5.

KEEPING TRACK OF INCOME AND EXPENSES

Besides the loose-leaf notebook, the provider also needs a ledger (see Figure 6). This can be bought at any dime store or stationery store and is the best way to keep a record of expenses and income.

		September 1992	Income	Direct Business Expenses			
				Meals & snacks	Household Supplies	Day Care Supplies	Transportation
9	4	fee - Marian	45 00				
9	4	fee - Willie	45 00				
9	4	fee - Mercedes	45 00				
9	4	A & P		61 90	18 71		
9	4	Woolworth's				13 03	
9	5	fee - Eunice	45 00				
9	5	taxi					4 25
9	5	U.S.D.A.	27 00				
9	5	Cleaning					
9	6	Fruit stand		6 42			
9	6	Driver's license					
9	9	Water bill					
9	8	Elec. bill					
9	8	Rent					
9	8	Telephone					
9	8	Hardware			52 50		
9	14	fee - Willie	45 00				
9	18	Large blocks					
9	18	Fruit stand		3 75			
9	18	Hardware (paint)					
9	18	fee - Mercedes	45 00				
9	19	Dr. fee (TB test)					
9	19	A & P		77 04			
9	25	fee - Marian	45 00				
9	25	fee - Eunice	45 00				
9	25	A & P		41 50			

Figure 6.

Care Business

Repairs Maintenance	Equipment	Other	Utilities	Repairs Maintenance	Other Home Expense	Home Equipment
					Related Business Expenses	
					27	50	
					4	50	
			14	82			
			21	20			
					232	90	
					16	88	

38	50						
					6	75	
		12	00				

Setting Up a Ledger

Income Ledgers have 12 columns on a double page. In column 1 all *Income* is recorded. A date must be written by each item recorded in the ledger, for instance: *Sept 4, Fee for Marian, $45.00*. On Mondays when each child's weekly fee is paid, the child's name, the date, and the amount received are written in the ledger. If an agency pays for some of the children's care, or all of it, the payment is written in on the same page in the same column. If a parent provides money for formula, or a trip, or if money is received from the USDA for the children's food, these too are recorded in the income column. Each item is dated and explained.

Direct Business Expenses The next seven columns are for the direct business expenses. Across the top of these seven columns write *Direct Business Expenses*, on top of column 2 *Meals and Snacks*, on column 3 *Household Supplies*, on column 4 *Day Care Supplies*, on column 5 *Transportation and Field Trips*, on column 6 *Repairs and Maintenance*, on column 7 *Equipment*, and column 8 *Other*. (Other is for everything that does not fit anywhere else.)

Meals and Snacks (column 2) is usually the biggest ongoing expense in family day care. Whenever the provider shops, she enters the amount she spends for her family day care program in the correct column. The total of all food goes in column 2. Cleaning supplies, paper napkins, soap, toothpaste, baby oil, light bulbs, and so forth, go in column 3. It is sometimes easier to separate the food from the supplies when shopping in the supermarket (food in the top of the shopping cart, supplies below). Then the checkout person can ring up two totals. This will save the trouble of adding and subtracting later.

The cost of everything bought specifically for the children is recorded in column 4. This includes things like sheets, blankets, washcloths, a first aid kit, art materials, toys, puzzles, and books. If the provider buys plastic dishes for the children, that expense goes in column 4. The date of purchase and exact descriptions of each thing are included.

All travel and other trip expenses are recorded in column 5. A provider who lives in the city might pick the children up from school in a taxi because of bad weather. The cost of the taxi goes in column 5. A provider who lives in a smaller town might take the children to visit a farm. She should check the mileage in her car before leaving and when she arrives. If the trip is 12 miles one way, for instance, she doubles that distance and figures 24 miles round trip. Figuring 25¢ a mile, the trip costs $6.00 in transportation. If she goes to a museum or zoo where there is an admission charge, the total for herself and the children is put in column 5 along with the cost of transportation. If she takes the children on an all-day trip, the lunch she packs goes into the food column, but anything she buys on the trip such as ice cream or milk goes into the trip expenses (column 5).

Column 6 is for all expenses from repairs and maintenance that are for the business and not the provider's family. This includes repairing anything the children break. Fixing, painting, refinishing, or repairing expenses such as new nuts and bolts for a wagon, replacing a glass broken by one of the day care children, and repainting the shelves would go into column 6.

The cost of equipment should be listed in column 7. *Equipment* is considered anything that lasts more than a year (*Household Supplies*—column 3—are things that last less than a year). A fence, a cot, a large cooking pot, and an infant seat are all counted as equipment. Items in this column must all be for the use of the day care children.

The direct expenses that do not fit anywhere else should be listed in column 8. These expenses might include membership in the local day care association, the National Association for the Education of Young Children, a subscription to *Day Care and Early Education* or *Parents' Magazine*, books on child care or nutrition, or attending courses. Day care insurance costs also go in this column.

Related Day Care Expenses The next four columns are labeled *Related Day Care Expenses*. These are expenses that cover both the business and the provider's personal life. *Utilities* should be written over column 9, *Repairs and Maintenance* over 10, *Other Home Expenses* over 11, and *Home Equipment* over 12.

Utilities include gas, electricity, water, telephone, and in some locations, sewerage and trash removal. Each one should be entered separately in column 9 with the date and the amount. This information is needed for tax purposes as well as for figuring expenses.

In column 10 go all expenses for repairing things that are used by both the day care children and the provider's own family (for instance, if the television needs repair, or the hot water heater needs a new valve, or the house needs painting).

Column 11, *Other Home Expenses*, is the place for rent or mortgage payments, insurance on the house and its contents, and any other home expenses that are not repairs, such as a newspaper subscription.

Home Equipment expenses are listed in column 12. This includes a new refrigerator, lamp, television, or lawn mower. The cost of a vacuum cleaner would go here, but a broom is considered a maintenance item and would go in column 10.

How to Use a Ledger

At the end of the month, each column is added separately (a small calculator is very useful here). All of the direct business expenses are added, columns 2 through 8. After column 2 has been added, the total can be divided by the number of children in day care (not including the provider's own) to get the cost of food per child. If the total for the month was $238.40 and the provider has five children in day care, the cost of food for each child is $47.68 a month. If she receives USDA reimbursement for any of the children, she can subtract that and figure out her own costs.

She then adds columns 4 and 5 and divides by the number of children she has in order to know how much she is spending per month on activities for each child. This is an important figure to have on hand when discussing the fee with the parents.

All totals in columns 2 through 8 are then added together and subtracted from the total income. This gives the provider a good idea how she is doing financially. Columns 9 through 12 are also part of the business expenses, but they are only figured in when preparing taxes.

The Effect of Welfare, Food Stamps, and Income Tax

The government agencies that control welfare, income tax, and food stamps have something to say about how much money the provider makes. Figuring out how much effect their regulations can have and how to manage these can be tricky, especially because they change frequently.

Welfare There are two ways that the welfare department affects family day care. The first involves accepting children who are receiving welfare. (This was discussed in the earlier section on licensing.) Sometimes, the agency pays the provider directly each month. In other places, the agency sends the check to the mother who endorses it over to the provider.

Another way in which the welfare department has an effect is when a person is receiving welfare and decides to become a family day care provider.

Each state has different rules about welfare, and these rules change according to the politicians in office, so providers have to find out what current rules are in effect. Whatever they are, it is now clear why the ledger is so important. Unless the provider has a record of all of her expenses, she cannot figure how much income she will have nor whether she can apply for assistance.

Food Stamp Program If the provider has been receiving food stamps when she begins her day care business, her food stamps will cost her more or she may no longer be eligible. The local office will have the latest regulations.

Income Tax Providers who take only welfare children have sometimes in the past been free from income tax through an agreement between the licensing agency and the Internal Revenue Service (IRS). The idea was that the provider was not in a profit-making business, she was simply being reimbursed for a service to a government agency. For a long time providers in many places were content to go along with this arrangement.

As family day care becomes recognized as a child care profession, however, providers want to be free to earn money, pay taxes, and save for the future. They want to have the same rights and benefits as other child care professionals, including the right to make a profit. Because they can deduct so many expenses from their income, they will find that they will not be giving up all of their profits to taxes, and indeed, even with the USDA food reimbursement, they won't have less after-tax income.

The family day care provider must use Form 1040 or 1040A and *also* Schedules C and SE. Schedule C is for people who have their own businesses, and schedule SE is for people who make more than $400 a year. Schedule SE entitles the provider to Social Security. Schedule C is the most important because it allows the person who has her own business to deduct expenses. Taxes are paid on *net* income, income after all expenses are subtracted.

The provider first deducts all her *direct* expenses (see the ledger described above). Then to deduct *indirect* or related expenses, the provider figures how much *time* and how much *space* she uses for family day care. This is how it works. If she has 6 rooms and uses 4, she divides 4 by 6 and gets 66.6%, or 67% of her home is used by her business. Then, if she has the children 10 hours a day, 5 days a week, she figures 50 hours a business week. The whole week is 168 hours (24 hours times 7 days). Now if she divides the family day care time (50 hours) by the whole week (168 hours) she gets 29.7%, or 30% of the time her home is a business. Now she must multiply the 67% space by the 30% time, and she gets 20%, which is how much she can deduct of her related, or indirect expenses. These include rent or mortgage, home repairs, insurance, cable TV, property taxes, and utilities. Finally, she can figure *depreciation on her home and furniture*. To do this, she must figure out how long her equipment is expected to last. Then the total cost of the equipment for the children is divided by the number of years it should last. There is a simple formula for doing this. For easy-to-understand instructions, write to Wildwood

Resources, Inc., 9085 E. Mineral Circle, Englewood, CO 80112, and ask for *Dollars and Cents*. This booklet also explains why participating in the USDA Food Program and declaring the income leaves family day care providers with *more* after-tax income than *not* declaring it.

Figuring out taxes is a tough job, but there is help. One thing providers need is a booklet called *Business Use of Your Home*, publication #587, which is available from the IRS office. With that help, and the booklet *Dollars and Cents*, the provider will most likely find that paying a little tax on a profit is not nearly as upsetting as not making a profit. And *not* paying taxes is becoming less and less of an option as parents declare their child care expenses and the USDA declares its food reimbursement.

Almost all family day care providers are women. It has always been difficult for women to become independently self-employed, even when the service they offer is as important as day care is, and women have long been trained to let someone help them with money matters. Providers soon realize that one way of assuring that family day care is regarded as a profession is by showing that they are able to manage their business in a professional way. Keeping records is not difficult. The effort is rewarded by having control over one's income, knowing one can make a profit, and deciding how to use the profit to improve one's business and personal life.

There is a great deal to be said for providers becoming independent, self-reliant business people. Certainly anyone who can solve the kinds of problems that caring for children present can also solve any problems that a small business might create.

Beginnings and Endings in Family Day Care

IN THE BEGINNING

Everyone knows the old sayings about the importance of first impressions and getting off on the right foot. These sayings could have been invented with family day care in mind. The first interview with the parent and the way in which the child is introduced to family day care will make the provider's first days with the child easy or difficult and will have a great influence on how the parents feel about placing their child in the family day care home.

Why is the beginning so important? For one reason, family day care is a service that involves human relationships, and human relationships are based on what one person *expects* of another and whether that person lives up to those expectations. It is necessary that the parent, the child (depending on the age of the child), and the provider have some idea of what to expect of one another. If these expectations are fulfilled, everyone involved will feel secure and confident; if they are not fulfilled, however, there will be feelings of anger, disappointment, and dissatisfaction. It is possible to improve on a relationship that gets off to a bad start, but the cost in time, energy, and emotion is great. For everyone's protection therefore, the provider should make very clear to the parent exactly what family day care offers and exactly what will be expected of the parent.

THE FIRST INTERVIEW

There are three main goals to be accomplished in the first interview. First, the provider must decide whether the child will fit into the day care family. Second, she must find out if the parent is someone with whom she can work over a period of time. One interview is usually enough to make a good decision on both of these points. Finally, she must give the parent the security and confidence of knowing that his or her child is being cared for by a competent and knowledgeable person.

Where To Have the First Interview

Although it is a good idea for the provider to visit the child's home at some point, the first interview should take place in the family day care home, where the child will be spending his or her days. It should be scheduled when there is enough quiet (nap time, in the evening, or on a weekend) for the provider to give her attention to the visiting parent and child. The parent should be asked to bring the child along to the meeting.

A Good Beginning

The provider can begin with a few simple questions: How did the parent hear about the provider? Does the parent live nearby? How many children are there in the family? How far away is the parent's place of work? Has the parent lived in the same place for a long time?

These questions should help the parent relax and begin talking easily. Everyone likes to talk about himself or herself, and one or two questions are usually enough to get the conversation started. While the parent is talking, the provider can get a good look at the child. She can ask herself how this child will fit into her home. Is the child alert, interested, looking the place over? Does the child seem healthy? Does the child respond to the provider's smiles? Is the child relaxed or nervous? What sort of relationship does the child appear to have with the parent? If she has not done so already, the provider should give the child something to do. She can offer paper and crayons, scissors, paste and old magazines, or small toys. There should be a place for the child to sit nearby. She may also offer the child a glass of juice or milk, an apple, or raisins. If the child is an infant, the provider might put a pad on the floor with a few toys or, if she has one, let the parent place the infant in an infant seat or a bouncy chair. The purpose in presenting an activity is to see how adaptable, responsive, and independent the child is. It also permits the provider to continue her conversation with the parent while keeping an eye on the child.

Once the child is busy and contented, the provider can ask some questions about the child's history. Is this an only child? Is the child in school? Who has looked after the child so far? What are some of the child's interests, likes, dislikes? If the child is too young to follow the conversation, the provider can ask about the child's personality. If the child is old enough to understand (that is, 2 years and older), there should be no questions that should not be answered in front of the child.

Accepting the Child

At this point, the provider can decide whether to accept the child or not. If she decides not to, she should tell the mother that she cannot take the child and end the interview. She might offer the parent some suggestions for other sources of child care—the licensing agency, other providers whom she knows, or a day care center in the neighborhood. If she decides to take the child, now is time to tell the parent a few things about herself and what she offers.

Explaining about Family Day Care

Being open and straightforward sets the tone for future dealings with the parent. The provider can describe her own family and the other children in day care, and talk about how and why she decided to offer family day care. Any questions the parent has should be answered honestly because the provider expects the parent to be honest in answering *her* questions. The provider does not need to answer questions that are too personal, of course.

During the first interview the parent should be told about the terms of the family day care contract (see Figure 7). The parent can take a copy of the contract, questionnaire, and list of responsibilities to read at home and bring to the next interview. It is helpful to have all of these in writing because people often forget details or else do not listen carefully enough to remember what was said. Later, misunderstandings can occur that easily could have been avoided.

Individual providers can include whatever terms they want but the basic items need to be covered. If the child's fees are to be paid by an agency, a contract with the parent is still a good idea. In some places the agency provides the contract. Even then, the provider may want to have her own contract with the parent. All contracts must contain fees (including overtime) and the hours the child is expected to arrive and leave. The effect of absences on fees should also be spelled out.

In addition to the contract, the provider will give the parent a list of responsibilities and a questionnaire. The list in Figure 8 is an example of some of the items of responsibility that the provider might include (this can be adapted to each individual provider's needs). The provider must have a list of telephone numbers where the parent and other family members can be reached during the day.

The final document is a questionnaire that is used to get a history of the child (see Figure 9). It is a good idea to have a form like the following to check off each item. It saves making a lot of notes while talking, and points out anything the provider might want to find out more about. When the parent returns the form, the provider can check if there have been any un-

---

CONTRACT

This is an agreement between _____
                                              (parent)

and _____ for the day care of
              (care provider)

_____ for 5 days a week,
              (child)

Monday through Friday. The parent will bring the child not before 8 am and will pick the child up not later than 6 pm. The fee will be _____ per week, payable on Monday. If the parent cannot pick the child up by 6 pm, the parent will telephone by 2 pm to tell the provider and will reimburse the provider _____ per hour overtime. The parent will inform the provider if anyone other than the parent will pick the child up. If the child will be absent, the parent will inform the provider the night before. If the child is absent 1 day, the fee is the same. If the child is absent 2 days in a row, the parent will not pay for those days. The parent will give the provider proof of a complete medical check-up and current immunizations. After the child has been ill and absent, the parent will give the provider a release from the pediatrician before the child will be accepted back into day care.

Agreed upon this _____ day of _____ 198___.

_____
                              (parent)

_____
                           (care provider)

Figure 7.

usual events such as an illness, a move from one city to another, or anything else about which she wants more information.

By the end of the first interview, the child has had time to get used to the place and feel comfortable. At this point the provider should try to make friends. Having an interesting toy handy helps. A young child is easily overwhelmed, especially in a strange place, so the provider needs to approach the child slowly. Merely talking to children, even to infants, is often enough to get a smile and some response. Children around one year of age are usually uncomfortable with strangers, and it may be best to offer a toy and a smile and watch the child's reaction. Toddlers and preschoolers usually respond to an interesting toy and some conversation. If the child has

RESPONSIBILITIES	
Care Provider's	Parent's
1. The provider will take care of all of the child's daytime needs.	1. The parent will provide an extra set of clothes for winter and summer.
2. The provider will not turn the child over to anyone but the parent unless the parent requests it.	2. The parent will inform the provider is she will not be at her usual work place.
3. The provider will take the child for medical check-ups once the child has been accepted into care.	3. The parent will inform the provider the night before if the child will not be in day care.
4. The provider will take the child for dental check-ups once the child has been accepted into care.	4. The parent will not bring a child with a fever, severe cold, diarrhea, or any other contagious illness.
5. The provider will give complete reports to the parents on the child's condition, progress, and any recommendations from the school, doctor, or dentist.	5. The parent will provide formula or any special foods for as long as the pediatrician recommends.
6. The provider will tell the parent a month in advance of any days when she will not be available.	6. The parents will provide disposable diapers or diaper service (or stroller, crib, etc.).
7. If the provider is ill, she will make other arrangements for the child for the first day, after that the parent is responsible for finding a substitute.	7. The parent will meet with the provider within a reasonable time whenever the provider requests it.
8. The provider will inform the parent in advance if she is taking the child on a trip.	8. The parent will keep the provider informed of any changes in her work or home telephone numbers.
	9. The parent will tell the provider one week in advance of removing the child from the provider's care.

Figure 8.

HISTORY

Child's name _____
Address _____
Home telephone _____
Parent's name _____
Parent's work address _____
Parent's work telephone _____
Family member to be called if parent cannot be reached _____
_____
Family member's telephone _____
Has a car? _____
Second family member to be called if first cannot be reached _____
_____
Second family member's telphone _____
Has a car? _____
Child's birth date _____

1. The delivery. Difficult? _____ Long? _____ Easy? _____
   Did you have any problem? _____
   Did the child? _____
2. Infancy. What kind of newborn? _____ Quiet? _____
   Active? _____ Often hungry? _____ Sleepy? _____
   Fussy? _____
   What problems did you have in the first few weeks? _____
   _____
3. Infancy and early childhood. Any illnesses? _____
   Hospitalizations? _____
   Surgery? _____
   Changes in the family? _____
   Changes in the home? Moves? _____
4. Any allergies? _____
5. Any physical problems? _____
6. Weaned? _____ When? _____
7. Toilet trained? _____ When? _____
   Nighttime? _____
   What word does the child use for urine? _____
   For feces? _____
8. Is there anything the child especially likes? _____
   Dislikes? _____
9. Are there any words the child has for things that I may not be able to understand? _____
10. Where is the child's medical record? _____
    Where should the child be taken in an emergency? _____
    Clinic? _____
    Pediatrician? _____
    Who has the child's immunization record? _____
    Is it up to date? _____

Figure 9.

already been playing with the materials offered, the provider can simply sit down near the child and talk while the child continues the activity.

Older children are usually able to answer questions about their friends, their teacher's name, their favorite game or television show. The provider can tell the child something about the kinds of things she does with the children and then ask the child what he or she likes to do and likes to eat.

THE FAMILY DAY CARE HOME

The next step is to take the parent and child for a tour around the home. The provider can tell the parent and child what sorts of things are done in each room, where the toys are kept, where each child keeps private things, and where the new child will eat, sleep, and use the bathroom. If the other children are in the house, the provider can introduce them. If not, she can tell the new child their names and ages and how long they have been with her.

Before the parent leaves, another appointment should be made for the parent and the child to come for a visit. The purpose of the second visit is for the child to get to know the provider and her home better and to give the parent a chance to ask any other questions she might have. At the second visit the parent should bring back the contract and both copies can be signed. The parent should also return the questionnaire and discuss it with the provider.

Before the second meeting a few things can be prepared to make the child feel like he or she belongs to the group. These might include adding the child's name to all of the places that already have the names of the other children (hooks for clothes, box for belongings, washcloth).

When the parent and child arrive, the provider can show the child what she has prepared and take the child to the toy shelves to choose something to play with. Once the child is busy, the provider can serve tea, coffee, or juice. The parent may have questions she has thought of since the last visit, and the provider may have some about the questionnaire that the parent has filled in. Once these have been answered, a date for the child to begin family day care can be set. At this time, it is a good idea to tell the parent that it would be helpful for him or her to come with the child for the first few days and stay as long as possible. Often parents have to go to work and they are not free to take off the necessary time. If they can stay, however, it is reassuring to both the parent and the child.

THE FIRST FEW DAYS

The first routine to establish is the daily greeting and exchanging of news. The parent should be greeted every morning, asked how he or she is and how the child is, and the provider should expect and encourage answers. Some parents are slow to talk about themselves at first. They may be afraid the child is revealing the family's private affairs. Once they come to know and trust the provider, however, they appreciate being asked how they are every day.

Managing the child's first days away from the parent differs depending on the child's age. Being away from home is hard on all children, and although much can be done to ease it, every child can be expected to show some distress and worry.

The different behaviors that can be expected from different ages of children are discussed in Chapters 8, 9, 10, and 12 and to some degree in Chapters 13 and 14. This chapter discusses children's reactions to separation from their parents.

Infants up to 10 Months

This is probably the easiest age for a child to be put into family day care. Although there may be more crying, fussing, difficulty in feeding, and general sadness for a week or so, these infants can be soothed and comforted by holding, rocking, or singing. It also helps to have the parent bring a favorite blanket or toy, as well as the familiar bottle. Providers should not worry that they are spoiling the infant; they are really building trust, the kind of trust that will make later teaching much easier.

The older children in family day care need to be told that the baby is missing his or her Mommy and Daddy or whoever used to take care of the baby. The older children will probably remember when they first started in day care and understand that the provider must devote a little more time to comforting the new baby. They can be encouraged to play act or pretend that they are spending their first days in day care and they can talk about what they remember about their first days.

For the first few days almost constant care and comforting is needed, and then occasionally there may be a bad day, until finally the baby gets used to the family day care home and the daily separation from the parent. It should also be expected for the baby to cry when the parent comes at the end of the day. The parent needs to understand that during the day, the infant may be distracted and forget for a while that Mommy or Daddy or Granny is not there, but the moment that person reappears, all of those sad feelings come back. Some children are so overwhelmed with sadness when the parent returns, that they turn away from the parent.

Toddlers from 10 Months to $2\frac{1}{2}$ Years

Children of this age suffer intense fear and sadness when separated from the person who has always cared for them. They are not yet old enough to carry the memory of the person they love with them, nor can they remember from minute to minute that that person is coming back. A 1 year old or 18 month old will ask for "Momma" again and again. Each time the provider will say, "Yes, your Momma went to work, she is coming back to get you soon." The toddler will continue to say "Momma," until he or she is able to accept the provider's reassurance.

At this age children are afraid that they will never see that loved person again or have the comfort and safety of being held by that special person. Until the child becomes attached enough to the provider to be content with her comforting, life can be sad and miserable. This can be helped by asking the parent to stay as long as possible for the first few days. The child can get used to the new place while having the security of the parent there. It is also reassuring to the parent to see the provider at work. As she explains the child's behavior to the parent, she demonstrates her knowledge of child development.

If, because of a job or some other reason, the parent is unable to stay an hour or so for a few days, the provider must manage alone. The moment the parent leaves, the change in the child will be evident. Playing usually slows down or stops completely.

Some people think the best way to handle the situation is to distract the child from the person he or she is missing. *This is not true.* The child is reassured by everything that reminds him or her that Mommy is working but will come back soon and that in the meantime the provider knows how much he or she is missing Mommy. Avoiding the subject makes the child think the provider *wants* Mommy to be gone and then the fear and sadness become greater. Talking to the child about Mommy—where Mommy has gone, why Mommy must work, when Mommy will come back—builds a connection to that loved person and makes it easier for the provider to be loved and trusted as well.

It is important to be open and honest with the child. The more the child can trust the important adults in his or her life, the easier it is to manage that life. This is one reason that the parent must *never* sneak out. From the very first day, the parent must say good-bye, even when it causes crying and struggling to hold on to, or to go with, the parent. The provider's job is to help both the parents and the children manage these difficult days in ways that teach courage and respect for each other and for each others' feelings.

The parent can be asked to leave something that belongs to her or him with the child. A picture of the parent in the child's box of special belongings often helps. The provider should talk to the child about the parent and anyone else she knows who is a member of the child's family. A telephone call to Mommy is a big help. It reassures the child that Mommy is not gone forever and will return soon.

While the child is adjusting to being away from the parent, interesting activities often help. Anything the child can do and enjoy not only interests and amuses him or her but builds confidence. Confidence in one's competence and the ability to get over the sadness of separation are closely connected. New skills are especially important at this time. Toddlers can learn to string beads, build block towers, climb stairs, or do anything else that catches their interest. Learning anything new will help, and is the best treatment for the pain of separation that a provider can offer.

It is very important with toddlers as well as older children to expect very little of them during the period of adjustment. It is natural and usual for children who have been toilet trained to have accidents, and to revert to wetting or soiling themselves for a while. Babyish behavior is also natural. Toddlers and even older children want to be fed, or rocked, or even given a bottle. They will snatch toys away from other children, or hit at other children, or have tantrums. It often appears that they are using all of their strength just to deal with the sadness of missing the parent, and therefore have no strength left to act their ages. It helps in managing all of this undesirable behavior for the provider to say "I know you must be missing Mommy. I know you're going through a sad time." It does not help to punish or scold. The provider should simply clean the child who has wet or soiled himself or herself and cheerfully say "You'll soon be used to being here, and then you'll be able to make it to the toilet when you need to." The child who is snatching toys or hitting other children should be removed to a chair or the couch to sit quietly with the provider and talk about how hard it is to play nicely when one feels sad and lonely. The provider needs to be very helpful with the child who acts helpless and cannot feed or dress himself or herself. Showing tenderness makes this period pass more easily and quickly. Making demands makes it worse. The kinder the provider is, the sooner she can get the behavior she wants from the child.

With toddlers and even more with older children one can expect some of the other children to make fun of the new child's distress. Seeing the sadness of the new child reminds the other children of their own feelings during their first days in family day care. Often they can deal with those feelings best by laughing at them. They sometimes show off the fact that they now feel at home by saying things about cry-babies or by complaining about the new child's behavior. *They should not be permitted to hurt the new child's feelings.* They need to learn to show sympathy and understanding. The provider's example will help but it may also be necessary to say "It's hard to think back and remember how sad you were when you first came. It will help _____ (the new child) get used to us if we remember how it feels and be extra nice." The older children can be asked at different times to help the new child with something, to show the new child something. They need and will welcome help in dealing with their own feelings that are aroused by the new child's unhappiness. The provider might say to the other children " _____ (the new child) is doing this because he (or she) is not yet used to this place and to us. Remember when you first came, you weren't able to be yourself for a while either."

Finally, dress-up and pretend games allow the new child to play act feelings. Once these feelings are acted out, they become more manageable. Simple games like peekaboo and hide and seek are ways of pretending to go away and come back again (just what the child wants the parent to do). Dressing up with a hat or purse or briefcase or coat lets the child say goodbye then go away and then come back. When one acts out a story of the return it makes the story easier to believe in and the time pass more quickly until the parent does return.

Three Years and Older

Children of 3 years and older have the advantage of being able to talk about the pain of being away from loved ones. When one can talk about something, that thing always becomes more bearable. The provider can talk with children 3 years and older about what the parent is doing, what they want to remember to tell or ask the parent about. At this age, children seem able to remember through a long day that the parent *is* coming back to get them. These children, therefore, have an easier time adjusting to the first days away from home.

At the same time, there is a new problem that only begins when children reach 3 years and older. These children often feel that they are in day care because they are being punished for something they have done wrong or something they did that made the parent angry. Beginning at about age 2 when adults have to say "no" to children, the idea of being bad or being punished begins to worry children. Even children who are *not* punished worry about making the person they love angry. When the child and parent have had a bad morning, are very rushed, or get angry with each other, the child can feel all day that the parent is angry and therefore will not come back. Sometimes these feelings come out in pretend play. If not, the provider can just reassure the child, and when the occasion arises, say how helpful, good, or smart he or she is. Feeling good about oneself is good medicine for feeling sad.

Even 3 year olds go back to babyish behavior when under stress, and should not be expected to be well behaved in their first days in day care. Just as with the toddlers, the time to learn the rules and routines comes later. The first days should be devoted to building trust and confidence.

Throughout life we have to accept being away from people we love. No matter how old we get, we still feel the pain and it still helps to have someone reassure us that we are cared for and cared about. With help we can learn to live through these painful times.

Saying Good-bye

When it comes time to say good-bye to a child who is leaving the day care family, the whole process of beginning has to be done again in reverse. Endings need as much preparation as beginnings need adjustment, and it is just as important to end things well as it is to get off to a good start. This is true for the child as well as for the adult, and it is important for the family day care business.

There are many reasons for ending the care of a child. Some children leave the family day care home because their families have to move to another part of town, or because the mother stops work, or because the child simply outgrows the need for care. These reasons are not too difficult to deal with, nor are the preparations for them very upsetting.

The provider's main job is to show the child that even though they will no longer be seeing each other every day, they do not have to lose touch. If possible, the provider and child can plan to telephone each other from time to time, or if that is not practical, write letters. It also helps to have daily discussions about what the child will be doing after leaving day care. Plans for future meetings and visits can be made and everyone can join in the preparation of a good-bye party. After the child leaves the provider must call the child or write a card. Follow-through is very important. The first few days and weeks away are the hardest and the time when reminders are most needed. Having the other children take part will also help them prepare for the time when they, too, will have to leave the family day care home.

Other Reasons for Saying Good-bye

There are other more difficult reasons for a child to leave the family day care home. The provider may have agreed to take a child into her home and then later found that the child could not adapt or had severe personality problems or needs that the provider was unable or unwilling to meet. It may be difficult for the provider to admit that she, a professional, is unable or unwilling to keep a certain child. No one likes to admit failure, and to admit to oneself that a certain child is too difficult or too demanding to cope with is too close to admitting failure. There may also be the feeling that someone else could help this child. The provider may wonder what will become of the child, and even fear that the parents may criticize her to others.

There are actually only a few important questions to ask when considering telling the parent that the child must leave the day care home. Is the care of the other children suffering because of this one child's needs? Is the provider suffering as a result of trying to keep the child? If the answer to either of these questions is yes, then the child's parents must make other arrangements for their child.

The situation should be given careful consideration. Was the child given plenty of time to adjust? What are the child's real needs? (See Chapter

18 on recognizing special needs.) Is there any way that the days can be planned to meet the child's needs more adequately? Was the parent aware of the child's special needs before? Have any of these difficulties been discussed with the parent? Has the parent offered any helpful ideas?

Before termination is mentioned, a few conferences with the parent need to be scheduled in order to give her a chance to make suggestions and get used to the idea that it may be necessary to find other day care for the child. The provider should not say she will dismiss the child if things do not improve. She has two aims to accomplish. The first is to figure out whether she *can* work out a way to keep the child, and the second is to help the parent do the best she can for her child.

The first step is to arrange a meeting with the parent when the provider can talk with her alone. (Chapter 6 describes how to organize and conduct these meetings.) Then the provider can ask the parent about the child. If the parent does not mention any of the behaviors that are a problem, the provider will have to ask the parent about the particular behavior, when it began, and what the parent feels is the cause. The parent may claim never to have had the problem. The provider must then say that she had hoped the parent would be able to help her understand these behaviors so that she could keep the child. This should make the parent want to help in order to have the child continue in day care. The provider should offer any ideas she has. If she gets no cooperation or if she feels (after reading Chapter 6) that these problems will take too much time and effort to resolve and will interfere with her care of the other children then she should schedule another meeting with the parent. She should not announce her purpose in advance, because the parent may either put off or avoid the meeting. The provider should simply say that she needs to have another talk with the parent.

The second meeting can begin with a very clear and uncritical description of the child's needs as the provider sees them. She can explain how difficult it is for her to meet these needs and those of the other children in her care. She should have a few suggestions ready to give the parent. It is not a good idea to leave the parent with the feeling that she has no place to go or that no one can help. Perhaps this particular child needs the care of someone who has no other children to look after. Perhaps there is a community mental health clinic that could help (see Chapter 18 for more ideas). The provider can offer to keep the child for one more week to allow the parent time to make other arrangements. All of these suggestions show concern for the parent and the child and leave the parent feeling the provider is a caring person and not a person to be angry with or to criticize.

The provider should try to figure out what the parent's reaction to the first meeting is going to be. Some parents may go home and tell the child that he or she will be punished if there is any more trouble. The provider wants to make sure that the parent understands that her child needs help, lots of help, not punishment. The provider should try and find out if the child is being punished or threatened, and, if so, quickly arrange another meeting or simply take a few minutes to talk with the parent and make sure he or she understands that the child can not cure the problem alone, and will need the help of the parent and the provider.

As soon as an agreement has been reached with the parent, the child should be told about it. Unless the child is under 3 years old, the situation needs to be explained carefully and often. The child can be told that because the provider has so many children to care for, she cannot do certain things for him or her that seem to be needed. The parent will find someone who can help with these special needs until the child can get over them. The child will naturally be angry and upset with the provider. This is to be expected. The provider can explain that she understands and that she feels bad, too, but that she is sure that the parent will figure out a better arrangement for the child. The provider needs to be as supportive of the child and the parent as she can, for the sake of child, the parent, and herself.

The End of Each Day

The end of the day is the time when everyone is tired and most apt to come apart at the seams. This is the hardest part of the day to plan for, but some of the problems that arise can be avoided by careful planning. It is important to remember that every good-bye is difficult, even little daily good-byes. The children are excited to see their parents after having been away from them all day; but they are also sorry to leave the games and friends and the provider. These feelings are upsetting and make it easy to be irritable and cross. As with all feelings, they are easier to manage if they can be talked about without worrying about being criticized or laughed at. It helps to remind the children to tell Mommy about a particular thing they enjoyed or did well, or what is planned for the next day. It also helps to give them something to take home to Mommy—a picture, a cookie, a poem neatly copied or made up.

Learning to live with others is never easy. Learning to say good-bye is even harder.

4

Providing Room for Family Day Care

Everyone has his or her own particular ideas about space and how space should be used. For some people, all empty spaces need to be filled, and two families of three generations each will often decide to share a small house out of *choice*. For other people, it is difficult just to share a bathroom with the other members of the family. In some parts of the world when people talk to each other they stand so close together that their noses almost touch. In other parts of the world people may be so upset when someone stands or moves too close that they either back off or shove the other person away. The degree of closeness to others that we allow is called our "life space."

There are times when we want the ones we love to be close, to be in our life space. Most people do not feel that babies invade their life space; indeed, we pick them up and hold them close. When toddlers lean against our legs or climb into our laps we do not feel invaded. At some point, however, we begin to realize that children are grown-up enough to have their own life space and to respect ours.

The space we live in—our home—is, in another way, our life space. How we organize it and maintain it depends on our own ideas about space as well as what we have to work with. When we decide to take children into our life space we have to take into consideration more than just our own or our family's needs. Our home then becomes a work place.

ORGANIZING FOR FAMILY DAY CARE

How a provider organizes her own place depends a great deal on the place itself. In planning how she is going to use it, whether it is a house, an apartment, or a trailer, she needs to think about four things: 1) safety; 2) efficiency; 3) independence; and 4) comfort.

Safety

It is a fact that more injuries occur in the home than anywhere else, including automobiles, planes, and all other vehicles combined. Most, if not all, of these injuries can be prevented. There are several kinds of home injuries.

Poison *All poisoning can be prevented.* The provider should begin in the kitchen and make sure there are no cleaning materials where young children can reach them. The usual place for dishwashing and other cleaning equipment is under the sink. When there are young children in the home, all cleaning materials should be placed in a high cabinet, and unbreakable refrigerator containers, waxed paper, plastic wrap, and other harmless items put in the low cabinets.

The kitchen should also be checked for other dangerous edibles. Vitamins or other medication belong in cabinets out of sight and out of reach. A kitchen closet in which supplies are stored should be kept locked at all times.

The bathroom has as many possible poisons as the kitchen. All medicines must be locked up. Any cabinet under the washbasin or otherwise within children's reach should be checked to make sure that there are no possible poisons. The other rooms in the house are less apt to contain poisons, although they should be checked for vitamins, medicines, or cosmetics that children are likely to eat or drink. What children will eat or drink is as amazing to adults as some of the things adults eat and drink are to children.

Finally, a provider is not expected to repaint her entire home, but if there is any peeling paint, it should be scraped and repainted and she should make sure she is using lead-free paint. All toys, cribs, and other furniture should be checked. The law requires all toys for children to be free of lead paint, but old toys may need a coat of lead-free paint.

Cuts and Burns The kitchen is, of course, the biggest hazard. All knives and breakable cookware such as Pyrex and oven-to-table china must be kept in the top cabinets. Plastic glasses, plates, and cups are safe and practical and do not break easily. The provider should take a tour of all cabinets that are within a child's reach. In the bathroom, there may be bottles, razors, or glasses within children's reach. These must be put away. Paper or plastic cups should be used in the bathroom as well as in the kitchen.

Next, the provider should consider the possibility of burns. There are four major sources of burns: 1) the stove; 2) heaters; 3) hot water and electrical appliances; and 4) wiring. If she is cooking soup or something else that cooks for a long time, it should be put on a back burner with the handles of the pot turned to the back of the stove. (Even when she is in the kitchen, the provider should keep the handles of the pots turned to the back of the stove.) Hot food should never be carried to the sink to drain when the children are nearby. Finally, even older children should not be allowed to do any cooking unless the provider is in the kitchen.

Radiators and heaters are another common source of burns. Radiator covers can be bought cheaply and will protect children from burns. Heaters are a bigger problem. It is better to put extra sweaters and socks on children than to use portable heaters. If necessary, the bathroom can be heated before bathing the child and then the heater can be removed when the bath is ready. Children can be covered well in the bed rather than have the bedroom very warm.

A plumber can adjust the hot water so that it is never hot enough to scald a child. If scalding hot water is needed in the kitchen, a mixer can be installed in the bathroom washbasin so that the children can develop good hand-washing habits without the risk of burns.

It takes imagination to think about all the ways in which electrical wiring can cause injuries. Burns, shocks, and falls are common. Furniture should be placed in front of wall plugs when possible. Socket covers can be bought at the dime store for unused wall outlets. Wires from lamps, radios, televisions, toasters, and other electrical appliances should not lie where people walk or infants and toddlers crawl. Little children are captivated by the idea of "off" and "on" and cannot resist making things such as "light" and "dark" happen. Once they have seen how you turn a lamp off and on, it will occur to them one day to give it a try. If the toaster is within reach, it may be too interesting to resist. Each room can be checked for electrical hazards and made safe for little children.

Matches and cigarettes or other smoking equipment are unhealthy for everyone and a serious source of burns for children. Matches should be kept out of sight and reach at all times.

Falls The most common accident in the home is a fall. For children, falls are part of growing up. There are even some old wives' tales about how every child must have at least one fall. It was probably invented to comfort a mother. If all bad falls could be prevented, children would benefit immensely. Preventing falls cannot be done simply by arranging space. Children will climb; it is, in fact, a necessary experience of early childhood. The only way to keep children from climbing would be to remove all furniture from the home. Because that is not practical, the next best way is supervision. Although it is not possible to watch all of the children all of the time, one can keep an eye on the child in the high chair, the infant or toddler on the couch, and the child running on a slippery floor. Scatter rugs, step ladders, and straight chairs that tip easily should be put away or given away. Windows need guards so a child cannot fall out. If there are stairs in the home, gates are needed at the top and the bottom until all of the children in the home are old enough to walk up and down safely.

Finally, breakables should be removed to high places for their own sake and for the sake of the children. Some adults seem almost to enjoy saying "no" to children all day. They pride themselves on teaching their children not to touch certain things. Professional child caregivers are more interested in having children learn what they *can* do than in what they can*not* do. Children respect an occasional "no"; they become deaf to a day filled with "no's." A safe home offers very few "no's" and is easy on the child's and the provider's nerves.

Efficiency

Everyone knows how pleasing and relaxing it is to be in an attractive, neat home. It is also known that a well-organized business with everything that is needed close at hand runs efficiently. The provider's job is to combine the two. She wants her home to be pleasant, comfortable, and, at the same time, organized so that her work is easy and efficient. To do this, she needs to plan and arrange every room very carefully so that every square foot serves at least one purpose and, often, two or three.

The first step is to look at what her work needs are. The provider must be able to provide eating, sleeping, and play space for as many children as she plans to care for. Because the easiest part is apt to be the sleeping space, the provider might begin there.

Sleep Space Children up to age 6 need a place to take a nap. Babies take more than one nap a day; very young infants spend a good part of the day in their cribs. Ideally, all of the sleeping arrangements should fit into one or two rooms so that these rooms can be darkened and controlled for noise. Having a quiet room for nap time also makes it clear to the children that when they go into the room they must be quiet.

Children no longer in danger of rolling out of bed can sleep in adult beds. If the provider uses her bed or the bed of someone in the family, she needs a sheet and blanket reserved for each child who uses the family's beds. The sheet can then be spread over the bedspread, and the child can be given a blanket or other cover especially for his or her use.

For the infants and children still in cribs, it is necessary to provide either cribs or beds with sides. Portable sides that tie onto a bed are not practical because they are not secure and are too small once the child is 1 year old or a little older. A crib—which can be used until the child is toilet trained at night and is no longer in danger of rolling out of bed onto the floor—is practical and takes up very little space. If a crib for each infant in day care will fit in the same bedroom, only one area needs to be darkened and kept quiet. Cribs should be placed away from windows unless the windows have guards or are screened and are not drafty and have no blinds with cords hanging. Many of us have heard stories about a child who was hanged or strangled by window blind cords.

The bedroom has other uses as well. Children often need a place to be alone, to calm down, or just to play quietly away from the other children. The bedroom is the place they can go to look at a book, or play a quiet game alone, or even just sit and think. If there is an infant, however, who sleeps much of the day in the bedroom, it is necessary to find another quiet place and make the bedroom off limits for the other children. Some children have a greater need to be quiet and alone than others and should feel free to go into a quiet room whenever they want to. There can be a shelf or box of books to look at, quiet games to play with alone, favorite sleep things (blanket, stuffed animals, etc.), and each child's sheet and blanket. Finally, for soothing infants, comforting children, having a quiet time with each child alone, or simply as a place to sit and relax, a rocking chair is ideal.

Bathroom If there are infants or toddlers, and if the bathroom is large enough, a changing table should be close to the bathroom sink. It is easier for the provider to wash the child and her hands after changing the child if it is close to the sink. If the bathroom is too small, she may have to arrange the changing table just outside the bathroom or near the kitchen sink. For sanitary reasons and to save steps, the diaper pail (or garbage can for disposable diapers) should be in the bathroom close to the changing table.

Living Room Unless the provider has a very large home, her living room is apt to be the children's playroom as well. The toys, games, and equipment for non-messy activities are best kept on shelves in the room in which they are used. The furniture can be arranged to divide the room into several play spaces—a space with a rug or carpet for blocks, another space for pretend games with a basket of dress-up things, a low table and chairs, shelves for puppets and dolls and other pretend equipment, and, finally, a safe place with a table for projects, games, and homework away from the younger children. The dining table is perfect for this. It should have a large plastic cloth to protect it and to wipe clean easily. (Messy activities like painting, clay, Play-Doh, pasting, and cutting are best done on the kitchen table.) How the room is divided to provide different spaces will depend upon the size and shape of the room. However it is arranged, there should be a comfortable chair for the provider with a good view of all of the spaces. (If she has an infant, this might be a good place for a rocking chair.) She can then keep an eye on the various activities, make comments on their progress, offer suggestions or ask questions, and be available to answer the children's questions or step in before a dispute gets out of hand. She needs a place to put an infant seat so the infant can observe the older children and she can observe the infant. If the baby is crawling or learning to creep, she will need to protect the older children's games. Even if there are toys on a blanket on the floor, the infant will want to join the older children, always more interesting than even the most creative toys. If the older children are busy playing and the infant is awake and sociable, an infant seat, bouncy chair, or swing (depending upon the infant's age) is safer than the freedom of the floor. Infants are rarely content in any of these for more than a few minutes, however and should not be left for long periods of time. After a short while, the provider will need to arrange a space for the infant which is away from the children's games, but which allows the infant some freedom to move about.

Independence

Helping children become independent is an important part of the professional provider's work. Since the drive for independence is already present from infancy, the provider's job is to arrange the space and the equipment in such a way that the child's natural drive can be encouraged. Beginning at a few months, babies try to hold their own bottles. Infants try to feed themselves (usually with their bare hands). Toddlers want to dress themselves, pour their own milk, wash their own faces. Some adults interfere with these natural behaviors because the child's efforts are too messy, too slow, or even sometimes because the adult enjoys doing things for the baby and does not want to give up that pleasure. Providers, however, should be happy to see the young children in their care become independent and encourage their efforts by being patient and tolerant. Space can be used to encourage independence and make the provider's job easier at the same time.

The Bedroom—A Quiet Place There should be a place to keep each child's sheet, cover, pillow, nap toy, or blanket so that it is available to the child without help. The provider should introduce each child to a routine for nap time so that she does not need to give directions or interfere. Each child's shoes and socks should always go in the same place.

The Bathroom Each child's washcloth, small towel, toothbrush, toothpaste, and soap should be within reach, including toddlers who may need help with the toothbrush and toothpaste even with a step to stand on at the sink. Toddlers will need a potty chair. A potty seat that must be put on the toilet each time the toddler needs it makes extra work for the provider and does not encourage the child's independence.

The bathroom should have low, very steady stools by the toilet and sink for the small children. Toilet paper should be easy to reach for even a very small child. Hooks for each child's wash cloth and towel should be placed low enough for the children to reach and rehang their cloths unaided.

The bathroom should have a mirror in which the child can easily see themselves (best of all is a big door mirror) to check for clean faces, to comb hair, or simply to admire themselves. This encourages good grooming, and self-help skills, and it helps children learn about how they look.

There should be no lock on the bathroom door so that it is not possible to lock it from the inside.

The Kitchen This room as much as any other is rich in opportunities to learn independence, but it requires a lot of planning in order to encourage self-help and, at the same time, simplify the provider's job. If the kitchen is too small for a table and there are enough chairs for everyone, the provider can put the table in an area next to the kitchen. The table can then be used for eating, preparing food, and doing messy art work. The floor can be covered in linoleum or something else that is easy to clean with a damp mop.

There are many meal-related jobs that children can do, should do, enjoy doing, and learn from doing. If the table setting equipment is kept in the low cabinets, small children can set the table for meals and snacks. Older children (tall enough to see into the sink) can clear the table after meals. The children can take turns washing and drying dishes if they are unbreakable. This is the best possible water play.

Five year olds and up can prepare morning and afternoon snacks with no assistance at all unless everyone is going to have tea or chocolate or something else hot. Even 10 to 12 year olds should not cook on the stove unless the provider is in the kitchen supervising.

Once the children have learned the simple skills required, they can do a great deal of food preparation. It adds to their independence, their competence, and the provider's free time. Spreading sandwiches, breaking and beating eggs, grating cabbage and carrots, rolling all kinds of dough, beating and spreading frosting—all of these and lots more are entertaining learning experiences for children. If each activity is introduced carefully, the children can do it with little mess or risk of accident.

The kitchen is also the best place for painting, clay work, and cutting and pasting. The kitchen table and the floor under it can be sponged clean. For 2, 3, and 4 year olds, the floor is usually a better place to paint. Little children cannot work on a table unless they are in a chair and then they are apt to become so interested in the painting that they can fall off the adult-sized chair. Unless the provider has an easel, the floor spread with newspaper is the best place for the paint pots, paper, and brushes.

Clay is stored in covered cans and kept with the other supplies (paint, paper, scissors, paste, and small dishes or cups to pour paint into). The children can learn how to set up an activity such as painting by themselves, beginning with newspaper spread on the table or floor. They can also learn to put everything away and then sponge off the table and, if necessary, the floor. Besides the many activities that take place at the kitchen table, there are important social events as well. During and after meals, art and cooking activities, or games when everyone or a small group is seated together, the situation is ideal for talking over plans, ideas, thoughts, or events. Often the kitchen table is the place in the house where the most important exchanges take place and where people sit after the meal is finished to continue a discussion. The provider can encourage this kind of socializing by allowing plenty of time, by not rushing to clean up, and by sitting with the children, relaxed and interested in what they are saying and doing.

Living Room–Playroom When asked what comes to mind when they think of children's play, most adults would say "a mess!" which is true unless the children are able to clean up when the play is over. Having children learn to put things away is a matter of making it easy and pleasant, not making it a painful job. Even little children can put things away if there are places to put them that are easy to reach.

After the furniture in the room to be used as a playroom has been arranged into three separate areas, storage space for equipment in each area needs to be found. The most practical places for encouraging independence are on low shelves. These can be made from planks and cinder blocks or bricks, or can be bought unpainted or in sections. Once stained and varnished, they are very attractive. For the toys that are not simply stacked on shelves (like blocks), boxes or baskets are needed. Baskets are becoming cheaper all the time and are very decorative. Boxes can be cartons covered with the contact paper that looks like finished wood. These are also very attractive. The boxes should not be so large that once they are full they are too heavy to lift. Smaller boxes or baskets that hold only one kind of toy each make putting things away easier and encourage children to sort things by category.

BLOCK AREA Blocks are the most useful of all children's toys. All ages play with them differently, but enthusiastically. The area reserved for block play should have a rug or piece of carpet to cut down on the noise of falling blocks.

Other toys in the block area should include some cars, trucks, trains, boats, planes, people, animals, and small furniture. These should be kept in smaller boxes. Sorting them to put them away is an important learning game.

PRETEND AREA The most important furniture here is a child-sized table and chairs. This serves dozens of pretend uses. It can be a table in a restaurant, in a Wild West saloon, in a home, a desk at school, the check-in desk at a hotel or an airport, the counter in a store, and, turned on its side, can become a stage for puppets. The other main furniture prop is a doll bed large enough for a child up to about age 3 or 4 to get in. Kitchen furniture is *not* important and teaches roles less suited to today than to farm life 50 years ago. The real kitchen offers all of the opportunities for kitchen activities needed.

Also needed is a basket of costumes for pretending—hats, purses, briefcases, ties, high heels, capes, and any other old clothes from the closets of adults. Other pretend equipment includes a box for pads and pencils, a tablecloth, napkins, dishes, and pillows and blankets for the doll bed. The doll bed also needs a few dolls, at least one for each child (girls and boys). Doll clothes for each doll add to the play and also teach dressing and undressing skills.

GAMES AND PROJECTS   The third area in the living room–playroom is centered around the dining table and is mainly for the use of school-age children. If there is not enough space for a dining table, the kitchen table area will do. The equipment for this area can be stored in cabinets, out of sight. It should include board games, puzzles in boxes, paper and crayons, pencils, felt tip pens, toothpicks, glue, paper dolls, sewing and knitting equipment, and equipment for hobbies of the older children (these might be model building, shell or rock collecting, or whatever the children's current interests are).

The board games and puzzles are self-contained. The other things require boxes. Clear plastic boxes from the dime store (sold in the closet department) are excellent for the rest of the equipment. These boxes and games can be stacked in a sideboard, closet, or cabinet.

Other Storage and Hang Up Areas   Each child needs a place to put outdoor clothing, coats, hats, boots, mittens, and personal belongings. Hooks, arranged at eye level in an entry way or in a closet with each child's name above one hook, are fine. A box for each child's private and personal belongings should be kept where the child can get it. The provider can put the child's name on it; then, each child can decorate his or her own box with drawings, pictures cut out and pasted on, or contact or gift wrapping paper, according to individual taste.

Comfort

Being comfortable in one's home takes much more than a big soft chair. Even the softest chair with pillows and a footstool is not comfortable if one does not feel relaxed. Only after all safety precautions have been taken and each room checked for hazards will the provider be able to relax.

Unless the home is efficiently arranged, however, the provider will find herself jumping up every few minutes to get or to do something. If each room is organized so that everything that is needed or that the children are using is close at hand, then the provider's work will be easier and she will have the leisure time to sit, observe the children, and take pride in her work.

Efficiency requires regular changes, of course. As the children grow older or new ones come, what was an efficient arrangement before no longer is. New ideas to suit new children's needs or merely to improve on the old arrangement will occur from time to time. As the children master the skills required for the old routines, the provider will be able to plan new and more efficient arrangements. As these ideas occur, they should be noted in the planning book so that when the time comes, the provider will be able to refer to them and remember what changes she thought of making.

To be comfortable one needs to feel one is doing a good job. When the provider has created a space in which children develop independence and competence, she can be satisfied about that part of her job. A sense of independence and competence spills over into other parts of the personality and makes for general feelings of well being. The pride and pleasure she takes in each child will be communicated to that child and, more than any praise she offers, will give that child a sense of contentment. That and her own contentment and satisfaction with the job create a general sense of comfort for everyone.

The Effects of Comfort When the children are busy playing, resting, talking together, or reading and the provider is sitting in her comfortable chair, relaxed and rested, she can do some very important things. She can, for instance:

>   Have a face-to-face conversation with a child
>   Dream up a great project for the child who does not have one
>   Read a story to a tired and cross child
>   Catch up on recordkeeping
>   Sew a new dress for a doll
>   Read an "Advice to Parents" article in a magazine
>   Discuss with a child how to make friends
>   Get someone started knitting
>   Pay some bills
>   Listen to someone's reading homework
>   Work on next week's shopping list
>   Talk with a child about what she or he wants to be some day
>   Look at each child and think about the child's possibilities and how she is making these possibilities become realities

A Learning Place One of the people who has contributed the most to our understanding of children, Sibylle Escalona, once said that it just is not possible for a day care center classroom to provide for a young child the variety of learning experiences that the ordinary home can and does. More than the games, activities, and projects that are provided, the variety of things that are done with and around children each day in the home make it the richest learning place an infant or toddler can have. The everyday activities of the home that children experience include:

    Helping sort laundry
    Listening to adult telephone conversations
    Going to the supermarket
    Helping fold laundry
    Helping prepare food
    Listening to the provider's conversations with the parents
    Helping vacuum and polish furniture
    Watching the provider hem and mend and then learning how
    Learning about the provider's hobbies and interests

Many day care centers try to imitate the home. They have "housekeeping corners," and they organize trips to stores or cooking projects. There is one big difference, however. These activities are not for real. They are pretend. What the children in family day care observe, discuss, and do are all real-life experiences that teach them how to get along in the real world. As the provider explains what she is doing and why and answers their questions, the children are learning how people function in the real world, what it takes to get along with people, how to succeed at what you set out to do, and understand what is happening around them. No other setting, no matter how well planned, can equal the richness of a home for infants and young children. The light switch that goes off and on, the faucet that turns the water on and off, the cover to hide under and then peek out of, the cabinet to crawl into, the kitchen pots to stack and bang, the couch to crawl around and hide behind, the older children to watch and imitate, the telephone to make noises into, and the millions of other possibilities all together make a rich world for an infant and toddler to learn in. The learning experiences of each age are discussed in the chapters devoted to each age. All of these possibilities are found in the home, the place our civilization has invented to give the best possible beginning to the citizen of tomorrow.

5

Providing and Planning Activities

Everyone has had the experience of going to the store without first making a list and forgetting to buy something important, like salt or paper towels, and having to make a second trip or else having to do without. The time spent making that second trip could have been spent doing something useful or restful. It takes very little time to make a plan, and it saves a great deal of time. If one is going to make a pie and gets all the ingredients together first, it is quickly and easily done. If, instead, one has to run around in the midst of trying to put it together to look for one missing ingredient, it is very likely the pie will not turn out as well, and it will surely end up taking much longer to make than if it had been planned ahead. Planning saves time, effort, and, most important, wear and tear on everyone's nerves.

A PLAN FOR EVERYBODY

The provider is responsible for meeting the needs of several different people. The only way to schedule time to accomplish this is to plan how and when. This might include time to have a talk with one of the children about a family crisis, time to take another child to the dentist, time to help another with a homework project, and at least 30 minutes of rest for the provider each day. All of these needs can be accommodated, but only if the provider has figured them out in advance and has made a master plan.

THE MORE PLANNING, THE MORE POSSIBILITIES

When dealing with other people it is not possible to know exactly what to expect, and one needs to be able to change plans easily. A child may develop a bad cold, so the day care family cannot go to the park as planned. If the provider has another at-home plan ready, she can respond to the children's disappointment with an alternate activity. The provider may have bought the ingredients to make cupcakes at home before learning that a child has to be picked up from school later than usual. If she has thought it out in advance, she can give everyone a small box or jar and take the day care family for a walk to collect leaves or rocks on the way to the school. These ideas are hard to come up with on the spur of the stressful moment, but if the provider has spent a little time writing down the ideas that occur to her and a list of what she needs to carry them out, she is ready for anything. Planning multiplies the possibilities.

CRISIS PLANNING

In even the best organized life there are crises—a child becomes suddenly ill or falls off the jungle gym; there is a power failure and no electricity, or there is a storm and the water is cut off. The provider needs a plan in order to function well in time of crisis. For illness or accident, she needs to know what to do immediately, without having to go to a first aid book. If she has studied Chapters 16 and 17, she will know by heart what to do in case of illness or accident. She will also have the telephone numbers she needs in case of an emergency on the wall by the telephone, and she will have a plan for what to do with the other children while she is occupied with the emergency. All of this requires split-second timing, which is impossible without advance preparation. When her plans require the help of others (as in dealing with an emergency), she needs to have a couple of rehearsals with the other people involved. If she depends on the services of the local hospital emergency room, she should make an advance trip to find out the routine and to introduce herself to the guards and the people at the front desk. She needs to know how to get the quickest possible help. Planning saves valuable time when minutes count (see Chapter 17).

ONLY THE WELL-ORGANIZED BUSINESS SUCCEEDS

There is one final reason why the provider needs to plan—no business can succeed without adequate planning. Both short-term and long-range planning are necessary.

SEPTEMBER

SUN	MON	TUES	WED	THURS	FRI	SAT
					1	2
3	4 Dan-wash Sarah-dry Todd-set table	5 Ricci's class day	6	7 P's brownies	8 Make cookies for tea	9 Tea with Sis' parents
10	11 George-wash Todd-dry Dan-set table	12 Take children to hear band in park	13 Library	14 P's brownies	15 G's grandmother to visit	16
17 Church supper	18 Sarah-wash Dan-dry George-set table	19	20 Library	21 Dentist for G. + T. P's brownies	22	23
24	25 Todd-wash George-dry Sarah-set table	26	27 Library	28 P's brownies	29 All day picnic if weather good	30

Figure 10.

Providing and Planning Activities

HOW TO PLAN

Plans should be recorded in two places: 1) in a book such as school teachers use for lesson plans or in a large appointment book with plenty of room to write plans, notes, shopping lists, and other reminders for each day; and 2) on a large wall calender with plenty of space for the provider *and* the children to write several things in each day's space (Figure 10). This should be hung on a wall where everyone can see it and write on it. A pencil on a string hanging from the same hook as the calendar encourages everyone to make notes.

PLANNING BOOK

The Business

The business should be taken care of first. In the planning book, the provider writes everything that must be done each month, every 3 months, and every year. This includes paying rent or mortgage, telephone, gas, electricity, insurance, and taxes (most people who are self-employed must make payments every 3 months). If the provider is part of an agency, she has reports (such as attendance) to send in and, if USDA money is available, menus as well. It helps to have a reminder noting when these are due. Any scheduled visits from agency staff such as annual fire or health department inspections or visits from the family day care supervisor should also be in the appointment book and on the wall calendar. That way, whatever preparations are required can be made well in advance.

The provider should check when holidays will occur and make a note to speak to the parents about whether the children should come on those days. Each child's birthday should go in the book and on the calendar with a reminder a week in advance. As soon as vacation plans are made, they should be entered and the parents given plenty of warning. If the provider is taking 2 weeks in August, she should tell the parents in the spring so that they can make their plans match. The provider needs to make a note to schedule her own dental appointment every 6 months and her complete medical checkup once a year. Finally, she should write a note to remind herself to make an appointment with each child's parents for a private meeting once in the fall and once in the spring.

Having taken care of the long-range planning, she can look at the week ahead. Some errands such as going to the cleaners, laundry, grocery store, post office, and drug store occur regularly, and the day can be planned in advance. If only one or two of these errands are done at a time, it is possible to take the children along, making it an outing as well as a learning experience.

Providers who live in cities may walk the children to school, in some towns they may take them in the car. Either way, shopping and doing errands can be done on the way home. She can write in her planning book which errands she wants to do each day, keeping in mind the problem of carrying packages. She may have to arrange deliveries for some of the shopping and only bring home the things that will spoil or are needed immediately. An important part of planning is having enough supplies on hand to be flexible about which day to shop. Bad weather, a child with a bad cold, or an expected repairman may mean changing plans. If the provider has a closet stocked with supplies such as tuna fish, powdered milk, cocoa mix, ingredients for corn bread, biscuits, cookies, or cakes, canned fruit, and so forth, she can put off shopping when other things need to be considered. Project supplies such as paper, paste, ingredients for cookies, and paints should also be kept on hand to bring out when a planned trip has to be cancelled or a special treat is in order.

It is a good idea to make shopping lists for food when planning the week's menus (see Chapter 19). These menus and lists will include the provider's own needs and her own family's as well. When shopping, she should remember to keep a record of all the food costs for the business, save the slips in a box, and write the totals in the ledger. All other business-related expenses (drug store, hardware, laundry) should also be recorded in the ledger and the slips kept in a box.

The Children

Many things that the children do every day are part of each day's routine and therefore do not need planning. Nap time, setting the table, bathing the children, cleaning up, and snacks are some of the things that are done the same time every day and are part of everyday activities. Children need these routines and adapt to them easily. Even new children quickly learn to expect what happens next and feel secure in knowing what they will do and when. From time to time a schedule of these routines can be made to see how much time they take so that free time can be planned carefully. Figure 11 is a sample of a day's routine.

Once the routines are running smoothly, the provider will know how much time she can plan for. Special activities such as a child's trip to the dentist or to the health clinic, a school fair, an older brother or sister's performance in a play will take the place of the planned activities from time to time. The daily routines will change, as well, when an infant goes from a feeding every 4 hours to three meals a day, or a toddler gives up a morning nap (which meant the family stayed home), or the preschooler becomes a first grader and stays in school until 3 p.m., or the school-aged child joins the girl scouts or tries out for the school band and has practice after school.

MORNING SCHEDULE

	Before 8	8-9	9-10	10-11	11-12
Lanny (infant)	Greet, change. Down for nap	Nap—	Bathe then cereal and bottle	In carriage	Home around 11:45 - Nap in carriage
Cheryl (age 2)	Breakfast. Begin special activity	Washes dishes while I clean house	Snack time. C. helps to prepare	Outdoors for everyone. Walk to playground then errands on the way home: get supplies for D+H's building	Everyone cleans up and helps with lunch
Dennis (age 4)	Building large school with blocks	Continue building	Return to building		
Herbie (age 4½)					
Jenny (age 9)	Breakfast then leave for school	. . . . .			

Figure 11.

The routines also change when one child cannot go outside for a few days or another child needs help with a big school project. These changes are taken into account when the week's plans are made. Although the time allowed for each activity varies according to the kind of activity, the kinds of activities do not vary. They include outdoor, indoor, active, quiet, art, music, literature, social skills, self-care skills, school readiness, homework, getting to know the city, community, or town, physical culture, group games, private conversations, and individual projects. These activities overlap. For instance, an outdoor activity can be active, involve a group, and include physical culture, all at once. An indoor activity can be quiet, be an individual project, and include music. The more kinds of activity involved, the better the plan. Including all kinds of activities gives the children a rich and interesting life, and makes the provider's more interesting as well.

Each day should include some active, noisy games as well as some quiet, soothing activities. Quiet times are scheduled when infants or toddlers

AFTERNOON SCHEDULE

	12-2	2-3	3-4	4-5	After 5
Lanny	Watches the children	Lunch and play time	In carriage to walk to school	On floor or in seat	Feed - Ready for home
Cheryl	Lunch if awake, otherwise later	Smack, then help with putting things away.	Everyone to park to play on gyms. Stop in at police station on the way home.	Play with paper, crayons and paste	Read to all the children. Cheryl needs toy to be quiet. Plan for another day's activities
Dennis					
Herbie					
Jenny	Here for lunch then back to school	Walk to meet Jenny		Talk with J. about school - help with homework	

Cont.

are napping, and just before going home. Active play should include some time each day spent outside playing the games that demand and develop physical strength and coordination. In every week's plan a new skill should be introduced or time allowed for the mastery of an old skill. Most importantly, each child's special interests and needs should be taken into account. The chapters on each stage of development (Chapters 9 through 14) describe the particular needs of each age. Only the provider, however, can know the current interests of each child in her care as well as the developmental needs of each one of the children. Each week's as well as each day's plans should take these into consideration. Plans are made for people; people are not made to fit into plans. As the provider considers each kind of activity, she must think about which children will benefit most from each, and which will suit the special needs of each child. An activity planned with a particular child in mind can also interest several other children. At other times the children's interests will vary so much that two or more activities will be needed at the

Providing and Planning Activities

same time. This can work well if the activities are organized so that the provider is available to assist or make suggestions to each child when needed. The following is a description of the kinds of activities to include in the weekly planning.

OUTDOOR ACTIVITIES

As a nation we are overweight, and many of us are in poor physical condition. We love sports—but mostly on television. Our schools are full of children who are already overweight and physically lazy, and are well on the road to a life of inactivity and all of the illnesses that inactivity and overweight bring. What is the cure? The cure is to care for our bodies. This means not only taking care of our bodies, but also caring for them in the sense of being proud of them, and liking them very much. This should begin when toddlers first become aware of their bodies. Pediatricians now believe that if toddlers are not allowed to become overweight the chances are that they will not become overweight as children or even as adults. (In Chapter 19 on nutrition there are suggestions for menus and snacks that are healthy and low in calories.)

Good physical condition, however, requires more than being slim. It includes developing muscles and learning to be strong and coordinated.

Children of all ages can enjoy the physical exercise of playing in playgrounds. Slides, swings, see-saws, and jungle gyms appeal to children of all ages. Older children can jump rope, run relay races, and play tag or dodge ball. Some may prefer team sports. If the school offers these in the afternoon some children may want to join. The provider can find out how the parents feel about lessons in sports, and if possible, encourage them. If there is a "Y" or other club nearby, the parents may permit tennis, swimming, or judo lessons.

The provider can do two things to make sure her children are in good physical shape. The first is to encourage the children to take an interest and pride in their bodies. She does this by talking with them about their bodies—how the body works, what food it needs to be healthy and strong, how to develop certain muscles. The children can be measured regularly and a record kept on a chart where they can see it. Not only their height should be measured, but also the size of their chest, upper arm, and thighs, when they are relaxed, then again when they "make a muscle."

The second thing the provider can do to show the importance of physical exercise is to take the children out every day if possible. She can take them somewhere where they can play *hard*. She may need to help them to organize games that require real effort. If she gives lots of praise for *effort*, and not just for skill, they will enjoy trying. When the weather or something else keeps the children from going outside, the provider can organize exercises on the carpet, such as sit-ups, jumping jacks, or running in place. The children can take turns suggesting exercises, or everyone can watch an exercise program on television to get ideas. Each child can then suggest one exercise for a particular part of the body. Even toddlers should be encouraged to join in, and when they do, everyone should be cautioned not to laugh at their efforts. They will soon be able to do the same exercises and to "make a muscle," too. In the meantime, they are learning with the other children that they only get one body to last for a whole life and they had better take good care of it.

Getting To Know the Community

There is another important kind of activity one does out of doors which involves several kinds of activity. Getting to know the community can include activities such as music, art, and literature. There are several things to think about in making plans to learn about one's hometown or city.

The best place to start becoming a community expert is the library. The librarian will know if there is a book about the city or town. (In most places, at some time, someone has written something about his or her hometown.) The librarian will know how to get a guide to all the places of interest. Sometimes one book will include only one kind of place, such as the historical buildings, or the churches, or the public buildings. The provider can then make a list of all of the places she finds and get some information on as many of these as possible. It is usually not much fun to visit a place without knowing something about it beforehand. One can get a list of the addresses while in the library or from the phone book of places to visit:

Fire department	Political party	Dance studio	Garage and
Police station	office	Jail	service station
Bakery	Courthouse	4H Club	Clinics
Farm	Record shop	Cleaner's	Elks
Restaurant kitchen	Moving	Church	Kiwanis
Factory	company	Laundromats	Shoe repair shop
Fish store	Florist	Boat yard	Poultry market
Bicycle repair shop	Warehouse	Telephone	Vegetable market
Dairy	Pet shop	company	Tool shop

The provider can then decide where to start. Everyone loves visiting the fire department. There are several steps to take, however, before going for a visit. First, the provider should telephone the local fire station about a week in advance to say she wants to bring the children for a visit. She can tell the fireman in charge the names and ages of her children and ask what times it would be convenient to come for a visit. She should get some books from the library about firemen, and, using them, talk about firemen, their equipment, their dogs, and what they do besides put out fires. Then the children can think up questions they want to ask the firemen when they visit. (The provider should write these down so as not to forget any, and then go over them on the way to the fire station.)

After the visit, the children should write a thank-you note, each child writing something or drawing or painting a picture to send. Each child can sign the note; toddlers can make an X or a squiggle. Good manners are always appreciated and make the children welcome the next time. This same procedure can be used for any trip.

The Library

Many libraries have storytelling times. Some show slides or movies. Some of these are entertaining and others are not. If the local library has a program, it is worthwhile to give it a try. The provider may find that it is too old or too young for any of her children. On the other hand, it may just suit one or two of them. If any of them enjoy it, the provider can encourage that child to attend by getting a schedule of the programs and taking the child regularly. It may be necessary to come up with an idea for the other children while waiting for the child who is at the library. They may enjoy looking at books and checking one out, or they may prefer to play outside. If the child who is attending the program does not begin to feel left out of the group and enjoys the program, the other children may want to attend as well.

Every child who is old enough should have a library card and should be encouraged to take out a book each week. Because each child needs to be responsible for his or her book, one at a time is enough. There should also be a special place in the family day care home for library books to be kept so that they do not get misplaced or left at home and cause a fuss. If the children take their library books home that becomes one more thing for the children and parents to have to think about in the mornings when they are rushed. It is usually better to keep the library books in one place in the family day care home to be looked at and read during the day.

Art

The city or town the provider lives in may have a museum and art galleries, or, if not, the library may have some sort of art program for children. If there is neither, the provider is on her own and will soon become an art expert.

If there is a museum, she can telephone and ask to have a brochure describing the museum's collection mailed to her. When it arrives, she should study it with the children and decide what everyone wants to see first. It is never a good plan to try to see a whole museum in one visit. The most one can look at is one or two rooms at a time. That allows everyone to talk about what they have seen, and learn the names of some of the artists shown. Whenever one sees too much, one can remember neither what one saw or whether one liked it. Libraries usually have books on the art or artists in the museum. Before going the provider should look at books with the children, talk about the pictures, ask which they like best and why, and everyone should learn the names of some of the artists. During the visit, the children can talk about their favorites. They will enjoy the game: "If I could have *any* picture I have seen today to hang in my room, I would want _____." Older children can take trip boards (see below) along to write down the names of their favorite pictures and artists. After they get home, they can make lists of their favorite artists, or try drawing in their style. By praising their choices, the provider can encourage the children's interest in painting, sculpture, and drawing.

The children's favorite rooms in the museum should be visited often. As children really begin to enjoy looking at art, each picture becomes a dear old friend. Each child can decide who their "dear old friends" are. Some museums loan out prints, others sell inexpensive copies. It may be possible to get a small print of each child's favorite for the child to put in a place of her or his choice.

If there is no museum in the town, the provider will have to find other ways to introduce her children to art. The library will have children's books on art. The provider can bring home one that she thinks will catch the children's interest. Cave paintings are often a good start. Many libraries have interesting children's books about different artists' lives. There are several, for example, about the artists called the "impressionists." These appeal to most children. The more familiar we become with paintings, sculpture, and drawings, the more we enjoy looking at the same pictures or sculptures over and over. When children begin looking at the same paintings or sculptures two and three times, they are well on their way to becoming art lovers.

Music

Modern jazz, rock, and pop music cannot be avoided in our society. Indeed, this music is sometimes played so loud that hearing problems are beginning to develop as a result. Classical music on the other hand is more difficult to find, listen to, and learn to know and love; yet knowing something about classical music is necessary to an educated person. Because concerts are expensive and, in many places, rare, the provider may have to rely on records. Many towns and cities have a lending library of records because very few people can afford to buy all of the records that their children might enjoy.

The best time to introduce classical music to children is in infancy. Babies love to listen to soothing music. It quiets and calms them, and played softly, will help them fall asleep. A good start is "Sheep May Safely Graze" by Bach. Bach and Mozart piano music is pleasing to all ages, and particularly to very young children. The more it is played, the more interesting it becomes. Toddlers and preschoolers usually love Ravel's "Bolero." They begin to dance as soon as they hear it, turning around faster and faster with the rhythm of the music. Khachaturian's "Sabre Dance" is another favorite for dancing. The provider can make paper soldier hats and play records of Sousa marches. She can give everyone a scarf or a square of soft material and then play a waltz. Soon the children will choose which records they want to hear, and request marches, waltzes, or dancing music.

Many records made for children are poor, the voices are hard to understand, the stories are silly, and the music is trashy. The provider should try to find those that are well-recorded, clearly understandable, and pleasing. "Peter and the Wolf," "A Child's Introduction to the Orchestra," "Carnival of the Animals," "The Sorcerer's Apprentice," and "Noye's Fludde" are all good to start with. The librarian can probably suggest others from the library's collection. If available, the provider can get a picture book to go with the record and sit with the children, turning the pages and listening with them. (There are probably six different books about "Peter and the Wolf." The provider can decide which one she and the children will like best.)

Older children enjoy listening to arias from operas, ballet music, folk music, spirituals, and gospel music. To some degree, the provider will have to rely on what is available in her library. She can supplement with music programs on educational television and classical music radio stations. She can look at the program of the local radio stations in the newspaper and then plan to listen to one particular thing at a time. The more the provider herself enjoys music, the more the children will. As they become used to other kinds of music, they may find the single rhythm and few repeated words of popular music less interesting.

A Word on Taking Trips

Taking children on trips requires more than simply deciding to go to the library, the zoo, or to a museum. In order for the trip to be fun *and* safe, the provider has to plan carefully. Some of the planning will apply to every trip and become routine. Some of it, however, will depend on the nature of the trip, and will take some thought and organization.

Routine Planning The first consideration is the number and ages of the children. The provider must think carefully about how she can manage the group. If she has four or five children, and one or two are school age, she can probably manage her group easily. Children who are cooperative and who get along well with each other and their provider will do as well on trips as they do at home. School-aged children can hold a toddler's hand or push an infant's stroller. Preschool-aged children will have learned to amuse themselves close by the provider while she feeds the infant. Only in the case of a day care family of three or four very young children does it become difficult to plan a trip. Because there are few trips of interest to very young children (the zoo, the park, the playground, a farm, perhaps the firehouse), the provider can make special arrangements. A teenager in the provider's family or neighborhood or an older sibling or relative of one of the day care children could accompany the provider and help out with the little ones. In any case, the first thing the provider needs to arrange is adequate supervision of all of the children.

The second routine concerns trip supplies. On every trip the provider needs a small bag containing a first aid kit, tissues, safety pins, change for telephone calls or transportation or cold drinks. This could be kept packed and ready to go on any trip at any time. Each child needs identification on every trip that includes their name, address, phone number, and person (and phone number) to contact in case of emergency. Toddlers and preschoolers can wear their identification pinned onto their clothes. School-aged children can carry theirs in a pocket. Children enjoy making their own, the little ones can decorate theirs. If the identifications are put away with the trip kit, each child can take his or hers whenever the day care family goes out, if only to the store or the park.

The provider will have obtained consent forms from the parents for all trips (see Chapter 3). For each trip parents will be told in advance where the children are going, and if a phone number is available, the provider will have given it to the parents.

Some trips require special clothes—a bathing suit or extra sweater. The provider will need an easy-to-carry sack to put these in, along with a bottle for the baby and snacks for the other children.

Planning for Each Trip One of the first considerations is the time required to make the trip. Often the going to and coming home take so much time that the trip is impractical or exhausting. The provider needs to begin by looking at the transportation and how long it will take. This may limit the trips she can take simply because the school children have too little time in the afternoon.

If the provider has a friend who also offers family day care, arrangements can be made so that one provider will keep the infants while the other takes the older children on a trip, or, alternately, the school-age children go to one provider because the other has taken the younger children somewhere for the day. This kind of planning requires a clear understanding in advance on everyone's part—the children, their parents, and both providers.

Providing and Planning Activities

The appropriateness of each trip must be considered when planning for children of different ages. Children of all ages can get *something* from any experience but it requires some attention to each child's interests and abilities. The provider must decide how long she will spend at the zoo or park; and if each child wants to see a different animal or go on a different ride, she needs to work it out *beforehand* so that tantrums or tears are avoided. It is always better to quit *before* doing everything planned than to drag tired children along because they have not seen the elephants yet.

Finally, children should be encouraged to take along paper and pencil, to sit and make drawings, to list what they like best, and to copy the names of what they see (animals in the zoo, paintings and artists, or on neighborhood trips, addresses, names of shops, whatever they want to remember). This makes it easy later to write stories about the trip, have discussions, or put together a scrapbook to show the parents.

Trip Board Children can make trip boards for recording their observations. All that is needed are a square of heavy cardboard cut from a carton, taped around the edges, and sheets of paper attached with paper clips or stapled on. Then with a pencil in hand, the children have a hard surface on which to write, standing or sitting. The boards can serve for several trips by adding more paper. This kind of note taking allows the children to think about what they have seen, develop collections of drawings and souvenirs, write reports, and extend the ideas gathered well beyond the trip.

INDOOR ACTIVITIES

Literature

Reading is another combination of many activities in one. It is not only literature, but school readiness and often homework help as well. It is indoor, quiet, and can be a group activity. Music, art, self-care, and social skills can also be the subject of the reading.

Literature provides more than reading, however. It also offers a way of becoming familiar with ideas and the famous people who help us to understand the world and the people we know. There is very little that we do today that has not already been done by people in history and people in literature. Knowing what happened to them helps us to understand what happens to us and why. Literature also gives us new ways of thinking about our lives, ourselves, and others.

For children who are trying to understand why things happen the way they do, the old stories offer ways to understand both their feelings and their experiences. But literature delights children because it entertains as well. Very young children love the Mother Goose rhymes. Babies less than a year old love to be bounced on one's knees to "Ride a Cock Horse to Banbury Cross." Stories with repeating lines like "The Little Red Hen," "The House that Jack Built," and "The Little Engine that Could" give toddlers a chance to join in.

Books like *Goodnight Moon, Waiting for William,* and *Caps for Sale* are loved by all young children and they want to hear them again and again. *Johnny Crow's Garden, Peter Rabbit, Angus and the Ducks,* and *Where the Wild Things Are* can be found in most libraries. Children ask to have them read over and over until they know them so well that they can turn the pages at the right moment.

Reading aloud should not stop when the children are old enough to read to themselves. About 15 minutes each day should be saved for reading aloud to older children as well as the young ones. The provider can begin with one chapter a day of *Charlotte's Web, The Wind in the Willows, Stuart Little, Alice in Wonderland,* or one of the *Tin-Tin* books. A good time to read aloud is just before the children go home. The provider can read a chapter, then the children can talk about it and anything else on their minds while sitting quietly.

By the time children are 10 years old, they are ready to hear some of the classics. Someone once said that if one wants to know everything there is to know about God, one should read the Bible, and if one wants to know everything there is to know about man, one should read Shakespeare. There are some readable versions of Shakespeare's plays for children and there are collections of children's classics in most libraries. These are best read aloud. If the provider enjoys the story, the children will, too, and if she does not, it is certain they will not. Among those that everyone enjoys there will, of course, be favorites and discussions about everyone's favorites are often as much fun as reading the stories. The provider may sometimes reread the children's favorite parts, or the children might take turns reading aloud their favorite sections or speeches, and talking about why they think a certain character did what he or she did. Everyone can join in, each telling what he or she might have done in the same situation. This kind of story reading can make some of the world's famous ideas and characters a part of the children's lives, and the provider's as well.

Just as very little children enjoy learning Mother Goose rhymes and saying them over and over, older children enjoy learning short poems by heart. A generation ago, all school children learned several of the world's best known poems by heart. Today poetry reciting has disappeared from the curriculum of most schools, and children miss learning something that children of a generation ago learned, remembered and enjoyed all their lives. Just as it is easier to learn the ABC's if they are learned as a jingle, poems are easy and fun to learn. If the provider reads the children's favorite poems often enough, both she and the children will learn some of the lines by heart and be able to recite them together.

Social Skills

Social skills are usually learned indoors, and then taken out into the world. They are learned so that we can go anywhere, be at ease, and know what to do. There are three ways in which children acquire social skills. The first is by watching others—not only family and friends, but the people on television, in the movies, and by learning from people in books. Although some of us may never attend a charity ball or a political banquet, we would all like to feel that we know how to behave in such a situation. Reading about social events gives us clues to guide us through the social encounters of our everyday lives.

Another way children learn social skills is by play-acting or pretending. All children love to have tea parties and luncheon parties. They love having a pretend birthday party, making a game of greeting the guests, the guests' parents, giving the present, eating ice cream and cake with elegant manners, and, on leaving, thanking the birthday child and the parents. They also love to pretend to go to a restaurant, order from the menu, figure the tip, deal with the hat and coat check person, and make a reservation. Going to a hotel, checking in, tipping the bell boy, and ordering from room service are not only entertaining games, but, with the provider's guidance, also teach the children how to go through these experiences in the real world with confidence and style.

These rehearsed skills can one day be used in a real situation. The provider is unlikely to be the person who accompanies the child to a restaurant, or on an airplane, or to dinner at a relative's home, but she can encourage the children to tell stories about the things they have done. These real experiences then become models for more pretend games, letting each child take a turn organizing an activity with which he or she is familiar.

Children learn social behavior in other ways as well. From watching the provider talk to parents, to neighbors, to salespeople, and by listening to the provider talk on the telephone, the children learn how to deal with people and how to make their wishes known in such a way that the wishes are granted. When little children ask adults why they said something, they want to know what was really going on. They want to learn how to ask for things in such a way that they will get what they want. When the provider says to someone, "You've always been so helpful with this . . . ," the child learns that she is asking for help again, and, furthermore, is asking in a way that will make the person he or she is asking want to help. The child then will learn to ask for help when needed in a way that will get help quickly and cheerfully. The child will also learn how to ask another child to share a toy, to let him or her join in a game, to give him or her a turn. The provider must be a model, however, and must explain how to ask, and why it works better to ask one way rather than another. Once children have learned how to ask for things, they will have a fair chance of getting their way reasonably often, and will then be able to more easily accept *not* having their way all the time.

Everyone needs social skills, not only in public but in private dealings with people as well. Some children seem to pick these up with ease, others need to be shown, over and over, how to ask for help, for a toy, for a turn. Mostly, we learn how to get along with people by having good models. The provider can point out good models using examples in public life and in the child's world. Most of all, however, the provider must be a model herself by using her best skills with the children. If she is polite to the children, they will treat her and others with the same respect.

Self-care Skills

Toddlers learn with enthusiasm how to "do it myself." They are eager to try to dress themselves, feed themselves, wash themselves. When they do not succeed, they are frustrated and angry. Encouraging toddlers to do things themselves requires patience—patience with their slowness, with the mess they often make, with their temper tantrums. The goal is worth the effort, however, and one can help the process along by playing games of buttoning and unbuttoning, zipping, tying, toothbrushing, and washing faces and hands.

Children who have received encouragement as toddlers go on to acquire more and more self-care skills. Preschoolers can set the table, prepare the snack, dust the furniture, sponge the table, comb their hair, hang up their clothes. Most of these skills are learned in the course of the day's routine activities.

As the children become older, there are new skills to add. School-aged children can wash their own hair, polish their own shoes, give themselves a manicure. Pre-teen girls enjoy experimenting with various hair styles, wearing nail polish, trying out make-up. With guidance, these activities help the children develop a personal style, a personal look, and a sense of their own attractiveness. If the provider approves these activities, the children will usually accept her guidance. If she disapproves, however, the children will not accept her suggestions willingly, nor will they give up their interest in their appearance. They will continue to experiment on their own, most likely. Our society rewards being sexy in advertisements, films, and on television. If the provider treats the children's efforts to be attractive as vain or vulgar, the children will merely reject her guidance and help along with her good taste.

The purpose of all this self-care is the sense of competence and self-reliance that it encourages. The more people can do for themselves, the more independent they become. When parents or providers insist on doing everything for children, the children's natural desire for independence is frustrated. They may even suspect that something is wrong, and they will certainly not become as independent, competent and self-confident as they might. Children who are capable at home, furthermore, are capable at school, and those who can do things well are admired by other children.

School Readiness

Activities that encourage school readiness are discussed in full in Chapter 13.

Homework

Chapter 14 covers the activities of school-aged children, and includes help with homework.

Wall Calendar

Part of learning independence and self-care is taking responsibility for one's own needs. The wall calendar encourages that responsibility. It should hang where all school children and preschoolers can see it and reach it. School children can then write reminders to themselves about the day they need to bring a bag lunch, return a book, go to scouts. Every Friday, each child can write his or her name and a letter that stands for the job he or she has the following week. For instance, Billy writes his name and a "T" by it to remind himself and everyone that he will set the table. June writes her name and "P" for the plants she will water. The person who will wash dishes will write "W" by his or her name, and the person who will dry will write "D" by his or hers. School events, teacher conferences, dental appointments, someone's grandmother who is coming for a visit, a trip planned or a friend invited, can all be recorded. The calendar then becomes a picture of things to come, letting everyone know what is expected.

EVALUATING THE PLANS

When the last parent has come for the last child and the provider sits down and puts her feet up, she has time to take a minute and think about how the day went.

First of all, did the routines work well? Was there enough time for everybody to do what he or she wants or needs to do? The general mood of the children is the best way to tell. If the children are calm and reasonably contented then they are not being rushed or pushed and they are not bored or restless. The chances are that in every day there are some rough spots that need attention. Are there some interesting things for the toddlers to do while the baby is fed or bathed? Do the preschoolers have time to finish their painting or block building before they have to clean up for lunch? Are there any children who are having a hard time getting along, and need to be given separate activities for a while? Is there enough time to spend some with each school-aged child in the afternoon? What is the general mood at the end of the day? Is everyone frantic and fussy? Or reasonably calm and collected?

The timing of each day is also important. Are there enough active times? Are they balanced by quiet times? Is something both calming and interesting planned for the end of the day so that the children are able to leave in a good mood?

It may be that one particular child is not playing with enthusiasm, or is fighting with the other children, or is complaining a lot. If this occurs, the provider may need to spend some time with that child before she can figure out what the problem is. It may be a problem in the child's home, or it may be a problem in the child's adjustment to family day care, to the other children, or to the routines of the day. Until the provider spends some time with that child, she will not be able to figure it out or plan for the child's particular need. It may just be that the child needs a quiet place to go from time to time to get away from the other children. The provider may need to be close to that child for a while and, in spending quiet moments together, help the child feel safe and watched over. Perhaps a place for that child can be made at the kitchen table while the provider prepares lunch or feeds the baby and the other children are busy with games. That allows the child and the provider to talk softly together.

One of the best ways to evaluate plans is to have a conference. At the end of the day or during snacks or lunch, the provider can plan a business meeting with all of the children, even the little ones. She can ask for their opinions on the activities, the routines, the food, or just ask what they would like to say about the day. At first, young children will have a hard time looking at what they do from the outside and saying what they think about it. It will help to give examples such as: "I thought we stayed too long in the park today and everybody got too tired. What do you think?" or "Making carrot cake took so long today we had no time for story reading. Was that OK with you, or did you miss the story?" Soon the children will learn to think about what they are doing and how they feel about it. This encourages independent thinking, self-expression, and respect for others, regardless of age or size. It is an example of what democracy is all about. Having a conference teaches children how to listen to others, say what they think, then put the question to a vote. It is the best way to be sure the day care plans are working for everyone concerned.

6

The Provider and the Parents

The parents of the children in the provider's care are her clients, and a successful business requires that she get along with them in a friendly and cooperative manner. To do this, she must ask herself what the parents want from her. Superior care for their children is not their only requirement. The parents want to be sure they have done the right thing in entrusting their children to the provider. Parents have beliefs about what one needs to know and how one needs to behave in order to make it in this world. If they feel that the provider's beliefs and values are like theirs, they will feel comfortable about her influence on their children. If, however, they feel that their children are not learning the same values and behaviors that they themselves have, they will be worried, anxious, and insecure. The provider will be able to tell from their behavior toward her. They may get angry over little things or be cold with her, or they may simply be uncooperative. Any of these behaviors will affect the child's sense of well being and make it hard for the provider to be supportive of the parents and for the parents to support her. When two people share in child rearing, they must try to share their values and beliefs about the world as well.

There is another reason to be friendly and cooperative with the parents. Children are very sensitive when adults distrust and dislike each other. The provider and the parent are so important to the child that any open disagreement between them can make the child unhappy. Moreover, if the provider and the child's parent cannot figure out how to get along with each other, how can either of them ever teach the child to get along with others?

GETTING TO KNOW THE PARENT

Beginning with the first interview (Chapter 3), the provider learns things about the life-style of the family of each child in her care. During the first interview she will have heard only good things about the child and the child's home life. Each day she will learn something more about the child's family and about the parent's beliefs, strengths, and weaknesses as well. Knowing these will help her to understand what the parent thinks is important in life.

There is, of course, some danger in knowing about the personal life of others. The danger is that one may feel that one is better than another person is, look down on that person, and even let it show in how one acts. With this kind of attitude, one cannot work in partnership. No one can bear being looked down upon, and no one can ever like someone who makes him or her feel bad. Most parents worry that they are not doing what is best for their children, that their children will suffer because they have to work, study, or train for a job. The provider must try, therefore, to reassure them, to encourage them as parents. This not only helps them to be better parents, but also helps the provider to be a better provider and helps the children as well.

There is also the danger that the parent will feel so uncomfortable about what the provider knows about his or her home life that he or she will avoid her or decide to look down on her. (There is an old saying that the best defense is a good offense. Many people never heard of the saying but behave as though they had.) Either way, these attitudes can make it very difficult for the provider to get along well with the parent.

What providers do with information about the parents and their home life has a great effect on the business and on their professional reputation. If ever they are tempted to tell a friend or a relative something they know about how a child is treated or about what goes on in a child's home, they should remember that even if the child and the child's family never find out they said it, they will have behaved unprofessionally. As much as friends or relatives may enjoy hearing the stories, they know that it is unprofessional to talk about clients.

THE PROVIDER AS SOCIAL WORKER

In Chapter 1, the many jobs that the provider performs are listed. One of these is the job of social worker. We have already said that the first social work job is to win the trust of the parents so that the provider and parent can work together for the child's welfare. Before the parent can trust the provider and talk to her, however, the parent must have confidence that she *will* help, and not use the information against him or her. The word *confidentiality* comes from the word *confidence*. It means simply that a person will keep all the information she gets to herself, in confidence. The job of providing is like the priest's or the doctor's in this respect. The provider can be trusted to listen and help but never tell others.

Sometimes this is very difficult. Suppose she knows something that she thinks should be reported for the protection or welfare of the child. Before she reports anything, she must think through exactly what will happen after she has made her report. Step by step, what will happen to each person involved? Will it be the best thing for the child? The truth is that sometimes these agencies are not much help. It is unfortunate that sometimes social service agencies do something in the beginning but then do not offer continuing help. Sometimes a case is reported, and the person to be helped gets referred from agency to agency without ever receiving any real help in the end. It is important to be sure that after a report is made on a person, the help that person will receive will be worth the possible distress to everyone concerned. It is therefore necessary to be realistic about what agencies can and cannot do, and to find other ways of helping each other and ourselves if the agencies fail.

Some of these problems may be serious. Unfortunately, child abuse, wife beating, drug and alcohol abuse, and violence of many kinds are all too common in our society. Although there are many agencies set up to deal with these, not many are having any real success either in helping individuals or in making these problems less common. In the case of children, agencies are often even less help than in the case of adults. Even in severe child abuse cases, the battered or burned child is often sent home with the abusing parents. More than a few of these cases end in the death of the child. In every case, the child is physically and psychologically injured for life.

Why are there so few agencies offering any real protection for the abused child? One reason for this is built into the American way of thinking about things. We believe that our children belong to us in the same way that our car does, or our television does, or our home does. No one can tell us how to treat our own things. Americans have the attitude that what we do with our own belongings is our own business.

There are two things wrong with this attitude when it applies to children. The first is the notion that one person can own another person. Our children are not slaves; we do not own them. Children are their own persons. No one has to have a child. If we *choose* to have a child, we are assuming the responsibility for the care of the child until the child is grown up enough to take care of himself or herself. Children are on loan, in our care, until they are ready to go out into the world. Then they become our contribution to the future, and, in a way, our immortality.

The other thing wrong about the notion of owning children has to do with the treatment of children. People have to be crazy to beat up on or batter their television sets or their cars or anything else that they own. Why then does the feeling of owning children allow one to beat up on or batter children? The only time people feel like kicking the television or the car is when it *does not work right*. Children are battered when parents feel that *they are* not working right—when they are crying, or wetting their beds, or whining, or acting "bad."

If there is a child in the family day care home who is punished often or severely, the provider should talk to the parent. She might, for instance, ask the parent what the child is being punished for. She can explain to the parent that children who are punished do not then behave better or "work right"; they become angry and hurt, and begin to think of themselves as bad.

If there is a problem of child abuse in one of the day care families, the provider is faced with deciding how to act to help the child. Her first step is to notify the local agencies (there is usually an emergency telephone number in the telephone directory for child abuse). There may be times when the provider feels she can help in an emergency to protect a child. Sometimes another adult or an older brother or sister can assume responsibility for getting the child who is about to be abused out of the way in time. If there are no other adults or children to protect the child, the provider might suggest that the parent call her when she feels she might abuse the child. In some cities there are hot lines for potential abusers to call.

The number of cases of child abuse on weekends is far greater than the number during the week. This is probably partly because the parents are tired after a whole week of work, and partly because the child is there all the time. If there is a problem with one of the day care families, the provider may want to suggest that the child spend some time with another member of the family, such as a grandmother, aunt, or cousin. If there is no other family, however, she may have to act on the child's behalf. If she decides to take the child on weekends, she will have to be reimbursed for her time and work. If the parent cannot afford it, the local agency may have emergency care funds for child abuse cases. If there is money for child protection, the parent should be the one to apply. With support and encouragement, the parent may be able to take on the responsibility and obtain protection for the child.

HELPING PARENTS THROUGH DIFFICULTY

There are some problems the provider can do little to help. If there is a drug or alcohol problem in one of the families there is not a great deal that the provider can do. If the problem is wife beating, it may help the parent to talk about it. In some cities there are telephone numbers to call for help for battered women. If a family has a severe problem, and if the family has failed to get help, the provider has to be realistic about trying to assist it. After she has suggested places to go for help, the most she can do is be sympathetic and supportive when necessary.

When asked about raising children, most people would say they want to be *better* parents then their own were. Why is it then so difficult for parents not to repeat their parents' mistakes? One reason is that as we grow up, our parents' behaviors become part of our own behavior, and then when we have children we repeat those behaviors, naturally and without even thinking about them. Often the behaviors that we hated in our own parents become part of our ways of reacting. We say, however, that we do the things we do because of the way we are, and we go on doing what our parents did, not really thinking about it, because that is the way we are.

Using Examples To Help Parents

The most important and most basic way to help parents is to be a model of the kinds of behaviors we want them to adopt. In helping parents, one treats them the way one wants them to treat their children. One way to do this is to listen, instead of talking. That may sound easy, but it is not. Listening is more than just not talking. Listening includes looking at the person who is talking, nodding encouragement, showing interest and concern, smiling sympathetically, and, when needed, asking a question. This kind of listening is also the best prevention of any disagreement with the parent. If the parent knows the provider listens, then the parent will feel like her wishes are being understood. Whether the provider really agrees with what the parent says or not does not matter too much. If she listens to what the parent is saying, does not disagree, she is showing she can understand her viewpoint, and the parent will be reassured.

Suppose that a parent tells the provider that she wants her to force her child to clean his or her plate at mealtime. The provider knows that forcing a child to clean his or her plate is poor child care technique. She does not say so, however. Instead she asks, "When you were growing up did your parents make their children clean their plates?" The answer, 99 times out of 100, is "yes." Then she says, "Tell me why you think it is important." When the parent has answered, the provider simply says, "That is very interesting. I'd like to talk with you some more about it." That reassures the parent that the provider understands her view. The subject is still open for discussion and no promises have been made. Another time the provider could say, "I was thinking about our interesting conversation about finishing food, and I remembered a cousin of mine whose mother made her clean her plate. She grew up to be a person who not only eats everything on *her* plate, but finishes other people's food, too. The only trouble is that she now has a hard time keeping her weight down to normal." Another time the provider might say, "It's funny about the business of cleaning your plate. A neighbor of mine has a child who's a poor eater. She makes him eat all of his food, even if he sits for hours! The odd thing is that the child is getting thinner, not fatter. In fact, mealtimes are so disagreeable that it looks to me like the whole family is getting thinner!" Regardless of the subject under discussion, the provider can usually think of some real-life examples to use to put over her ideas without letting the parent feel that she does not share her view, and without appearing to argue. If she cannot think of any examples from her own experience, she can always invent a few.

Paying Attention Next to listening carefully and encouragingly, the most important part of being helpful to parents is giving them some attention. If the provider gives the parents uncritical attention, they are unlikely to disagree seriously with her on any issue. In fact, if they feel that she likes and respects them, they will probably go along with her even when their own values are different.

There will be times, of course, when the provider has to deal with her own feelings of disapproval of a parent's ideas about child raising. There will never be a parent (including the provider's own) with whom she is in perfect agreement. If, however, she can show concern and interest in the *person* (if not in their beliefs), she can manage to get along with most parents. Just as with children, adults are usually eager to please the person who they know likes them.

Getting the Parents' Confidence It really takes very little to show concern for another person. In the morning, the provider can ask the parents a few questions such as, "Were you able to sleep through that terrible storm last night?" or "Did you see that woman on TV last night who won the lottery?" or whatever else comes to mind. The question is not important; listening to the answer is. Then, even more important, she should say something to show she is paying attention to the parent's response.

Once a parent becomes convinced that the provider cares about him or her and his or her child, the provider will be able to talk about the child's needs. When she feels she has a parent's confidence, she can begin to work on the problem: "Troy has been so sleepy lately. Is it hard for you to do all the things you have to do in the evening and still have enough time with him? I know you want to spend time with him, and that makes it hard to get him to bed early." If the parent says that she tries to put him to bed but he has napped so long during the day that he does not want to go to bed, the provider can say, "That *is* a problem. I guess Troy hates to go to bed because he wants to be with you as much as possible. He would rather sleep when he's with me, and be awake with you. Why don't I wake him from his nap tomorrow so that you can get him to go to bed more easily?" Then if the provider finds that waking the child turns out to be upsetting to him, she does not have to continue it. The parent will know that she is willing to cooperate. She will probably find ways to do all that she wants to do with her child and still get him to bed earlier. Once the pressure is off, the child will probably be ready for bed earlier anyway.

The provider's main goal is to convince the parents that she cares for them and their needs, and that she wants to help them do what is best for their children. As long as she does not act as though she thinks she knows more about the children than the parents (even when she may think she does), she will not cause the parents to feel jealous and angry. If she wants to discuss something about a child that concerns the child's behavior in the day care home, she can say, "You know Sharon so much better than I do, tell me what you think makes it so hard for her to stay with the rest of us when we go out for a walk?" This way, instead of having the parent answer: "I don't have any trouble with Sharon when *we* go out," the parent may say something like: "She probably wants to hold your hand all the time. I always hold on to her." (More about solving behavior problems in the next chapter.)

Showing Respect Along with listening to parents and giving them some attention, the provider wants to show the parents she respects them. The best way to get reasonable behavior from people, adults or children, is to make them feel they are capable of reason, of thought. Since most parents and providers have very different life-styles and work, it can be difficult for each to show respect for the other's choice. The provider will find that if she shows respect for the parent's intelligence and knowledge the parent will not only respect her in return, but cooperation between them will become easy.

As she gets to know the parents' interests, the provider can ask questions related to these. When she finds an article in the newspaper or in a magazine on a subject that she thinks will interest one of the parents, she can save it and give it to him or her at the end of the day. By exchanging ideas about general subjects in this way, the provider is laying the groundwork for reasonable and respectful discussion of important issues around child care when they come up.

Sharing the Pleasure We are never expected to share something that we *do not* want. Sharing is something done when two people want the same thing. This is especially true when sharing a child with his or her parent(s). The provider needs to think of all the pleasures, the funny sayings, the new skills, the silly games, and the good times that the parents would like to be able to share. Too often the parents only hear about the problems or difficulties. "Lois was really cranky and cross all day." "Donald didn't eat any lunch." "Shirley won't play nicely with the other children." Many of these things need not be reported to the parents at all. When there is something the provider really wants to tell the parent, she can say it in a positive way. "Harold wasn't sleepy at naptime today so he may want to go to bed earlier than usual." "Tyrone will probably be very hungry at supper. He didn't like our lunch very much today." Unless she has some reason to think a child may be getting sick, it is better not to report crankiness, crossness, or whiny behavior. Those are better dealt with by planning activities that interest the child, by spending time with the child, and by figuring out what the child needs or what is troubling the child. In the afternoon when the children are getting their things together to go home, the provider can be sure they have whatever they have made or brought from school to show their parents. When the parent arrives, she can say, "Dorothy has something lovely to show you."

If there is any real problem, it should not be presented to the parent at the end of the day when both parent and provider are tired. The provider should ask the parent when they can get together for a talk. A meeting date should be arranged when both have plenty of time to talk together. In the daily contacts, the provider should exchange good news and share pleasant and amusing events, so that the parent will look forward to her few minutes with the provider. If that is the pattern of the exchange, when the provider does have to introduce a problem, the parent will be able to cooperate because she will not be protecting herself from more bad news.

Limits to Being Helpful

The provider's efforts to establish a partnership with the parent can go too far. There are parents who need to have limits set, because they find it difficult to meet their responsibilities and are only too willing to let others do things for them. If the provider finds that a parent is bringing a child who is still in the diaper he or she slept in, or is coming late regularly, or is failing to bring diapers (or anything else that is expected) with her, it is *not* wise to accept the behavior and say nothing. Often providers will simply care for the child and decide the parent is not very competent or mature. This will only make it worse for both parent and provider. The parent needs to assume responsibility for her half of the bargain. The provider should remind the parent gently. If that fails, she can bring out the list of responsibilities (see Chapter 3). If that fails, she needs to make an appointment to sit down and talk to the parent. She can tell the parent that she knows how hard it is to get to work on time and also get the child ready. Then she can say that she was willing to help out and overlook the problem at first, but because it has not improved, she feels she must tell the parent that the parent will have to fulfill her half of their agreement. If the parent is not willing or able to, the provider will not be able to keep the child. At this point the parent will usually agree to mend his or her ways. This may not be the end of it, however. The provider may have to remind the parent a few months later. Once the provider has made it clear that she will not be imposed upon, however, the parent will usually come around.

The reason it is so important to keep the parent to her share of the agreement is that if she does not, the provider is creating a barrier between herself and the parent. At first, it seems easy to do what the parent has failed to do, but as time goes on, the provider cannot fail to resent it, and deep inside herself feel angry that the parent is taking advantage of her. That anger will not just go away, and it will make it more and more difficult to get along well together. By holding the parent to her agreement, the provider is actually showing respect, showing she thinks the parent capable of doing what she has agreed to do.

VISITING IN THE HOME

It probably means more to the child that the provider visit his or her home than it does to either the parent or the provider. It builds a bridge between the two parts of the child's world. It is a sign of the cooperation between the provider and the parent. It is also useful for the provider to see the child's home life, and to meet the people the child lives with and talks about.

It will be easier for the parent to have the provider come for a visit if he or she has already been invited to visit the provider during off-business hours. If tea or coffee has been served and if they have talked together, the parent is more apt to feel comfortable about having the provider visit in her home.

The first visit to the child's home is not the time to discuss any kind of problem. Instead, the provider should be friendly and interested in the child's family. She might want to bring a gift to the parent—something the child has made, or a little plant she has grown from a cutting, or some cookies that she and the children baked.

One purpose of this visit is to learn how the child lives. If possible the provider should meet the child's family. More important, however, she can get an idea of the emotional atmosphere. What is the mood of the child's home? Is it calm and relaxed, tense and angry, quiet and controlled, easy and pleasant, or a combination of these? She will be able to pick up the mood easily from the parent's behavior and the behavior of the other family members that she meets. This will help her understand many things—what the child expects from adults, the moods that the child expresses, the way the child interacts with other children, and the child's response to direction or help.

LIFE-STYLES AND VALUES

This chapter began with the importance of values and beliefs in raising children. These values and beliefs determine our life-style. If we believe, for instance, that it is good to talk about our feelings, our life-style will be open, with everyone free to express happiness, sadness, and anger. For some people, this is a very uncomfortable life-style. They believe in self-control and in keeping their feelings to themselves. Some people value neatness and orderliness, and have a very organized life-style. They spend a great deal of time putting things in order, in place, and are not happy if someone upsets their organization. Other people value flexibility—being free to change their minds or change their direction. They do not like to feel pinned down or committed. These values and beliefs are easy to discover by simply observing a family in their home. They are important to understand when sharing parenting. Life-style affects our decisions about weaning, toilet training, self-care, neatness, cleanliness, and language; in fact, it affects almost everything we want children to learn in the process of growing up. Whether we feel children should be toilet trained by 18 months or feel that each child will learn when that child is ready, we are convinced that our way is right. It is part of the life-style we have learned, and if we really thought about it, we might realize that we think people who do not agree with us are wrong or have lower standards than we do. We believe that children must learn certain things in order to have "character," to be a "good person," or to be the kind of person who is going to make it in the world.

Once there is some understanding of the values and beliefs of each child's family, the provider will be able to deal with the parent in a positive and supportive way. She can take into account that particular parent's views whenever she talks with her. Knowing that values have an effect on how we see the world and how we see ourselves, there is no point in trying to change another person's view. Unless that other view is taken into account, however, there can be no hope for cooperation.

Suppose she has a child in her care whose parent's values and beliefs are very different from her own. What effect will it have on the child? The answer depends upon how she and the parent treat each other.

What is important here is not that the child's parent and provider agree about everything, but that they respect each other. Even a child's father and mother do not agree all the time. If they try to agree on everything, they create a very unreal world, with one person going along with the other in order to show a strong front or simply to keep the peace. That kind of arrangement usually breaks down sooner or later. In the end, it is better not to pretend to agree with someone else all the time, but also not to put down that other person's view. If we *respect* someone, we do not need to agree all the time. Just as we can love and respect more than one person, we can also love and respect people with different values. Only the weak or insecure have trouble with people who disagree with them. Strong people can take a variety of values in their stride and not feel uneasy.

Learning about different views, values, and beliefs make a child's life richer. Only if that child gets caught in the cross fire between adults who are fighting over their values can the child be hurt. If the provider listens to the parent, pays attention to her, and shows her respect, there will be no problem for the provider, the parent, or the child.

The child then will learn about the values and beliefs of both the parent and the provider. The child will also learn how people get along in the world, working cooperatively to achieve their goals—in this case, the care and raising of children.

7

Solving Problems in Family Day Care

Hardly a job exists that doesn't present problems to be solved. A chemist may have to cope with the side effects of an important new drug. An engineer has to find a metal that won't overheat in a rocket launch. The most difficult problems to solve, however, are those that humans present to each other. Providers deal with human problems. This chapter looks at the kinds of difficulties that can arise between adults who share responsibility for the care of children.

One of the reasons why these problems are so difficult to solve is that they deal with feelings, and feelings are hard to control and hard to understand. Solving something that you do not understand and that you cannot control is not only difficult, it is also upsetting. When people become upset they find it even harder to work things out. Feeling upset makes some people angry, others may manage to convince themselves that it is not important because they want to avoid bad feelings. In either case, the problem that is causing the distress is apt to go unsolved. When these are things that concern the daily care of children, leaving them unsolved can be hard on both the child and the adults. Finding solutions is less hard on everyone, and there are ways of going about it.

One of the reasons that feelings are so hard to handle is that often it is hard to know what they really are or where they come from. Everyone has had the experience of suddenly feeling sad without having anything in particular to feel sad about. Another common experience is the feeling of being uncomfortable and uneasy, and yet knowing that there is nothing to be particularly uncomfortable or uneasy about. For some people, these unexplained feelings are so upsetting that they find ways of shaking them off. They may get very busy, or go get something to eat, or get up and leave the room, or go for a walk. Our ways of dealing with feelings are learned from the important adults in our childhood long before we understand or recognize the feelings themselves. Although adults may not know themselves what feelings upset them, they act quickly to get rid of their own unpleasant feelings, as well as those they think the children around them might be having. Once we have learned to avoid certain upsetting feelings, we insist that our children learn to avoid the same feelings.

Because we know so little about our own feelings, how can we ever expect to understand other people's, the parents', for example? And if we don't understand our own or the parents' feelings, how is it possible to solve the problems that are bound to come up when two people feel differently about a job they share? The first step is to look at the kinds of feelings problems that the care of children can raise.

Chapter 6 presents some of the values and beliefs that affect our lifestyle. These values and beliefs are the source of some of our strongest feelings and have to do with what we want children to become when they grow up.

When parents are asked what they believe is most important in life, they give a lot of different answers. Some believe the most important thing is to be smart. Others believe that the most important thing is to be a good person. There are some people who believe in being creative. Some people are not sure. They may *say* they believe that being a decent person is the most important thing in life, but they really feel that unless you make a lot of money you will never be secure. The best way to find out what someone really thinks is important is to look at what he or she thinks children should learn and how children should be raised.

Most people believe that even very young babies are already learning about the world, and, therefore, the kind of care they receive will have something to do with what they learn. For this reason, the way people care for children indicates what they really believe is important. Sometimes these child care beliefs are individual, others are cultural, that is, almost all the people in a society believe the same thing. In either case, when more than one adult is caring for a child they need to come to an agreement about some of the ways that the child will be cared for. The following are some common examples of child care beliefs that can cause disagreement.

INFANT FEEDING

Because infants in family day care are usually bottle fed, the issue of bottle versus breast feeding does not usually come up. The issue that might arise between provider and parent over infant feeding concerns what an infant is fed and how often. What an infant is fed is often the recommendation of the pediatrician or nurse-practitioner at a well-baby clinic. There can be considerable disagreement about this because all pediatricians may not agree about the introduction of solid food, formula versus cow's milk, or the use of prepared baby food versus table food. The provider may have had different pediatric recommendations from those the parent is getting. In this case, the provider is obliged to follow the parent's pediatrician's recommendations.

The issue most likely to cause disagreement concerns how often a baby should be fed. There are some people who feel that infants should be fed when they seem to be hungry. Just as adults have different appetites and eat at different times, infants need different amounts of food on different schedules. Sometimes an infant will take an entire 8-ounce bottle and then be hungry again in 3½ or 4 hours; other times the infant will take less and be content for 5 hours.

Many people feel that the adult who cares for the infant must be sensitive to each infant's individual needs and feed the infant accordingly. There are adults, however, who feel that infants should be fed on a regular schedule regardless of whether it suits the infant's hunger. They will allow an infant to cry until the scheduled feeding time and then wake a sleeping infant when the schedule says it is time for a bottle. Why is making the infant fit into the adult's schedule so important to these people? Because of their feelings about what they think people must learn in order to succeed in the world. They are afraid of spoiling the infant or losing control over the infant and raising a child who wants to have his or her own way all the time. For some people it is important simply because they have little control over anything else in their lives and therefore want to have their own way with the infant.

Control also affects another issue in infant feeding, the issue of when the infant should be weaned (taken off) the bottle. Giving up the bottle is seen as a big step in learning to be grown up, in giving up babyish behavior. People who feel strongly about weaning may also object to pacifiers. For people who have had a hard life, teaching children how to give things up can become an important part of child rearing. Other adults encourage children to continue to take a bottle. They find they can often deal with a toddler's or even a 3 or 4 year old's demands for attention by substituting a bottle for a more personal response. Actually, either too much or too little attention to giving up babyish behavior can make for difficulties.

TOILET TRAINING

For many parents toilet training is an even more important issue than how and when an infant is fed because it involves not only self-control but feelings about cleanliness as well. Because this is a subject about which people feel very strongly, the experience of being toilet trained is probably very impressive to children, and the strong feelings that adults have about it are probably a result of their own experiences as very young children. (See Chapter 10 on toddlers and toilet training.)

INDEPENDENCE

At about the time children are becoming toilet trained, they are also learning to feed themselves, to help with dressing themselves, to brush their teeth, to wash their faces, and to put their toys away. While all this independent behavior is being encouraged, the child's other efforts at becoming independent can be very upsetting. It is at this age that children learn to say "no," begin to have temper tantrums, ignore what they are told, and generally appear to be out of control. For some adults, this is an extremely difficult stage. The child's efforts at independence and at doing things his or her own way can bring out strong feelings of anger in the adults. (Managing and encouraging independence is discussed in Chapter 10.)

LANGUAGE

For some people words have magical powers, both good and bad. *Please* and *thank you* have great powers of good, and curse words have equally great powers of evil. When children do not use the good words and do use the bad words, adults may have strong feelings of pleasure or of horror. Very young children figure this out and use these powerful words to get attention. They also learn that the people who object intensely to the use of bad words are often the very people who use those words when they feel they need them.

Another kind of language that is upsetting to some parents is what is called talking back or sassing. For some parents what the child says is often more important than what he or she does. If the parent tells the child to do something and the child "answers back" the parent will be upset even if the child has immediately done what he or she was told to do. Often the child will be punished, even if the job was done. These parents cannot put up with the least threat to their authority.

Other parents encourage answering back. They, too, believe in the power of language and words, but to them the power is for good not evil. They teach their children to reason by arguing with them about nearly everything, important or not, simply for the practice. To these parents the ability to reason, to think on your feet, and to persuade with words are required for any kind of success. They begin teaching their children these skills as soon as the children are able to say a few words. To other people these children may appear argumentative and disrespectful, but to these parents this is how people learn to use words to get what they want in the world. Finally, there are parents who are not consistent; sometimes they encourage answering back, regarding it as cute behavior. Other times they react harshly. The child often does not know what response to expect. (See Chapter 11 on language.)

AGGRESSION

The word *aggression* means many different things to different people. To some it means the wish to hurt a thing or a person. To some it merely means playing a game hard, or being pushy, or demanding attention, or working overtime. How people feel about aggression has a lot to do with how they define it. How they define it has to do with how they interpret certain behaviors.

Even before babies can tell the difference between themselves and others, they bite the nipple (of the bottle or breast), grab hair (of anyone near enough), kick their feet (against anything or anyone close enough), and poke their fingers into the faces of whoever is holding them. Adults interpret these infant behaviors in different ways. Some recognize that they are simply the different ways that infants examine their surroundings. Others respond to these behaviors as though they were intended to hurt. Some adults even fight back by slapping the baby's hand or calling the baby bad.

The ways in which adults react to infants' behaviors can encourage aggressiveness or discourage it. People who believe in their own strength are not often openly aggressive, and they are less apt to react aggressively. They do not feel under attack. People who feel they are not so strong or that they are easily taken advantage of will act aggressively and will encourage children to fight back. Because our feelings about aggression have to do with our feelings about our own power or weakness, they are very difficult to talk about or change. (More about this in Chapters 9 and 10.)

NEATNESS, CLEANLINESS, ORGANIZATION

These three are lumped together because they often go together. People can be neat without being clean, and they can be clean without being organized. Usually, however, people who feel cleanliness is important feel the same way about neatness and believe in being reasonably well organized. They also feel strongly about teaching children to be clean, neat, and organized. These people find a baby who needs a diaper change distasteful, and they interpret a baby's cries as "wanting to be changed." (There is actually no evidence that young babies are even aware of being wet or soiled until adults teach them to be.) They think toilet training is very important, and feel the same way about learning to put away toys or learning to keep their clothes clean. To many people these three things, cleanliness, neatness and being organized, mean being acceptable to others and feeling good about themselves.

Beliefs about how infants should be fed and toilet trained, how children should learn independence, cleanliness, even beliefs about aggression, are generally cultural, that is, most of the people who have grown up in the same area will have similar beliefs. If all of the parents of the children in a family day care home come from similar backgrounds, their beliefs will not be very different. Of course, no two parents will have exactly the same values or beliefs about child care, but these differences will be small compared to the differences found between one culture and another. For instance, in some cultures infants are carried inside the mothers' clothes so that they are able to nurse whenever they want. In others infants are left for long hours while the mothers go off and work. In some places infants are toilet trained by the age of 1 or 1½ years at the latest. In some places children are never toilet trained; they simply learn from watching older children. Whatever the child rearing practices in a given place, they are apt to be considered the best and only way to raise children.

Although the provider is unlikely to find any great differences in parents' beliefs about child rearing, differences will nevertheless exist and will have to be taken into account. In addition to the cultural beliefs, there will be personality differences between parents as well, and these can present more problems to be solved.

Within a culture, even within a family, different people will have different attitudes about punctuality. Some feel that being on time is very important and are very uncomfortable if they have to be late. These parents are never late to pick up their children. They can also be counted on to pay the fee every Monday morning. Other parents do not consider "time" very important. They come at different times every evening, and they may be equally unreliable about paying the fee on time.

People show individual differences in their attitudes about danger. Some parents see potential danger everywhere and spend a great deal of time protecting their children and teaching them to be cautious. Other parents give their children a lot of freedom from a very early age. They allow them to climb jungle gyms and trees, to play outside unsupervised, to go to the store alone. Between the parents who believe you can never be too careful and those who feel children should learn to take care of themselves, there are many degrees of cautiousness.

Some parents take very good care of their things. They believe that their children should learn to be just the same way. A broken toy, a missing button, or a broken shoelace all need to be taken care of immediately. Other parents are much less conscious of things, and although they may not have more money, they will replace something rather than spend the time fixing it or caring for it.

These are some examples of personality differences. There are many others as well, and all of these differences can create problems. How the provider solves these problems is important to her business, and to the feelings of all concerned. Because all of these possible problems begin with individual values and beliefs there are no right or wrong solutions.

PROBLEM PREVENTION

The easiest way to prevent problems is to come to an agreement on as many issues as possible before the contract is signed. Certainly, all of the business details can be agreed upon at the beginning. Once the parent and the provider know what is expected of each, many problems that could arise are avoided. If the time that the parent is expected in the evening has been agreed upon, and if it has been agreed that any time the parent must be late the parent will telephone the provider, then the only issue left is the amount of overtime due. It should be agreed at the outset that this overtime will be paid *at that time*. It is easier to pay for something when it is due; later it may seem less reasonable.

Other business details such as the things the parent agrees to supply (extra set of winter and summer clothers, formula or other baby food, stroller) can be agreed upon before the provider accepts the child. These should be included in the list of responsibilities of parent and provider. Other details such as who washes clothes, gives baths, takes the child to the dentist and doctor, meets with the teacher can all be settled and can even be spelled out in the list of responsibilities. These are concrete issues dealing with money or items of clothing and are easily settled at the outset. Other possible problem areas, having to do with beliefs and feelings, are not so easy to recognize or to prevent.

Once the provider has had an interview with the parent (Chapter 3), she should already have a good idea of where problems may occur. When describing the child, did the parent show any special concern or worry? Is the child sickly (frequent colds, earaches)? Does the parent feel that the child needs more attention than most children? Did the parent say that the child is stubborn and needs to learn to mind, to obey? What clues did the parent give the provider about her special feelings and beliefs about her child, and, therefore, about the care she feels her child should have? If the provider has an idea of what particular concerns each parent has, she can do some preventive work. When the parent comes to pick up the child she can mention how well the child seems to be, how well he or she ate, or slept, or played with the other children. She can remark on how helpful the child was that day or how good natured, whatever she feels will reassure the parent. This may not prevent problems altogether but it will make many potential problems seem less serious. As long as the parent feels the provider is aware of her concerns about the child, she will feel more secure, and will be less apt to come up with problems that have to be solved.

PROBLEM SOLVING

Having prevented all the problems that can be prevented and reduced the others to manageable size, what can one do with those that remain and that demand attention? The first thing to do is to decide if there is a real problem and what that problem is.

PROBLEMS FROM THE PARENTS' POINT OF VIEW

As soon as the provider begins to suspect that the parent is troubled about something, she should get to work on it. First, however, she needs to have an idea of what it is. Unless the parent is a person who says what she has on her mind, the provider may find it hard to figure out what the problem is. She can begin by listening carefully to the child. If the parent is talking to her family about what is on her mind, the chances are that the child has overheard. The child who loves the person he or she spends most of the day with, will talk about what he or she hears at home. If the provider gets no clue from the child, she will have to go to the parent. When the parent comes to get his or her child, the provider should ask outright if there is anything wrong. It could be that the problem is something in the workplace or at home. If the parent denies any problem, the provider should say that if ever there is anything she can do, to please let her know.

If, on the other hand, the parent says there is something wrong, that he or she is not happy about some aspect of the care her child is getting, then the provider should ask immediately for an appointment to talk about it. It should be made for the soonest possible date. Once there is a problem out in the open, it needs to be taken care of quickly. Often just being out in the open will cause the problem to grow. The appointment to talk should be made for a time when parent and provider can be alone, quietly, and in the provider's home, not the parent's. It is always better to be on one's own ground. The provider should have her notebook and pencil at hand to show a businesslike attitude. She should serve coffee or tea or some refreshment.

DISCUSSING THE PARENTS' PROBLEMS

There are two major principles in dealing with any problem. *Be friendly and be quiet.* This works for two reasons. First, it shows that the provider is not on the defensive and that she knows what she is doing. Her attitude should be that this is simply a misunderstanding and will be cleared up as soon as both parties know what the other thinks. Second, after the parent has said everything he or she wants to say and the provider has remained quiet and listened attentively, it will become clear that most of the parent's feelings will have calmed down. The provider should remain quiet and sympathetic looking. Letting the parent talk it out is often a cure in itself, and it is wise not to speak until the parent seems tired of talking and wants the provider to say something.

The next step is not as easy. This is the time for the provider to figure out what is *really* bothering the parent. Beyond the complaint the parent offers, there is usually a more serious problem. For instance, if the parent says that the other children pick on his or her child, he or she may really be saying that he or she is afraid that the child does not know how to defend himself or herself and that the provider is not helping the child to learn how. If she says that her child is becoming very whiny and cranky or exhibiting some other undesirable behavior, she may be worrying that the child is not as happy at home as with the day care family. If it is not possible to figure out what lies behind the complaint, the provider might ask the parent to tell her more, to give some examples.

At some point, regardless of whether the provider has an idea about what the real problem is, she will have to respond. *She should always be positive.* She should never say anything negative about the child. If she does, she will convince the parent that: 1) she does not like the child; and 2) whatever the parent fears about the child may be true. For instance, if the parent feels his or her child is being picked on by the other children and if, indeed, the child does sometimes annoy the others or interrupt their games, the provider should say, "Lenny is learning to play so nicely with the other children. He is joining in their games, even when the others are much older. It is hard sometimes for a child his age to play with other children, but he is really learning."

If it appears that the parent is afraid that her child enjoys being in family day care more than at home, the provider could say something reassuring such as, "Janet talks about you so often. She saw a blue blouse in the store window today and said that her Mommy has one like that, only prettier" or "Sam told me what fun you all had last weekend. He loved the bus ride." She should try to find something to say that will make the parent feel good about himself or herself, contented that he or she is still first in her child's affections and secure that the provider is not trying to win the child away.

As each provider gets to know more and more parents she will find that the things they bring as complaints are often really worries that their children are not getting the love and attention they would get at home, or that they are being allowed to develop some undesirable personality traits and that the parents are away from them too much to correct them. Providers must be reassuring and understanding. They should tell stories to show the parents how good, how strong, how kind, how smart their children are. They can ask the parents if there is anything special they would like done, and whatever it is, tell the parents that they will certainly try.

The meeting should end on a happy note. It helps to tell some story about the child or children that is amusing and that shows how much they are appreciated. As soon as the parent leaves, the provider should make some notes about the meeting in her notebook, describing whatever it is that the parent feels is a problem. That way, she will remember both to pay special attention to the child's needs in that particular area and continue to reassure the parent.

DISCUSSING THE PROVIDER'S PROBLEM

From time to time problems arise that the provider will want to discuss with the parent. These may be even more difficult to handle than the problems the parents bring. Parents are apt to be on the defensive about their children already, both because they have to be away from them so much and because they want to feel that their children are as smart, as well behaved and as attractive as any other children. Therefore, before the provider decides to talk to the parent about a problem with his or her child, she should be very clear in her own mind what she wants the parent to do about it. If it concerns some behavior in the child that she does not really feel the parent can change, it should not be brought up. The only time to bring up a problem the provider does not believe the parent can do anything about is when she has decided not to keep the child. (see Chapter 3).

The kinds of problems that need to be shared with the parents are those that require specific attention. Any health problem should be brought to the parent's attention—a lingering cough, a cold, diarrhea, pink eye, or a cut that does not heal. Any problem that might indicate some special needs, such as the possibility of poor vision or poor hearing, or a perceptual or coordination problem (see Chapter 18), requires the parent's cooperation. Any problem that is mentioned by the school must be shared with the parent. Finally, anything that might be going on in the home that the provider believes to be harmful to the child's physical or psychological development should be discussed with the parent. None of these, however, should be presented to the parent before notes on several occasions have been made describing in detail the behavior that suggests a problem. At the meeting, the notebook should be handy so that the parent can see the descriptions of the behaviors and the dates when they occurred.

Health Problems

These are sometimes the easiest problems to discuss because there is a clear-cut solution: the parent's permission or willingness to take the child for a medical check-up. Bringing up this kind of problem demonstrates the provider's concern for the child, and unless the provider makes the parent feel that he or she should have already done something, the solution is easily reached. Should the parent say he or she feels it is unnecessary to do anything about the problem, it will go away, the provider must say that she cannot continue to keep the child unless something is done to clear up the condition. Finally, a second meeting should be arranged to follow up on whatever treatment was needed and to make sure that the problem has been solved.

Special Needs

These are more likely to upset the parent than health problems because they may suggest to her that her child may be not quite normal. Before meeting with the parent the provider should have specific notes about what behaviors she has observed that suggest a problem (see Chapter 18). Then she should have resources for help listed, such as an eye clinic, or a hearing clinic, or some clinic that tests for learning disabilities or neurological disorders. She can offer to make the appointment for the parent, or, depending on the agreement she has with the parent, offer to take the child to be tested. In any case, cooperation in carrying out the suggestions is necessary, and the parent's willingness must be obtained from the very beginning. If the parent feels that the provider is being supportive and not critical, the chances are that he or she will be cooperative. Again, it should be made clear to the parent that it is the provider's professional opinion that the child should be checked so that if any special care is necessary she will be able to provide it.

School Problems

It is the responsibility of the family day care provider to share with the parent any communication received from the school, good or bad. If it is bad, it can become a problem. In this case, it may help to have some possible solutions ready to offer before meeting with the parent. If it is a matter of homework, the provider can offer to lend a hand in the afternoons. If it is a behavior problem, the parent should be told what was said and he or she should be asked for her ideas. It will help for the provider to have some of her own solutions ready, then the provider and the parent together can study the behavior problem to find out what it means in terms of the child's needs. (See the next five chapters for the developmental needs of each age child.)

Of course, any report of bad behavior will be upsetting to the parent. The best way to deal with the anxiety and distress that the parent has to feel is to come up with a good plan for action. The parent needs help to: 1) understand the meaning of the behavior; 2) figure out what the child needs at that moment; and 3) draw up a plan to meet these needs. A second date should be made after a week or two in order to get together for another talk. Both parent and provider will benefit from the support of the other, and the child will benefit from their united concern and effort.

Home Problems

The more serious home problems—child abuse, wife beating, drug and alcohol abuse—have been discussed in Chapter 6. The next level of home problems can be considered neglect. Like the more serious problems these usually represent such severe conditions that it is difficult, if not impossible, to do anything to help. If a parent neglects to feed a child, or dress a child warmly, or change a child's diapers, or if the parent leaves a child alone in the home, there is something so wrong that simply talking it over is not likely to have much effect.

Again, one has to decide if the child is being harmed, and if so, to what degree. If the provider feels there is real harm to the child she should think about what could be done for the child's protection. These possible solutions must be thought through carefully to make sure that they will indeed help. The provider will want to decide what she thinks is a possible solution *before* she meets with the parent. She needs to decide whether she thinks the parent is able to carry out the solution she proposes. If she decides that an agency might offer some help, she may want to discuss it with the parent first. There is a slight chance that the parent will be able to make enough effort to correct the problem. In this case the provider will need to offer that parent a great deal of support and encouragement.

There are no easy solutions to the problems that arise when two people must agree on how to raise children. Every problem demands some sort of compromise. Having to compromise can feel like having to give up an important belief about what people should be or what people *must* be if they are going to succeed in the world. These beliefs are also very personal. They have to do with what a person is and what that person believes is right. When two people do not agree on what is right, and a problem is seen as *me against you* or *you against me*, there is no way to find a solution. Finding a solution means taking the problem out of the personal—*my beliefs* versus *your beliefs*—and into the more general world of ideas. This is not easy, because by the time two people have already taken a position on one side of the issue, the problem has become personal. It requires real effort to step back, take a look at the problem from a distance, *listen* to the parent, remain quiet, and search for the real reason that the parent is upset (the value or belief that is the real cause of the parent's concern.) If the provider can manage that, she is well on the way to a solution.

Suppose, however, that finding the general idea that is behind the problem still leaves the provider and the parent holding two opposite views. The best thing to do then is to postpone the solution. The parent should be asked to explain her view, the reasons for it, where she got the idea, what she thinks is important about it, and why she feels it could be a problem. Then the provider can say how much she appreciates the parent's time and trouble, and now that it has been explained to her, she has a great deal to think about and they can talk again.

In this way, building trust and respect rather than agreeing about a particular belief becomes the solution. Within any partnership there will always be disagreements—often disagreements about important things. If these occur between respectful and trusting adults, they will not destroy the partnership. If both adults are secure enough to respect beliefs different from their own, and discuss them openly, they can usually agree on a solution, even if the solution is a compromise that simply shows their willingness to work together for the benefit of the child.

8

Providing for Growth and Development

The family day care provider is in the business of giving every child she cares for the chance to develop to the best of his or her ability. She is, in fact, a child development specialist. No other child specialist (pediatrician, teacher, psychologist, nurse, social worker, child psychiatrist) spends as much time or can have as much influence as the family day care provider. She cares for the total child.

The greater part of the child's day is spent with the provider. These hours spent with the provider are the important ones, the daytime hours in which the most learning takes place. Furthermore, the provider's influence extends beyond the time she spends with the children. She makes the connection for the children between their lives with her, their lives at home, and their lives at school. She helps them fit together all the pieces into a whole that makes sense.

There are a few family day care providers who have never had children of their own. The majority, however, have had their own children—some are grown and some are still at home. Most have learned child care on the job and enjoy it.

There is more to raising children than merely enjoyment however. The provider needs a *philosophy*. Doing anything well requires knowing what one wants to accomplish and how to go about it. Every parent and provider *has* a philosophy, although many people do not think about it as such. When someone decides to become a professional child care provider, it becomes necessary to think about what one is doing, what the family day care children need to learn and to be like when they are grown, what that will take, and how to prepare them to be successful in the future when they are finally adults. No one really knows what the future will bring, but we *do* know that the adults of the future will have to adjust to many things that cannot be predicted. Therefore, children must be prepared to learn, to have confidence in themselves and in their ability to make good decisions, and to know good from bad decisions.

The real question, then, is *how* to care for children to assure that they will have what they will need as adults. There is no recipe, of course. The best we can do is use all the knowledge that is available to us and then trust in our own good will and good sense.

The previous chapters have described the general things the expert in child care needs to know about caring for children at home. The next seven chapters describe children at every specific stage, from infancy through elementary school. With this kind of knowledge, a dependable, confident, and considerate person can offer children a fine beginning.

WHAT IS DEVELOPMENT?

The moment the human egg is fertilized, the development of a person begins, and until that person's heart stops beating, development of some kind continues. The fertilized egg develops into an infant who learns how to learn, the infant develops into a toddler who walks and talks. The toddler becomes a young child who develops reading and athletic skills and makes friends. The child becomes a teenager who develops an adult body and the ability to solve problems. The adult develops skills in making and managing money and in sharing his or her life with another person. The middle-aged person develops new interests to fill his or her leisure time and new skills to go with these interests. The old person develops wisdom, along with ways of dealing with physical problems and inactivity. How and what each person develops depends on two things: 1) what that person was born with; and 2) the experiences that person has in the course of growing up. For many years people have argued over which has more effect on what we become: what we are given at birth or what happens to us in our lives. In spite of all the study and all the discussion, we still do not know for sure. We only know that both play a part.

THE STUDY OF DEVELOPMENT

Human development only became a subject of study in the last couple of generations. Even now, we know more about plants and crops, mathematics, rocket building, and cattle breeding than we know about what human beings are and how they become that way. People often raise children with very little knowledge about what a child is and what makes a child do the things he or she does. No one would try to bake a cake without finding out first what goes into the batter, how much and when to beat it, how hot an oven is needed, and how long it should bake; and yet that same person will have a baby and without reading one book on the subject, decide what the child should eat and when, with what and with whom the child should play, what to do when the child is unhappy or in pain, and what behaviors the child should have and when. Raising children is more difficult than baking a cake, or assembling a car, or planting crops, or building a house. Why, then, do people feel that they can do it without any training? Most people would answer that because their parents did it, they can, too. And that is true. Furthermore, most of us, in spite of what happened to us as children, survived and grew up. Most of us are able to live reasonably contented lives and succeed reasonably well at what we try to do, all without our parents having learned a thing about child development. Why, then, should providers need to learn about how children develop? The reason is that providers are professionals in the field of child care, and being professional means knowing more than the average person.

KNOWING WHAT TO EXPECT FROM CHILDREN

How often parents say, "I don't know what makes that child act that way!" And because they do not know why children do certain things, they do not know what to do about it. Parents also say, "I don't know *when* that child will learn!" Not knowing when a child is ready and able to learn certain things can cause unnecessary frustration and misery to the adult and to the child. Providers cannot afford not to know how children develop, what to expect from each age, when to teach certain things and what to do when the child seems to be having some kind of trouble. They have to be able to help children over the rough spots and explain to the parents what the children are going through and why.

THE TROUBLE WITH NOT KNOWING

Problems develop between two people when one person cannot understand why the other person is behaving in a certain way. Everyone has ideas about how other people should act. When children do not behave the way we feel they should, we most often become angry. When their behavior suggests illness, however, we may become frightened. Both fear and anger interfere with the ability to understand and to act sensibly. When the reason for a certain behavior is not clear, it is difficult to know the best way to handle it.

When children behave in ways that are not understood or approved many adults feel that the children are spoiled, or contrary, or having a bad day. The adults may become angry and punish the child. Although the punishment may make the behavior stop, the reason for it is still there so it is not likely that the problem will disappear. In any case, punishment will only make it more difficult for the child to make the adult understand the next time he or she has some need that requires attention.

The family day care provider must know why children do certain things at certain ages and not at other ages. She needs to know how to tell that children are ready to learn certain new things. Knowing *what* to expect will allow the provider to be ready for certain behaviors. Knowing *why* children do the things they do will allow the provider to understand and to direct children's behavior. Knowing *when* children are ready to learn certain things will make the learning easier and more rewarding. Finally, knowing what is to be expected will allow her to recognize any signs that the child's development is not going as it should. She can then do whatever is required to correct the problem.

CHILD DEVELOPMENT—A NEW SCIENCE

Adults have been watching children grow up for thousands of years, and yet the idea of studying child development only occurred a couple of generations ago. Until recently, parents were mainly concerned with trying to keep their children alive. Even today, in many parts of the world, the death rate is high for infants and children. In those places, parents are struggling to feed their children enough and protect them from sickness and harm; they have no time to worry about anything more than their health.

Another reason that parents have not thought much about child development is that children used to be thought of as small adults. These small adults were too little yet to do the things big adults do, but their characters were thought of as already fixed and unchangeable. People said and still say things like, "He acts just like Uncle Arthur and, just like Uncle Arthur, he is hard headed!"

People thought that along with food and shelter, strong discipline and training was all there was to child rearing. Childhood was rather like army basic camp, lots of discipline and some on-the-job training. In the past childhood ended much earlier than it does today. Young children worked on the farm and in the factory. Girls and boys were expected to go to work as soon as they could be hired, and for many jobs this was even before they became adolescents.

As fewer children were needed in the work force, laws were passed to keep them in school longer. Education, instead of on-the-job training, became the work of childhood. In France, people began to be interested in why some children learned more than others. They decided that if they could figure out *how* children learned, they could see to it that *all* children learned. In America, the idea of equality as a basic part of the country's democratic system led people to think that equal education for all would give every child the same kind of preparation and an equal start. It followed that people would begin to learn more in the hope that if every child could be offered a very good beginning, there would be a world in which all people were equally successful.

This has not happened. One reason is that not every child has an equal start. Some children have more and better care, better food, better education, richer and more varied experiences, and more protection than others. Another reason is that experts still do not know how much of a role a child's early life experience plays and how much is determined by birth.

Finally, the idea of child development has not really caught on. Many parents today are so concerned with making a living that they have little time to think about what is going on inside their children. This is not true in only poor families. In middle-class and rich families there are parents more concerned with their own needs and interests than with their children's development. When children do not get the care they need, they grow up with problems that prevent them from being caring adults.

There are some parents who think of child development as a way of making something special out of their children. Instead of using the information about how children develop to provide their children with the best possible beginning, these parents often decide to do experiments on their children, just as scientists do on animals. Here are two famous examples. A violinist claimed that if he could have a child as a toddler, he could make the child into a fine musician. Enough parents were impressed to send him a number of children to work with. He gave these 2 year olds violins and after some years they learned to play. Neither the parents nor the violinist were very interested in the many other things that these children needed to be learning. As the children did not all become outstanding violinists, interest in this particular experiment has faded.

Another famous experiment was done by a well-known professor in a famous university. He created a box to put babies into at birth. The box was designed to provide a perfect environment—clean, perfect temperature, safe. In addition, the professor put into the box play equipment to encourage the child to learn what he thought the child should be learning. He found that just as it is possible to teach pigeons and rats in the laboratory to do what they need to do to get fed, children can also be taught to do many things. The only thing they can not learn about when kept in a box is the real world, and that is the business of child development.

WHY STUDY CHILD DEVELOPMENT?

Child development is like any other subject in one respect: the more you study it the more you find there is to learn. For instance, the more you know about what children learn and how they learn it, the more amazing it is that so many manage to learn so much.

The first thing that we learn from the study of child development is that children do not come into the world empty to be slowly fed with knowledge. For generations children were seen as empty balloons that had to be pumped full of things in order to take off. Their stomachs were fed food and their heads slowly filled with the things adults wanted them to learn. Crawling, walking, talking, feeding oneself, dressing oneself, counting, reading—all these learnings filled the balloon and as the child got bigger more was added. At a certain point, the child was ready to take off into the world.

Now we know that life is more like a cafeteria with many different kinds of food. Each dish is a way of learning, a kind of learning. As we grow up we take what we can use and need at each stage of life. As we have enough of one kind of food we move on to another kind. We outgrow some things and move on to something new. A big child will not eat pablum, and a baby cannot eat broiled lobster. Knowing what the mind can digest is as important as knowing what the stomach can.

If we look at life and learning in terms of providing what is appropriate at each stage we can quickly understand one of the important facts that child development teaches. It is that children not only know *less* than adults, it is that they know things *differently*. In other words, their understanding is not only less, it is completely different. The biggest problems in child rearing come from not knowing that the child's view is different from ours, and that it is not that the child *will not* see things out way, it is that the child *cannot* because the child's way of seeing things is dictated by the stage he or she is in. Only by giving the child a wide choice of experiences can we help her or him to grow and develop.

FOUR KINDS OF CHILD DEVELOPMENT

One can look at child development in four general ways: physical, social, intellectual, and emotional. There are other ways as well, but they can be seen as part of these four general categories. Each of these kinds of development is connected to each of the others. No part of a person makes sense without the rest.

Physical Development

As has already been said, physical development was for a long time the only kind of child development. For many people today it is still their greatest concern. This is understandable in families that have suffered illness or physical handicaps. In generally healthy families that can afford to eat good food and live in a place that is reasonably safe and free from disease and danger, children should be able to grow healthy and strong. They, of course, still need to be protected from illness with regular visits to the well-baby clinic to get immunized against childhood diseases and to make sure they are free of any conditions that could affect normal development. They need to learn to care for their bodies, to avoid danger whenever possible, to treat their illnesses before they become severe, and to exercise to build strength and control. None of that is very difficult; and yet looking at the people in the street, in the stores, in the schools, a very small number appear to be healthy, strong, and energetic. Many are overweight, many more are physically lazy, a number seem unhealthy. When asked what kind of physical shape they are in, few adults would answer "excellent." Yet in the richest country in the world, there is no reason why most of us are not in excellent health.

It is important to develop well physically because our physical well-being affects everything we do. To the degree that we are not feeling well, we cannot work well or play well. Children who must constantly fight off colds, sore throats, stomachaches, fevers, coughs, earaches, have little strength left to learn, to play, to notice the world around them.

Another reason that our physical development is so important is our sense of confidence. The first thing that other people notice about us is our physical appearance. If we feel that we are attractive then we can deal with other people with confidence and security. If not, we are at a disadvantage. People who take an interest in how they look usually look well and are able to deal with other people successfully.

A third reason that physical development is so important has to do with being competent, being capable. Little children, even babies, interact with the world in a physical way. They reach for things, shake them, bang them, and throw them. These are the ways in which they can make things happen. As they begin to crawl, then stand, then walk, they take great pleasure in what they can do with their bodies. They act out what they are thinking. As they begin to take over doing things for themselves they take pride in their ability. The more they can do, the more competent they feel. The more competent they feel, the more they will try to do and the more they will learn to do. A sense of competence may be the most important thing a child can have.

Finally, the physical development of the child affects the child's development socially, intellectually, and emotionally. As each of these kinds of development are described, the connection between physical and social, physical and emotional, and physical and intellectual will become clear. After all, we live in our bodies, we express ourselves with our bodies, and for all our lives our bodies express our most moving experiences.

Social Development

When we consider all we must learn in order to live in a civilized world, it does not seem that one lifetime could be enough. Furthermore, many of these learnings take place when one is very young, and, if for some reason they do not, one's future is in trouble. Why? And what are these early learnings?

Probably the earliest and most difficult things children must learn are the meaning of the word "no" and the use of the toilet. Both require the very young child to put aside what the child wants and accept what the adult wants. There is no other reason to do this except that the child is very attached to the adult and loves the adult so much that pleasing him or her is more important than having his or her own way. For most children, it is very difficult to accept these demands, and it takes quite a while before they realize that this is serious and there is no way out. Most children decide that the battle is not worth it, and settle for the approval and the praise of the loved person.

These are examples of the first big social demands on the very young, but there are many others. The child must learn to wait, to take turns, to share, to say "please" and "thank you" and to do what others say, even when it seems very unreasonable.

Finally, the child must learn to take responsibility for what he or she does, to be truthful, and to consider the feelings and needs of others. That is a large order for a 5 year old, but to the best of our knowledge these skills have been learned by age 5. The child will continue to learn new social skills in school, but the basic work has been done by the time the child enters school.

How well that work has been done can be seen at the end of first grade. The child with well-developed social skills will be a leader, have friends, and be a child that the teacher likes and enjoys helping. The child with poor social skills will decide that school is an unpleasant place and he or she does not belong there. For this reason, social skills have a great deal to do with school success.

Intellectual Development

In our country it is generally believed that to be successful one has to be "smart." The worst insult one can make is to call someone "dumb" or "stupid." One can call another person a liar or a cheat or a crook or almost anything else but if he or she is a *smart* liar or a *good* con man or even a *clever* criminal a certain amount of respect is given. And yet we have only begun to learn how a child becomes smart. In fact, almost everything we know we have learned in the lifetime of one man, Jean Piaget, who recently died in Switzerland. From him we know that children are born with the ability to learn, that at the time of birth they are ready to begin learning, and that these experiences of infancy are important to all future learning. We know that this early learning is physical and at the age of about 2 years, when the child begins speaking, thinking begins to take over from simply doing. These very early experiences have a great deal to do with how much children will be able to learn as they grow up.

The most important thing we have learned about intellectual development is that children understand the world *differently*. When it is difficult to explain something to a child it is not that the child is not intelligent and it is not that the adult cannot explain clearly, it is that the child has such a different view of the world from the adult that the adult's view and the child's cannot be placed in the same frame. Some adults think that children can accept the adult's view if they really want to, or if they just try. What they do not realize is that as children's minds go through stages of development, they learn and do things according to how they are thinking at that time. Adults who do not understand this end up making learning difficult or painful for the children they want to teach.

Emotional Development

As with the other areas of development, we do not yet know how much of our emotional development is determined by what we are born with and how much is learned through experience. Certainly we have heard people say that a certain infant began crying at birth and never stopped. Another baby is quiet and calm, eats contently, and sleeps peacefully. Some babies jump at the slightest noise and cry nervously. Others may startle and grunt and continue to sleep. Nurses who work in hospitals with newborns know that there are many differences in babies' behavior that are present at birth.

As we grow up we learn to handle our emotions; some of us learn to do it well and others less well. Although there is a great deal that we know we can do to help children understand, control, and enjoy their emotions, there is clearly an inborn difference in the strength of children's emotions and in their ability to deal with them. Some children need more help than others in learning how to cope. The number of people using drugs and alcohol as a way of avoiding emotional stress is frightening. What is even more frightening is that many of these drugged people are parents whose children are not only not learning how to deal with emotional stress but are suffering the added strain of having to deal with addicted parents. Among middle- and upper-class parents alcohol may appear to be a more common way of dulling the emotions than drugs, but tranquilizers are used as well. The combination of alcohol and tranquilizers is as efficient as any of the street drugs in blotting out one's feelings and one's surroundings.

Why has the emotional development of people suffered so much in recent years? It is clear from the advertisements on television and the radio and in magazines that Americans have permission to avoid distress. We no longer believe that we should suffer any discomfort, certainly not when "relief is just a minute away."

The idea that suffering makes a person strong and noble was a religious idea which has now become less popular. If suffering does not make one strong or noble, then why not avoid it? If it is physical pain and can not be cured, certainly there is no reason not to avoid it if one can. But if the suffering is emotional, it can often be cured and, better yet, it can be prevented. It can be prevented by teaching young children to understand their emotions and by helping them learn to manage them. To do this, adults must be good examples. To learn to manage our emotions we have to learn to believe in ourselves, to believe in our ability to do well and to be able to succeed at what we want to do. The most painful and destructive of all the emotions are self-hate, doubt, and fear. These can be prevented by good child rearing practices.

In the next chapters each stage of childhood and some of the developments of each are examined. The kind of care that gives children the chance to grow strong physically, socially, emotionally, and intellectually is described. As the provider learns about the behaviors of each stage of development, she will want to make notes about the development of each child in her family day care home. The notebook described in Chapter 2 will have a section in it for each child. It should be kept handy so that notes can be made from time to time. Any behaviors that show signs of growth, of a new skill, of a possible problem, or simply something to think about at leisure should be recorded. These notes will provide the material needed when talking with the parents about their children. They will also serve as a profile of each child's development as the provider learns more about the ways each individual child learns to understand, respond to, and act in the world.

9

Providing for Infants

The provider who cares for a child from infancy can influence the whole life of that person. For many years we believed that before infants walked and talked, nothing that happened to them made any real difference in their later personality. Now we know that what happens before children can talk, even what happens from birth on, has a great deal to do with both the success they will have and the problems they will face as adults. Long before infants can say a word, they are learning about being a person.

One reason that infancy has not seemed such an important time is that there are so few things that infants can do—they eat, sleep, look around, and cry. It is hard to believe that these few behaviors can have much to do with adult life; but in fact, the fewer things a person can do, the more important the doing of each becomes, and these simple behaviors are the beginnings of the adult person.

THE EFFECT OF EARLY CARE

To understand the effect of infant care on how the child grows up we must look at the basic kinds of learning that take place in the first 12 to 15 months—the learning about things, about people, about thinking, and about becoming a person. From birth to about 3 months, infants are mostly trying to adjust to the outside world and learning what to expect in the way of care. Then, suddenly, at about 3 months of age, babies become adorable, interesting little people. A great deal of learning goes on between 3 and 8 months. The last stage of infancy is the time from 8 months until the infant walks and becomes a toddler. Providers do not usually have infants younger than

8 weeks in their care. At whatever age the infant comes to family day care, however, his or her behavior will reveal a lot about what went on in those first weeks of life and what the infant has already learned.

BABY BOOK

When the provider accepts an infant into her family day care home, she needs to buy a notebook in which to keep a record of the baby's daily feedings and naptimes. Each day she will put the date at the top of a new page. When the parent comes to pick up her infant, she will look at the book to know how often, when, and how much her baby was fed, how much the infant slept, and any other information the provider has recorded. This might be a new behavior, like rolling over, growing a new tooth, noticing a hand, or grabbing a foot. When the infant is one year old, the book can be presented to the parent as a birthday present (and a new one started for the baby's second year).

PREVENTION OF ILLNESS

The care of infants requires special efforts to prevent the spread of illness. In Chapter 4 the arrangement of the bathroom for infant care is described. The provider needs a convenient place to change infants (and toddlers) close to water so that she can wash the child when necessary and her own hands after every change. A closed container for soiled clothes and a tightly covered can for disposable or cloth diapers are necessary so that germs do not spread and toddlers can not get to these items. From time to time the toys that infants and toddlers play with need to be thoroughly washed in hot soapy water and then carefully rinsed and dried. These simple precautions can make child care easier for the provider and prevent many of the runny noses and diarrheas that infants and toddlers may otherwise have.

EARLY INFANCY

The care of very young infants takes a great deal of time and often seems to be an enormous job. One reason is that in our civilization the infant and the mother or provider live quite separate lives. In other cultures, the infant and mother remain very close after birth and many of the infant's early needs are met with ease and comfort. Some Eskimo women carry their infants inside their clothes, keeping them warm and nursing them without effort; these infants never know the panic and pain of hunger. Some Indian women carry their infants around on their backs on a board or in a sort of basket.

Some African and some South American women carry their infants tied to their bodies with a shawl or large cloth. For these infants, the movement and the closeness to the mother are not so different from their experience before birth.

In our civilization, however, we usually place babies in cribs. For newborns who have been in a very tight place for 9 months, it can be alarming to be suddenly laid out on a sheet on a hard crib mattress. They often manage to wiggle into a corner of the crib where they can feel close to something, if not to their mother's body. Often a fretting newborn can be comforted simply by being wrapped in a blanket or soft cloth of some kind and placed in a carriage or other small place. Those arms and legs that are not yet under control are then held close and secure.

Movement

A few years ago it was found that if premature infants are put into a rocking bed they gain weight faster and develop better than if they are kept in a still incubator or bassinet. Being moved around as they have been before birth makes a real difference in their well-being. Babies with normal birth weights are also able to benefit from being rocked in a rocking chair, bassinet, crib, or carriage.

Key Care Ideas

- If a carriage is available, infants should be taken out in it, and allowed to nap in the carriage when at home.
- Small babies should nap in a carriage so that they can be gently rocked if they need help falling asleep.
- When the infant is wakeful, the provider should hold him or her in her arms in a rocking chair while watching over the other children.
- If the infant is fretful, an older child can be asked to rock the infant's carriage gently or jiggle the crib.
- It may be necessary to explain to parents the reason for wrapping young infants in a lightweight blanket or cloth.

Feeding

In the first few weeks of life, infants have to get used to the routine of feeding. Each infant has individual food needs and these needs change from day to day. It takes many weeks for the newborn's stomach to adjust to being filled up every few hours. The stomach has to learn how to digest properly. Colic is one of the ways that infants' stomachs protest being filled, sometimes too full and sometimes not often enough. Feeding newborns small amounts and often during these first few weeks makes it easier for those brand-new stomachs to learn to handle regular meals. Mostly, however, it is just a matter of getting a few weeks older. Colic, for instance, disappears naturally after a couple of months, once the newborn's body has grown up a bit and has learned to do the job.

It is not necessary nor is it a good idea to overfeed infants. The best way to avoid this is to keep a record of the times and amounts (number of ounces) the infant takes at each feeding. The average infant will take between 21 and 24 ounces of formula *a day* for the first few weeks; this can be increased over the next couple of months to about 32 ounces. The infant who cries after having had 4 or 5 ounces may be having trouble digesting (colic) or may be having trouble falling asleep. Gentle rocking in a rocking chair or a carriage can help the infant fall asleep. A pacifier will often soothe an infant who has a full tummy but is still fretting.

Key Care Ideas

- Feeding young infants smaller amounts more often will help the infant get regulated more quickly and easily than trying to keep to a schedule of every 4 hours.
- Keeping a record of the number of ounces taken and the times of feedings will help the provider decide whether the infant is getting enough.
- A lot of burping *will not* prevent colic. One gentle burping after the infant seems to have had enough is all that is necessary. Pounding on infants' backs can only make digesting more difficult. When infants are held so that their bodies are upright, any gas in their stomachs will come up naturally.
- Each day the provider should show the parent the Baby Book with the time of the last feeding and the number of ounces taken.

Sleeping

We now know that human beings are not born knowing how to fall asleep and sleep well. Like everything else, babies have to learn to fall asleep. This can take a few weeks or even more, depending on how much help the infant gets. Doctors who study infants' sleep have found that movement seems to help infants learn to fall asleep and then sleep well. In fact, movement seems to encourage the development of other behaviors controlled by the brain. Those mothers all over the world who carry their infants around with them are doing something that directly helps the development of their babies' brains.

Some 10 or 20 years ago, parents complained about their children's eating problems. Nowadays most of those eating problems seem to have been replaced with sleeping problems. These sleeping problems begin when the child is very small.

<u>Key Care Ideas</u>

- Gentle rocking in a rocking chair or a carriage, or gently jiggling the crib will usually help an infant fall asleep.
- Babies can learn to sleep through the noise of a radio, television, voices, and street sounds, but their sleep will suffer. Their later learning will also suffer. When infants have to shut off the rest of the world in order to sleep, they often have trouble turning the world back on. It is worth the effort to find a quiet place in the home where infants will not be disturbed by noise.
- Whenever possible, a sleeping infant should not be disturbed. Disturbing an infant's sleep is one of the main causes of later sleeping problems. When the provider knows that she will have to take the infant out (to meet the school children, for instance), she should put him or her down in the carriage so that she can gently take the carriage out without disturbing the baby's sleep.

Exercise

It has already been mentioned that newborns and infants are more comfortable and more peaceful when wrapped snugly and placed in a small, cozy place. For instance, the best way to comfort a crying newborn is to hold the baby in one arm and hold the baby's arms and hands close to the baby's chest with the other hand. Then speak softly to the infant. When the arms are under control, the infant is more easily comforted (see Figure 12).

For the first 6 weeks or 2 months of life, infants are apt to be more relaxed, more comfortable and less fretful if wrapped in a soft cloth or a light blanket (see Figure 13). In most of Europe, for instance, babies are tightly wrapped in lightweight blankets or squares of cloth all year round (see Figure 14). In some countries, their arms are free, in others the arms are wrapped inside the blanket. Babies carried in shawls, in the mother's clothes, and as papooses are also held close. In Russia, many mothers still wrap their babies so securely that they are like neat packages ready for mailing.

In America, wrapping babies is rarely done. One reason is that it is thought to interfere with the need for exercise. Babies *do* need exercise to grow strong healthy bodies; however, since they do not do a lot of exercising in their sleep, there is no reason why they cannot have the security of being wrapped. The ideal exercise time is during the bath. If the provider bathes the infant while the other children are napping or busy and not apt to need her attention, she can allow the infant plenty of time to kick and stretch and exercise in the water. After the bath is a good time to play a few exercise games.

Providing for Infants

Figure 12.

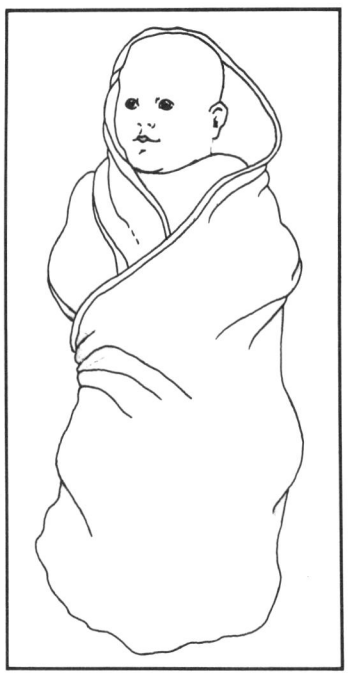

Figure 13.

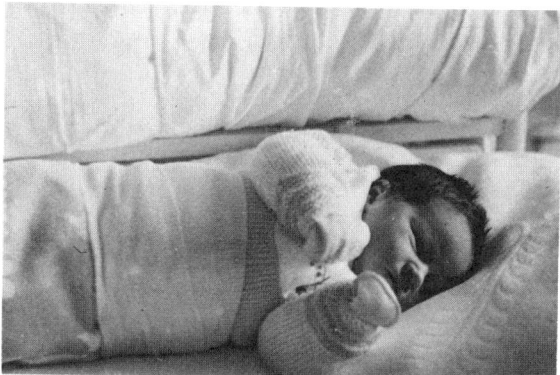

Figure 14.

Exercises

- After putting the baby on the dressing table, the provider can hold one of the baby's hands in each of her own. She can bring the baby's hands together over the baby's chest, then stretch the baby's hands out to the sides. This should be repeated a couple of times, talking to the baby continuously (Figure 15).
- The provider can also place her hands against the baby's feet and let the baby kick at her hands. It is a good idea to say something each time the baby kicks and successfully hits the provider's hands, like "You got me!" or "Hey Superman!" or whatever comes to mind. That way the baby can connect the provider's response with his or her own kick (Figure 16).

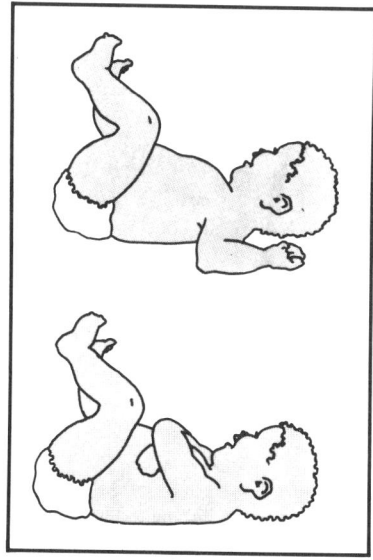

Figure 15.

Providing for Infants

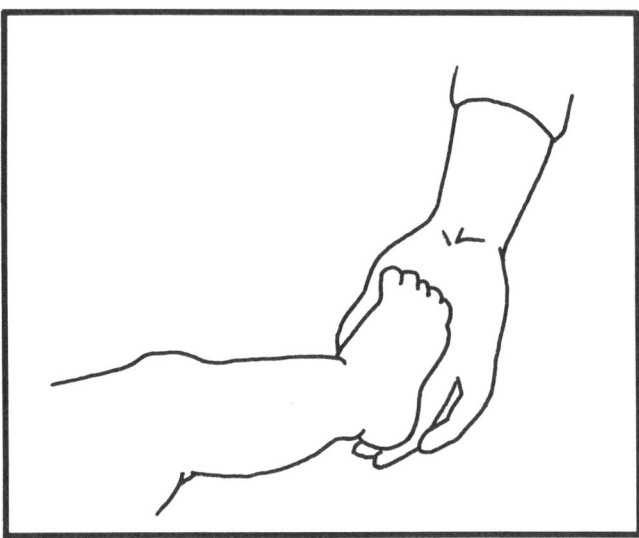

Figure 16.

Even in these first 12 weeks babies need a little exercise each day. The easiest times are the changing, dressing, and bathing times.

About People

Within the first 24 hours after birth infants are interested in other people. A day-old infant, when awake and not crying, will turn his or her head to the sound of a soft, gentle voice. A newborn can be comforted by being held and talked to softly. Within weeks the voice of that person who takes care of the baby becomes special and more comforting than all other voices.

Seeing other people is even more important to infants than hearing them. When nursing or being held and fed a bottle, infants will look directly into the eyes of the person feeding them if that person looks at the infant. Looking is so important that if the nipple is taken out of a hungry baby's mouth, as long as the baby is looking into the eyes of the person holding him or her, the baby will wait for the nipple to be returned. Of course, if the nipple is not put back in the infant's mouth, there will eventually be a protest.

Animal studies have supported the importance of seeing. Baby geese and ducks will follow the first moving thing they see after they hatch. If the eggs are taken away from the mother goose or duck and put to hatch near some other moving thing, the newly hatched gosling or duckling will take that moving thing for a mother, and follow it faithfully. Konrad Lorenz, who did these studies, found that baby geese would adopt him, a human male, as a mother. In one strange experiment, newly hatched ducks adopted a football as a mother. In every case, they continued to copy the movements of the man or the football until given to their real mothers who adopted them and taught them how to be ducks or geese.

Humans also need to be "claimed." The ways that humans make that first contact with their newborns are almost exactly the same the world over. They examine the hands and fingers of the newborn, touch the cheek with their fingers, stroke the infant's cheek with the back of their fingers, and touch the newborn's head with their lips.

Looking and touching are the first signs of sociability. Voices are also important from the first day. Within days an infant will smile at the sight of whomever cares for the infant, if that person looks into the infant's face, talks, and nods. By 8 to 9 weeks, hearing the voice of that person will often bring a smile to the infant's face. Within a few weeks, the infant begins to make sounds when someone puts her face near the infant's and talks to the infant.

By 3 months these "conversations" are very important and have a lot to do with the infant's later language development. Chapter 11 is devoted to language and describes the connection between babbling and later language development.

There is much disagreement about many things regarding the development of infants in the first 3 months. About one thing, however, there is general agreement. Infants crave touching, holding, looking at, and listening to a warm, gentle, calming person. This first contact is the beginning of learning how to be a sociable human being.

Key Care Ideas

- Everytime the infant is changed, dressed, undressed, bathed, and fed there should be some conversation. The adult can nod and talk with the baby, smiling and repeating some of the words or sentences.

- When about to pick up the infant she should say so, so that the infant gets used to hearing the provider coming and knows what is going to happen. This way, the infant learns to connect hearing the voice, then seeing, and then feeling the provider's touch.

- Those few short waking times should be sociable for the infant. While the provider is supervising the homework or playing a game or reading a story with the older children, the infant can lie in her lap and enjoy the company.

Thinking

We now know that in these first months infants are also beginning to learn about the world. They are learning the difference between a pacifier and a bottle or the breast. They are learning the difference between a thumb

Providing for Infants 119

and a hard toy. They are also learning the difference between a rattle and a toy that makes no noise. They can follow an object with their eyes, look around when they hear a noise, turn away from a bright light. They are beginning to learn about making things happen, whether it is making the water in the bath splash, making sounds with their mouths, or shaking or kicking a toy. They are beginning to reach for things. They can tell what is going to happen before they are fed, bathed, or picked up just from the sounds they hear. They will wait quietly as soon as they hear these sounds. All of these are the beginnings of thinking, the beginnings of learning.

At this early age the most important learning depends upon the person who cares for the infant. Before infants can become interested in things they have to be "turned on" by that person. At this point, they are completely dependent on the care and attention they get. They are not even aware as yet that they exist as separate from that person who holds them, feeds them, rocks them. They can become interested in a rattle or other toy that is shown to them, but it is really only borrowed interest, shared interest. They are ready to learn, but at this point, they must learn *through* that person who is still their "other self."

<u>Key Care Ideas</u>

- The provider can talk to the infant while getting the bottle or the bath ready saying aloud what is going on and what will happen next.
- Some time should be spent each day holding the infant, singing, talking, holding hands, and playing touching games.
- A cradle gym or some other toy can be tied with an elastic in the infant's crib or carriage. If the toy rattles or shakes, the infant will become interested. As mentioned above, objects are only interesting at this age when someone makes them so.

The Beginning of Personality

The care that infants receive has an important effect on their personality. If their body needs are taken care of promptly and tenderly, they will feel secure and safe and will have confidence in the world. Adults who have a sense of self-confidence have been well cared for as infants.

Infants crave contact with people. Without it they become fearful, retarded in their development, and unable to respond to other people. Cases of real neglect, such as in some orphanages or where children have been locked in a room by a crazy parent, are rare. More than *just enough* care is needed, however. Adults who are sensitive to infants, to their helplessness, to their need for company, to the way they like best to be held, will raise children who are strong and secure, who feel safe in the world, and who have confidence that they will be able to manage.

There are parents who feel that responding to infants too quickly results in spoiled children, that the world is a tough place and infants had better get used to that idea from the beginning. This is one of the many examples of the ways that adults confuse the infants' thinking with their own. Infants have no understanding of themselves as separate beings or what happens to them. When they are allowed to cry in desperation, the only thing that they learn is to be depressed. When their cries get no attention, infants become insecure, untrusting, and unhappy. To them the world is not a good place. In some of the films made in orphanages where infants are merely fed, bathed, and changed but otherwise ignored, the depression is so great that many of the infants no longer cry. They are past crying. Their sadness is so great that they make no sound, no movement. Many do not live to be 2 years old.

When babies' cries are heard, and their need to be fed or rocked or played with is understood, there are two outcomes. One is that the infants find a comfortable routine that suits their bodies' needs and the other is that they have less need to cry. Babies whose cries have been answered cry much less than those who have been allowed to cry unnoticed. This is why infants at this age cannot be spoiled. Because infants are not able to understand why things happen, the most they can learn is that the people who care for them will come when they need them. This kind of trust is directly connected to the later ability to learn, both at home and in school.

Another important part of infant care is protection from overstimulation. Just as infants are dependent on adults to protect their bodies, they are also dependent for emotional protection. All infants have times of distress and crying, every day, often from some reason other than hunger. Because it is hard to know what the cause of the distress is, it is often hard to know how to comfort the baby. If there is nothing obvious to do—the infant has been fed, is dry, is comfortably dressed—the best comfort is usually rocking, walking the baby, singing, or talking softly. The important thing to remember is that infants cannot decide not to cry or learn to be less distressed. They have to be helped. Letting babies cry and become more and more upset is not good child care. This kind of overstimulation does not help children become strong. Letting infants cry it out does not prevent spoiling. It only makes it harder for them to learn to control their own feelings.

As already seen in newborn nurseries, some infants need more protection from distress, tiredness, and excitement than others. They are less able to calm down, to relax, to be able to eat or sleep when upset. Because infants cannot decide when *not* to play, *not* to get too excited, and *not* to get overtired by themselves, the person who cares for them must. Otherwise, infants feel lost, overwhelmed, and out of control. When adults help infants learn to manage their feelings, the infants then learn how it's done.

Key Care Ideas

- When the provider is busy, an older child who enjoys babies can be a great help with a crying baby. Children often love rocking or walking babies. It lets them express tenderness and concern as well as their own competence and maturity.
- Because infants need to be protected from too much excitement and distress, the older children need to learn that they must not play too loudly or too long with the baby. The provider should watch for signs that the infant is becoming excited or jumpy.
- A pacifier will fall out of a very small infant's mouth until he or she has learned how to keep it in, but once used to it, a pacifier can be comforting to a fretting infant.

MIDDLE INFANCY—3 TO 5 MONTHS

By 3 to 3½ months newborns have become smiling, babbling babies who are very interested in things and people. Instead of sleeping most of the time, they have regular wakeful times and want to play. Their bodies are working well, and if they have had colic it is now gone. They eat, digest, and sleep more easily. They can also see and hear as well as an adult, and when they cry, they now have tears. Soon they can grab a toy that is held close and shake it, bang it, put it in their mouths. If there is no toy, they often study their hands or feet. Now they are strong enough to hold their feet up and they learn to grab them and sometimes pull their toes up to their mouths. They carry on long babbling conversations, they imitate what they see, and they are a pleasure.

A Word of Caution

Now is the time for providers to watch the reactions of the other children to the infant carefully. Little children especially are apt to be jealous. Toddlers who only yesterday were infants feel their place has been taken, that the attention they were getting is now going to another. The provider can prevent some of these feelings by finding time when the infant is sleeping to spend with these children. When feeding the infant she can talk with the other children about *their* interests or games, not about the infant.

Parents often deal with jealousy by asking the older child to "help with the baby" by holding the bottle or doing some other job. This is supposed to make the older child feel grown-up and protective. Actually, this frequently makes it more difficult for the older child, who is then forced to deny his or her feelings and pretend to enjoy the job. If the provider makes sure the older children have something interesting to do while she cares for the infant, then keeps an eye on them to make sure they are content, eventually they will want to examine the baby and help care for him or her. Then with *careful* supervision the provider can let an older child help. The main thing to keep in mind is that toddlers *can* hurt an infant when they cannot control their feelings of jealousy and therefore must be watched and kept busy and contented until they get used to having an infant around.

Movement

Babies at this age move a great deal on their own and therefore have less need to be moved about. Rocking is still comforting and sociable but not as necessary as it is for the newborn's brain development.

Feeding

By 3½ months infants have acquired a routine and eat at more or less regular times; colic symptoms are gone, and the baby's body is grown-up enough to manage eating and digesting. Eating has become a social event; most infants smile and babble contentedly during their mealtimes.

Key Care Ideas

- At this age the baby's feeding time does not usually fit with the older children's, which allows the provider to give the baby her complete attention when feeding him or her. She can make sure the other children are busy and contented so that there will be plenty of time to talk and play with the baby before and after the feeding.
- Solid foods are usually added around 6 months, depending on the wishes of the parents and the well baby clinic or pediatrician. Chapter 19 describes how to make sure these first solid foods are healthy.
- It is still important to record feeding times and amounts in the Baby Book to show the parent each day.

Sleeping

By this time most infants have learned to sleep through the night. Some still need some help getting to sleep, a little rocking or jiggling of the crib, but if they are put to bed in a quiet place and not waked by noise or otherwise disturbed, most infants at this age take two long naps during the day and sleep through the night. If the crib is placed where it is quiet and away from the noise of the other children (the provider's bedroom perhaps) and if the times when the infant is sleeping remain uninterrupted or disturbed, the infant will develop good sleeping habits.

Providing for Infants

Key Care Ideas

- Infants still need a quiet place to sleep. The provider still needs to tell the older children to play someplace away from the sleeping infant.
- Naptimes should be recorded in the Baby Book to show the parent each evening.

Exercise

By the age of 3 months, unless it is bitter cold, most infants no longer need to be wrapped. Even at 6 weeks, the comfort of being held close, of being wrapped in a blanket, is less necessary. By 3 months, babies enjoy the freedom to kick and turn to one side and the other. When placed on their stomachs, they can hold their heads straight up for minutes at a time. By 3 or 4 months, babies are eager exercisers. They bring their own hands together and hold them, fingers locked together. They move their clasped hands up and down. Kicking is another favorite exercise, and they kick at anything their feet can reach.

Key Care Ideas

- Plenty of time can be allowed for the bath so that the infant can play in the water.
- Exercises can continue after the bath while dressing the infant. When infants kick against the provider's hands, she can take the infant's feet and gently stretch out his or her legs. The same thing can be done with the infant's hands. The provider can gently stretch them up over the baby's head, and then out to the sides. She can hold the infant under the arms and allow her or him to "dance" on tiptoe on the table or on her lap.
- During a wakeful time of day, the provider can place the infant on a mat on her or his stomach. If the other children are nearby, the infant will watch them with great interest. This allows the infant to practice holding up his or her head and to develop arm muscles.
- Sometime between 3 and 5 months most babies learn to roll over from their stomachs to their backs. Rolling back is more difficult and usually takes more time. Rolling over is the first means of travel that babies acquire, some can go from one end of the crib to another, or quickly go from the middle of the mat or pad onto the floor.

About People

Babies 3 to 5 months old are usually very sociable. In fact, well-cared for babies at this age often seem happier than at any other time in their lives.

They smile at the provider, at the other children, at interesting toys. They babble when the provider talks to them, and when she plays games, such as "Peekaboo" and "So Big", they chuckle or give a big belly laugh. Although they are now very clear about who their favorite people are, they are sociable and have smiles and conversations for everyone. They are, in fact, adorable.

Key Care Ideas

- This is a time to take advantage of this lovely age and include the baby in group activities except when it is the baby's naptime. An infant seat gives the baby a good view of the goings-on. Older children enjoy talking to an infant and getting smiles and babbling in return. They are also amused to hand an infant the rattle that keeps falling and watch the infant shake, bang, and chew it, and then let it fall again.
- Changing and dressing times are still excellent for conversations. When the infant babbles or gurgles or makes some noise, the provider can imitate the sound. The infant will usually then imitate the provider. From about 2 months on infants love to engage in imitating games.
- At this stage, babies will grab the provider's hair or poke at her face when held close enough. This is also the time when some adults show their lack of understanding of infants. They may not realize sometimes that babies find faces very interesting, especially noses, eyes, and hair. Some adults get angry and act as if the infant's pulling, poking, and pinching was meant to hurt. Having no idea that what they do has an effect, babies often bite their own toes without knowing what they are doing. It will be a few years before they can begin to understand feelings—their own or another person's—or know that feelings have a cause.

Thinking

At this age babies develop intense feelings of curiosity. They are not happy just to look, they begin to reach out, to try to hit, grab, touch, stroke, taste, and chew on everything they can get their hands on. They become little scientists studying the world around them. The more things they are able to explore, the more they learn. At this age infant seats are alright if they are placed so that the infant can reach and play with a crib gym or mobile or other toy tied to something close enough to reach. Placing infants on their stomachs on a pad on the floor is still better because it allows them to study the toys around them as well as the pad itself or whatever they are on. Being on a pad also allows them to exercise. Before too many months the infant will be crawling.

Sometime after 3 months infants become good grabbers. Whatever they can reach, they grab and put through the usual tests—tasting, shaking, banging, and dropping.

Because at this age infants are awake about 6 hours total during the day, they can join in a lot of the family day care activities. The home is a fascinating place for infants. They enjoy watching the provider make lunch or snack (especially if they have some measuring spoons to play with), or the bath of the other children (with a squeeze toy or washcloth to hold), or the other children's games. Infants will often listen along with the older children to stories or to records. The family day care home provides much for infants to think about and learn from.

More about Becoming a Person

Babies of this age are such good company that they are easy to enjoy. Their first laughs are so pleasing that there is a temptation to overdo it. It is important to remember, however, that although adults can turn away when *they* have had enough, babies cannot. They not only become tired but they also overload their nervous system. Some adults discover that babies around 4 months can be tickled for the first time. If they overdo tickling, it becomes not only distressing but also frightening to the infants. This is also true of roughhouse games. Many people who do not feel easy with babies play very rough games of pretending to drop them or pretending to throw them over their shoulders. People who play this way with babies need to be shown other games, such as hiding a toy under a cloth and then finding it, making funny noises and faces, and playing imitating games.

MIDDLE INFANCY—5 TO 8 MONTHS

Two big things happen at this age: infants learn to sit up alone and they learn to crawl. Both make a big difference in their lives and in the care they need. They can join the other children at mealtimes and snack times in a high chair. They can no longer be put down on a pad on the floor near the other children's games since they can now try to join in, at which time it is the older children's interests that have to be protected.

Feeding

By 5 months many infants are on a three-meal-a-day schedule. This may make it harder to feed the infant and still attend to the older children's needs. It may help to feed the infant before giving the other children their meal. Once fed and content, the infant can have a piece of apple or a piece of toast and watch the other children eat, which gives the provider time to sit and enjoy eating with them. Infants want to feed themselves at this age and they begin to pick up and play with tiny objects like crumbs.

Key Care Ideas

- Infants can now have some foods that they can eat by themselves. They still probably need to be fed most of their meal.
- This is a good time to give infants a cup to drink from, one with a no-spill top is good for starters.
- Infants enjoy being in a high chair during the older children's mealtimes and enjoy the company. They should not sit until they become tired and cross, however, because the idea is for them to continue to enjoy being a part of the day care family.
- A record still needs to be kept of what infants eat each day in the Baby Book to share with the parents when they come to get their babies.

Sleeping

Most infants at this age take a morning and an afternoon nap. Errands or shopping should be arranged so that the infant can nap without having to be waked. If the older children rest in the afternoon, they can either use another room or have their rest at a different time. It is unlikely that they can share a room with the infant without disturbing his or her sleep.

Key Care Ideas

- The provider should tell the parents about any unusual nap times (a very long afternoon nap, or a very late nap, or no nap) so that they will know what to expect at bedtime. (Sometimes parents will glance at the Baby Book but not really notice something unusual unless the provider mentions it.)
- Outdoor playtime can be planned so that it does not interfere with the infant's nap time.

Exercise

By 5 months infants have well-developed muscles. They can now roll over from stomach to back and back to stomach. They will soon learn to sit up and to crawl. To do this they need space. A pad on the floor is the best, at least until the infant can crawl off the pad and into the other children's activities. Infants need no encouragement to practice rolling over, sitting, or crawling. They do all these with joy.

Key Care Ideas

- A clear carpet area or a pad placed on the floor allows the infant to practice the new physical skills that come at this age.

Providing for Infants

- Bath and dressing time can still double as exercise time.
- Any new behavior or skill learned is recorded in the Baby Book, along with the day's usual records of feeding times and amounts and nap times.

About People

Infants at this age are still wonderful company. As they understand more and more of what is going on, they become even more entertaining. Older children are usually very interested in babies of this age, and the provider has lots of volunteer baby sitters. They should be encouraged to play with the baby. At this stage, infants can begin to play games such as "Peek-aboo", "So Big", "Ride a Cock Horse", "This Little Pig", and "Where's the Baby?" (see Chapter 11). The older children may enjoy these games as much as the baby, especially the 3 and 4 year olds who played them only just recently.

A new behavior sometimes shows up toward the end of this stage. Around 8 months some babies begin to react to people they do not know very well, with shyness or even with fear. In other countries where babies are cared for by several people at once, this reaction to little known people may not show up. It probably depends upon how many different people each baby knows well and is used to. The infants in family day care may only be cared for by their parents and their provider, a small enough group for them to notice and react to strangers. Fearful behavior can be expected to continue for at least 6 months, and often longer. Strangers should not be allowed to pick up and hold the infant, unless it is necessary. If they are surprised that the infant turns away from them, or cries, the provider can say, "Babies this age often go through this kind of phase. It will soon pass and we'll see friendly smiles again." It is especially important to prepare people who expect the infant to be the same smiling creature he or she used to be. Grandmothers, grandfathers, regular visitors, like postmen, neighbors, the salespeople, all need some explanation for this new unfriendly character. It only makes it worse to force the baby to go to someone strange. Because babies do not understand their own feelings, adults have to be patient and understand that this is a stage that will pass and not a reaction to any particular person.

<u>Key Care Ideas</u>

- The baby should be included as much as possible in the activities of the other children.
- The other children can be encouraged to play the same games that the provider plays with the baby. They will quickly catch on to how much the baby enjoys imitating games. Because older children love imitating each other, they will happily play the same game with the baby.

- The provider should expect the baby to react differently to strangers, or even to anyone but the parents and herself. She will need to explain this behavior to everyone the baby reacts to, as well as to the parents who may wonder why their usually friendly child is suddenly shy.

Thinking

For the first time babies at this age begin to look for something that falls out of sight or is put out of their reach. They also try to make something interesting happen again, such as turning a light or faucet on and off. They are busy learning how things work. They continue to grab things and put them through all the tests they know—banging, shaking, biting, dropping. This can be a nuisance when they try to bite the face or nose of the person who is holding them, or when they drop every toy and every bit of food they have on the high chair tray. It is important, however, to remember that these are ways of learning, not bad behavior. Babies at this age have no idea about feelings or reasons, nor can they be forced to learn about them. They must first figure out how things work and what they can do.

<u>Key Care Ideas</u>

- The provider needs a couple of containers (plastic boxes or baskets) filled with small objects such as a ping-pong ball, an old washcloth or other piece of material, a clothespin, plastic measuring cups, empty spools, and plastic containers and lids from yogurt, cottage cheese, and so forth. These can be brought out when the baby is on the floor or in a high chair (the provider needs to be ready to play fetch as everything gets thrown on the floor). Having more than one collection allows the provider to vary the objects. Any that do not interest the baby can be discarded and replaced with something more entertaining. A favorite game is "Fill the can then dump it out."
- Babies love the experience of "making things happen." When sitting on the provider's knees playing "Ride a Cock Horse" or "This is the Way the Ladies Ride," the infant will bounce to show he or she wants *more*. If the provider plays some more, the infant will know she understands what he or she wants. Babies also love turning the light on and off, and turning the water faucet on and off. In the tub a squeeze bottle lets the infant make bubbles under the water, and squirt water out.
- These favorite games should be recorded in the Baby Book.

About Becoming a Person

The shyness or fear that some babies show to adults they do not know really well are the first feelings that babies direct to a person. The pleasure, delight, and joy they show to the person who cares for them hardly counts because those smiles of pleasure just mean contentment. The cries of rage of small infants are not directed to anyone in particular. They are simply cries of discomfort and frustration, not anger at another person. But when babies begin to feel shy or frightened at strangers, they are showing their feelings for another person. This is the first time their feelings have a reason. Babies need to be protected from this distress. If an adult persists in talking to a baby who is shy or fearful, the provider can ask that adult to turn his or her face to the side. For some reason, babies find the face with both eyes upsetting, but not the profile, not half a face.

Key Care Ideas

- When taking the infant on excursions, the provider should continue to be aware of any signs of shyness or fear. She can reassure the infant by talking about those nice people in the store or on the way. Given a lot of support this phase will soon pass, and the infant will be friendly again.

LATE INFANCY

This is the period that takes the baby from infant to toddler. In fact, once babies walk, they are actually toddlers, and most babies begin to walk at about one year. This is the biggest change in a child's life; once mobile, the whole world is there to be enjoyed. For the provider this is not as pleasant a time as the months of middle infancy. A crawling and walking baby is as demanding as an infant in the first few weeks. Even if the provider has prepared her home for family day care, she will have to look it over again in terms of a crawling, toddling baby. Wires from lamps, small objects dropped on the floor by the other children, doors that swing, cabinets with doors that can pinch fingers, anything that tips over—all these have to be removed or watched for. The temptation to use a playpen has to be resisted. This stage is not only a time of great physical growth, but also great growth in learning. A caged child will not learn very much. When parents say that their children are happy in a playpen, they are really saying that they have succeeded in turning their children off, mentally and physically. They have made them accept a boring life. Intelligent, healthy children will not stay happily in a playpen more than a few minutes. It is better to close doors to the room and give the baby the freedom to play on the floor. A room that has been checked for safety is the best playpen a child can have.

The other major change at this age is the beginning of language. At 8 months babies understand and respond to many words. By 14 months they are saying a few (see Chapter 11).

Babies now become expert crawlers and then stand and walk. The change in their lives, and the provider's, is enormous. Suddenly the business of child care becomes much more difficult and much more demanding. What children learn at this age has a lasting effect on what and how they learn the rest of their lives. The kind of life-style that develops between the baby and the person who cares for that baby most of the time will be the life-style the child uses with every important person for the rest of his or her life.

Feeding

At this stage babies are not only more interested in feeding themselves, they are also better at it. They can pick up bits of food and feed themselves nicely. Near the end of this stage they may begin to use a spoon. Using a cup also gets easier. The provider may still have to help with the feeding, but if meals are offered that an infant can handle (see Chapter 19) the job becomes more a matter of planning than of feeding.

Key Care Ideas

- Infants are now eating many of the foods that older children eat. They are also enjoying being with the rest of the day care family and copying them at the table. The provider should not worry if some pieces of food come out undigested in the baby's bowel movement. If the food is not hard, like nuts or bacon bits, it will not hurt, and enough will be digested to keep the baby healthy.
- Depending on the amount of milk infants manage to take from a cup, this is a good time to begin to cut down on the number of bottles. One or two a day provide plenty of milk.
- The greatest food problem that can arise at this age is *overeating*. It is very important to keep babies at one year from becoming fat.
- Fat cells collected at this age *never go away*. It is possible to starve these fat cells, but not to lose them. Healthy babies are *not* fat, and are not used to cookies, crackers, and other fattening and unnutritious foods.

Exercise

The physical skills infants are learning at this age provide all the exercise they need. All the provider needs to provide is the space. Because children this age have enormous curiosity, every square inch of the home is interesting. The only possible way to discourage their natural drive to learn would be to keep them penned up in playpens or cribs.

Key Care Ideas

- As infants begin to pull up on all the furniture, crawl, walk holding on, then walk not holding on, and climb, the provider will need all the help she can get.

The older children (8 or 9 years and older) can be a great help in watching an infant.

- A record should be kept of each new skill to share with the parents—the first steps alone, the first climb up on the couch without help, and so forth.
- To exercise their new skills and to encourage curiosity, infants must be able to move freely in space. This means preparing each room they use for safety and also being personally available to prevent the accidents that even safety precautions cannot avoid.

About People

This is the time when infants are most attached to the person or people who care for them and at the same time are most upset by strangers. The provider will get lots of smiles, babbling conversation, hugs, and wet kisses. Strangers will get frowns and sometimes tears. When infants are at home in a place they know well they are less upset by strangers than when they are in a store, a park, on the bus, or anywhere else that is not their home ground. The provider should keep in mind that the more their shyness is accepted, the easier and sooner this stage will pass.

The provider need not worry about an infant's strong attachment to her at this stage unless it upsets the parents. In this case she may need to have a talk with them about the meaning of attachment at this age. They can be reassured that it is only a stage, that it will pass, and that it does not mean that they love their parents less.

At this age infants are beginning to learn from parents and providers all the things they can and cannot do. As soon as they begin moving freely, they will find out that they can feed themselves, but they cannot pull on the curtains; they can take their shoes off, but they cannot take the knobs off the television. As infants become mobile, they are suddenly able to do many things that are either dangerous or destructive. How the provider manages these will not only affect her future relationship with the child but also that child's relationship with other people and *their* belongings. The chapter on discipline, Chapter 15, goes into this in more detail.

One of the most important social skills that children learn begins at this age. That is the skill of using adults for help when help is needed. Some children learn how to ask for help in such a way that help is given happily. Other children whine, pull on an adult's arm or skirt, get mad, even have tantrums; as a result, adults do not give help with much joy or interest. Whether children learn how to ask for help and get it or do not learn will decide whether they become spoiled or not. Whining, crying, and constant demands for attention are really the result of not knowing how to get adults to help. They are also the behaviors that most of us call spoiled. Once these behaviors take over, the child is not only spoiled but worse than that, the child has lost interest in things and become absorbed with people, in fact, with annoying people.

Finally, babies at this age still need a good deal of comfort and support. If they receive it when they need it, they can go on to become independent and busy. If they do not receive enough, they become more needy of attention and less and less able to entertain themselves. Adults who are available to soothe a baby who falls down, or fix a toy that does not work right, or hold a tired and weary baby end up spending much *less* time in these activities than the adults who are always "too busy" to take the time and as a result are constantly dealing with whining, fussing babies.

Key Care Ideas

- Babies still do not go to anyone they don't know. They are still in that phase of shyness with strangers. If the parents are worried that this phase will never pass, the provider should reassure them, it is not permanent.
- The affection of babies at this age should be enjoyed and encouraged. The other children will enjoy holding, hugging, and playing with the baby. Babies *can* be spoiled at this age, but not by affection or loving attention.
- Now is the time to begin teaching babies what is allowed and what is not. Chapter 15 suggests ways to accomplish this difficult job.
- When asked for help, it should be given as quickly as possible; the more the provider gives at first, the less the child will ask. If the provider cannot stop what she is doing to help, she should explain why and then give help as soon as she can. If she is in the middle of something that will take a while, she can ask an older child to help. The purpose of the help is to make it possible for the baby to continue whatever game or activity he or she was doing. To help support the activity the provider can say, "What a good game. Here are a few more blocks in case you need them" or "You look great in those clothes. Are you going to a party?"
- Babies need lots of affection, comfort, and protection. At this age they are so full of energy, curiosity, and interest, they often overdo it. They can become frightened, exhausted, or overexcited. The provider should be ready to do some rocking, holding, or just have a quiet moment.
- Because babies can now get into the other children's way and games, the provider needs to protect these older children and not let the baby loose where the older children are playing. Because babies love watching older children play, they will try to join in if they can. It is the provider's job to protect all parties.

Thinking

Babies are still touching, shaking, tasting, banging, and dropping objects of all sorts to learn how they work. Once they "know" all about something it is no longer interesting. Toys need to be replaced often. Keeping boxes of assorted objects in a closet is a good way to change them every now and then to keep babies from being bored. Too many toys are confusing and as overstimulating as playing roughhouse. The provider needs boxes of assorted toys in a closet to take out one at a time. It helps to change boxes and the toys in each box from time to time. Since babies still put everything in their mouths it is important to keep small objects that can be swallowed away from them.

Anything that "works" such as a jack-in-a-box, a toy that tips down and back up, or one that makes a noise allows babies to "make something happen." Hiding games are also excellent for this age. The provider can cover a toy with a cloth and see if the baby looks for it, or she can put something like her hand in front of the toy and see if the baby will try to get around her hand to get to it. If a piece of the toy shows it helps the baby to find it. Balls are fun because they roll away in unexpected places. Babies learn about space and direction as they go after their ball. Books with hard pages and simple pictures of animals, toys, and people are good, too. Babies will listen carefully as the provider or one of the other children names the objects in the pictures.

The freedom of the home rewards infant curiosity more than anything else can. These rewards pay off in later learning ability, in fact, there is probably no time in a person's life that offers more new learnings than that time between 8 months and one year.

About Becoming a Person

Babies now recognize themselves in a mirror. They are delighted to look themselves over and to study themselves and the person with them in the mirror. As they touch the provider's nose, then their own, touch her mouth and eyes, then touch her mouth in the mirror, they are learning about themselves and other people. This is the beginning of a sense of one's own body, one's self.

Babies are now eager to be part of the older children's games. This is often upsetting to them because babies are apt to "mess up" these games. Left alone, the older children may hit or push the baby away. As soon as the provider sees this about to happen, she must step in and take the baby away from the scene, and from possible hurt. Respect for other people is a lesson that begins in infancy. Babies can begin to learn to respect others with the provider's help. If they are pushed and hit and slapped, however, they will learn to be aggressive and to hit back. They will also learn to fear the people they live with and *should* be able to trust and respect.

About this time babies can become easily frightened. Now that they can get around they can also get into scary situations. As they are rescued they begin to learn how to take care of themselves. Children raised by adults who do not take enough care of them become careless of themselves. Care, like love, is learned on the job.

As soon as infants begin to walk, they become toddlers. If they have had a well-cared-for infancy, they will be ready to stand up and face the world. They still need someone behind them to lend a hand, to steady them, to show them how it is done. From time to time they will run back and crawl up into that person's lap for comfort and for strength, like refilling a gas tank. Then they are off again. How far they go depends a great deal on what kind of start they had, on their experiences in infancy.

10

Providing for Toddlers

Once infants stand up and walk an entirely new way of life begins, both for them and for everyone around them. It is something similar to what happened a long time ago when early man gave up walking on all fours, stood upright, and walked on just his feet. As soon as his hands were freed to do other things, mankind as we think of it began. Infants repeat this same process as they go from crawling to walking. Suddenly their hands are free, they can see all the things they could not see before without tilting their heads way back, and they are finally able to walk and hold things at the same time.

This is the time when adults suddenly expect a great deal of children. Infants are considered babies until they begin to walk, then overnight they become "children" and new demands are placed on them. These demands are partly a result of their new "grown-up" position on their feet, and partly a result of the dangers that come from all the things they can now get into.

There is hardly an adult who does not find toddlers difficult at times. For all the pride and pleasure that we take in watching infants learn to walk, there is the worry and fear that toddlers cause by running, climbing, reaching, grabbing, and pulling things down on themselves.

A toddler at home demands a lot of care and attention, but a toddler in a family day care home not only makes these demands but makes them in competition with those of two or more other children, sometimes close to the same age. The care of toddlers requires more skill than that of any other age and at no age does the kind of care have greater consequences. Toddlers, like infants, are learning what to expect from people and from themselves. What they learn they will use with other people all the rest of their lives.

WHY TODDLERS ARE SPECIAL

Toddlers are adorable. In old master paintings, the cherubs and angels are perfect examples (Figure 17). The round, dimpled babies of artists like Rubens on are typical toddlers. By this age babies legs have become longer and filled out and their heads are no longer so large in comparison to the rest of their bodies.

Toddlers are not only lovely to look at but they are suddenly capable of many new skills. They can feed themselves, turn on and off the television, take off most of their clothes, and blow out a candle or a match. Besides all that, they are beginning to talk, to put two or three words together, and to say "no!" to all sorts of requests.

Figure 17.

They are making their first revolutionary war of independence and at the same time regularly running back to the lap of their parent or provider. This independence is very fragile, like a tender young seedling, and must be handled just as carefully. In the effort to become a whole human being at no time do we have more at stake than we do as toddlers.

SPECIAL TASKS OF TODDLERS

The primary task of toddlers is to learn to manage themselves and the new skills they are learning. As soon as they begin to walk, they begin to realize that they are separate people. They must now learn not only what it is to be able to do things for themselves but also what it means to be a person. Like everything else we learn, we must also learn how to be a separate person.

For providers this drive for independence is not always welcome. Toddlers want to do things for themselves—feed themselves, dress themselves, undress themselves, go up stairs, walk alone, get in the bathtub, get out of the bathtub. Very few are able to do these things without help and fewer can do them safely. At the same time, toddlers find any kind of assistance upsetting. They keep on trying, even when they do not succeed. For providers it is difficult to deal with the frustrations that toddlers suffer in trying everything on their own, but more than that, there is the loss of time waiting while toddlers make these attempts. With three or four other children to care for, this time is very valuable and losing it can upset the provider's carefully organized schedule.

Mealtimes

The best way to manage mealtimes is to make a deal with the toddler. One should allow and encourage toddlers to do what they can, and quietly but firmly do the rest. For instance, toddlers enjoy feeding themselves, but because they also enjoy dropping plates and cups and spoons as well as decorating themselves and the high chair and floor with food, it is a good idea to give them only a few bites of food at a time on a small unbreakable plate. If the food is dry, it can be served in paper cupcake holders. If there is just a little food, it is more apt to be eaten than used as a plaything. As each bite or two is eaten the provider can add something more. Pieces of hard-boiled egg, fruit, vegetables, or hamburger will usually be eaten. The provider can pour only a swallow or two of milk into the cup at a time, then add another couple of swallows. Because toddlers are very interested in praise, as interested as they are in learning to do things for themselves, something should be said whenever possible about how much they seem to be enjoying the food and how well they feed themselves (see Chapter 19 for ways to avoid overfeeding).

Dressing and Undressing

Dressing and undressing toddlers is often the cause of major battles. Diaper changing is usually the biggest problem because as infants, they were changed lying down and now suddenly lying down is the *last* thing these new walkers want to do.

There are various ways to make a deal with toddlers on the question of dressing and undressing. All require both parties to give in a little. Providers who are good with their hands can usually manage to diaper a toddler who is standing up, that is, when the diaper to be changed is merely wet. When it is soiled, it is more difficult. Cleaning up in that case often requires washing and a trip to the bathroom. If it is very difficult for the provider to put a diaper on a standing child, the best way to keep toddlers reasonably still is to place them on their stomachs and keep one hand on their backs so they do not get up on their knees (Figure 18). A mirror can be placed at the end of the changing table to capture the attention of toddlers lying on their stomachs. Looking at themselves, they will usually permit a diaper change without too much twisting and turning.

Putting on clothes is much easier than diapering. Toddlers can "give you a foot" to put into a pants leg, or "give you a hand" for a sleeve. They can quickly learn that "skin the cat" means pulling a garment over the head. They will usually cooperate because they are taking part in an activity. By telling them what comes next, the provider is allowing them to do some of the job. When they must "hold still" in order to tie their shoes or button

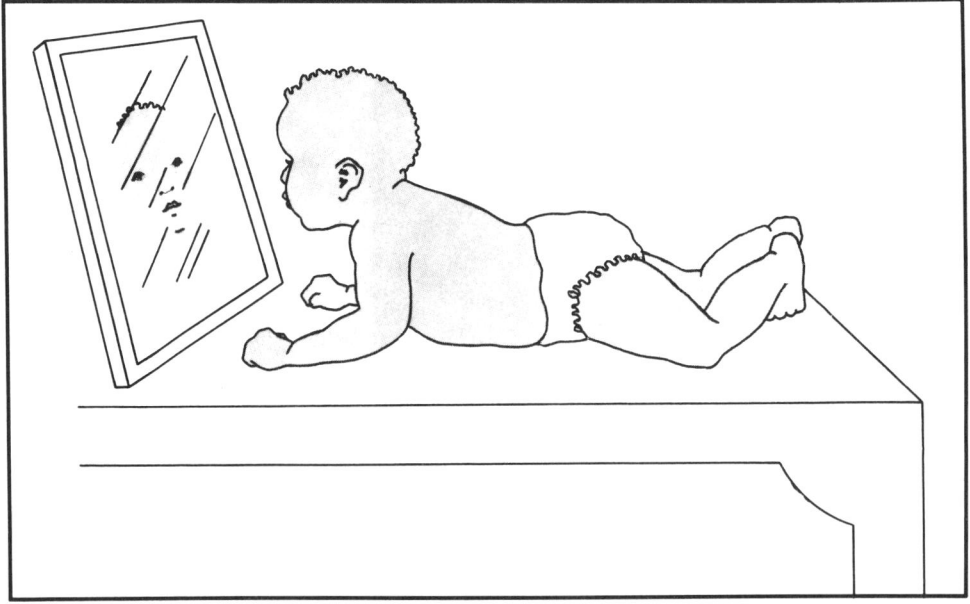

Figure 18.

their shirts, the provider should say so firmly. Then, if necessary, the provider can look very serious and say, "Now I'm going to tie your shoes, so you must hold still a moment." Toddlers are very sensitive to adults, especially those they are close to, and they will soon know that this is not a time for games.

Nap Times

Many children give up either the morning or afternoon nap sometime in their second year. For toddlers in family day care, this will depend in part on the family's schedule. If a toddler gets to bed around 8 p.m. at home and must be up by 7 a.m., two naps will probably continue to be necessary for a while. The question should be discussed with the parents so that the best time and the number of naps can be decided upon based on the toddlers' needs in their life at home as well as in day care.

As toddlers become tired their behavior becomes more and more disorganized. They become overexcited, easily frustrated, cross, and whiny. It is time to step in when this happens. As soon as the provider realizes that the toddler is tired, she should try to schedule a nap. This is not always possible, but she should be as flexible as she can be. If she is about to serve lunch, she can place the toddler in the high chair away from frustrations and excitement and calmly offer a very little bit of food. As soon as she has served the other children, she can take a moment and put the toddler to bed.

Tired toddlers often protest being put to bed. Again, firmness is the key. In a gentle voice the provider should say that it is time for a nap. The toddler's favorite blanket, animal, or loved object should be kept handy. The provider can then gently and affectionately put the toddler in the crib with the thing he or she loves and without hesitation leave the room. When toddlers sense the provider's seriousness and determination, they can more easily accept the decision.

Bottles

Toddlers need about 16 ounces of milk a day. Many will drink that much from a cup. If they will not and if the parents want to continue the bottle, a toddler can be given a bottle at nap time. Often a disorganized, upset, or overtired toddler will throw the bottle out of the crib rather than settle down quietly with it. If this happens a few times, it does not make sense to continue to offer the bottle. In this case, a loving, affectionate, firm attitude is the best way to put a toddler down for a nap.

Independence

Besides the ways that providers handle mealtimes and dressing and undressing, there are dozens of other events during the toddler's day that allow for the growth of independence.

From the moment the toddlers arrive in the morning they are intent on two things: practicing their new skills and keeping the provider's attention focused on what they are doing. Toddlers are torn between pushing away and staying close to the ones they love. Encouraging independence means giving that needed attention so that they know that it is there. It can then be accepted and not constantly demanded, and the toddlers do not need to spend time asking for it.

From time to time during the day toddlers need to make contact, to touch base. Even in the middle of a favorite activity, toddlers often stop and run back to throw themselves in the provider's lap or against her legs. A hug and a few words of praise are usually all that are needed and toddlers can go back to their business. Sometimes, however, they need the provider to add something to make what they are doing more interesting. She may need to return to the game with the toddler, sit down for a while to see what could make it more interesting, and, having come up with a good idea, return to what she was doing. As she does, she can keep talking to the toddler so that he or she feels the attention is not lost.

There are times every day when toddlers are tired or they have used up their interest in a certain activity, and they go back to being babies. This behavior should be accepted for what it is—a short vacation from independence. The provider should then sit a few minutes in a rocker or on a couch, holding the toddler and talking softly. A few minutes of comforting is all most toddlers need, then their energy returns and they scramble off.

It is sometimes difficult for toddlers to get involved in play without help. If adults check on them often, praise the activity, make a suggestion, encourage trying out a new idea, toddlers will learn by themselves to do things that keep their own games interesting. Preschoolers who are not able to stay with any activity without an adult close by have never had enough of this kind of assistance as toddlers. The moments spent helping toddlers get involved in an activity will grow into minutes and hours of attentive, individual, independent play.

AT TWO THE CHILD BECOMES A THINKER

Jean Piaget, who discovered a great deal about the ways children think, said that at 2 years children can begin to think about doing something before they do it. This is an important step. There is a big difference between doing something to see what will happen and *thinking* about what will happen if one does something. Until this occurs, it is not possible to choose between doing one thing or doing another, or even choosing not to do something at all. It is only at this age that children can choose not to touch something when told not to. Even then, their memories are too short to remember the next time, or even to keep the thought in their heads. It is, however, the time to begin explanations, not long descriptions, but short ones, such as "That tips over easily," or "If I put ice in now, it will spill out," or "It won't stand on just three legs," or "The big block needs to be on the bottom." At this age children have enough words to think about things. The time from toddlerhood to kindergarten is the time for putting all their actions into words and using the words both to remember and to try out ideas. Giving them the words they need is very important. Using the words to talk about everything that happens is the best way to help toddlers to go from infancy into the age of thinking.

The Importance of Words

Chapter 11 is about language—how it begins and how it works—in our thinking and in our behavior. There are two things toddlers do that are especially difficult to handle and both have to do with language. The first is the toddler's use of the word *no* and the second is the temper tantrum.

No It is rare for a toddler not to say *no* long before saying *yes*, and it is also rare to find another word used as often. Some toddlers do not say *no*, they merely shake their heads. Infants actually learn to shake their heads long before they understand the meaning of no. They turn their heads away when they have had enough, or when they are offered something in a spoon that they do not like or do not want. Shaking the head begins with avoiding food and goes on to refusing other things. The meaning of no gets connected to head shaking when adults begin saying *no, no* to infants, *no, no* to the sugar bowl, *no, no* to the magazine, *no, no* to the electric cord. Adults often shake their heads as they say it. Very early, infants learn that *no, no* stands for the same thing as head shaking. It is one more way in which words can replace actions.

Some toddlers say no more often than almost any other word, but then they also hear more no's than yeses or okays. The adults who object to toddlers' use of the word are often the very adults who use the word the most.

There are a couple of things to keep in mind when dealing with toddlers' use of the word *no*. The first is that toddlers often do not mean it. They are practicing the art of making independent decisions, of acting on their own. It is too early for it to work, of course, but it is time to begin practicing. There are times when one offers a toddler something like some raisins, only to be told *no* at the very moment that an eager hand is held out. In this case, as in many others, the toddler is really saying, "I *could* say no, I am a separate person with a mind of my own." The best way to deal with the many no's is with a lot of humor: "Well, maybe I'll just give you a few raisins anyway because I see a little hand open and waiting."

The other way to deal with the no's is to avoid asking questions whenever possible. One should not ask, "Do you want some grapes or a piece of banana?" "Are you tired? Ready for a nap?" "Will you give me that plate?" Instead, one should say, "Here are a few grapes. You can also have a piece of banana." "It's nap time, I can see you are tired. Let's go." "I'll take that plate, thank you." Words are quite enough for the toddler to manage, choices are too much.

When the provider says she is going to do something, she must *not* delay or wait for the toddler to join her or follow her. It is best not to make toddlers do things that are not really necessary, but when they are necessary, it is important to do what has to be done quickly, quietly, calmly. The provider should say what she is doing and why as she does it. Because one of the most important things toddlers do is put actions into words, this kind of talking while doing is very helpful.

Temper Tantrums There is a good reason for temper tantrums. Once on their feet, toddlers can do many things they could not when still crawling. They can try many things that are dangerous or destructive. All of this is both exciting and frustrating, and with frustration comes intense feelings. Tantrums are the easiest way to let out this tension. Even as adults, when frustrated we say, "I could just scream!" or "It made me so mad I could have kicked something." Most of the time we are too controlled to really scream or kick, but toddlers are not. In fact, they do not have the control even if they wanted to use it. They can only learn control as they learn what they can do and can not do and as they are allowed to borrow on an adult's control until their own develops.

Another frustration of toddlerhood is the shortage of language. Many times toddlers are not able to say what they want or what just happened well enough for adults to understand, even those who know them and their language best. If they are not understood after making a couple of tries, they become so frustrated that a tantrum is likely to be the only way they can let off steam.

Tantrums are *not* a cause for worry. A 2 year old who never has a temper tantrum *is*. Normal toddlers with normal interest in the world around them and in other people will face many moments of frustration. Emotional tension can only be released in a limited number of ways at this age and one of these is the temper tantrum. The absence of tantrums shows an absence of imagination or of interest, both of which are a serious cause for worry.

The best way to deal with a tantrum is to say to the child, "I know you're upset. Come to me as soon as you feel like it." As the kicking and screaming begins to stop, the child will need to be comforted. It is hard being a toddler. There is so much to learn and in the effort to do it all at once they become overexcited. They are then forced to release some of the tension. Imagine a house just equipped with lots of new appliances. When they all get used at once, a fuse blows. Having a tantrum is similar to blowing a fuse. One can often avoid a blown fuse by being that extra line that is brought in to help with the job. Later when toddlers have learned not to use all the appliances at once, the extra line will no longer be needed.

Fears and Nightmares

For the first time in their lives, toddlers learn what it is to be afraid. Some of their fears come from the new things they are learning to do and the dangers that go with them, and some come from new things that they do not understand and find frightening. Selma Fraiberg, in a wonderful book called *The Magic Years*, describes some parents who decided to make sure their child did not develop any fears. They never threatened their child or frightened the child or even allowed the child to see anything on television or anywhere else that might frighten him. They were surprised and horrified when the child began to have nightmares about monsters and wild animals. They finally realized that fears and nightmares have to do with the conditions of a toddler's life, and are not all a result of seeing or hearing scary things. They are also a result of the fact that toddlers are not sure about what is real and what is not. They believe there are real people in the television set, with guns, on horses or jumping off cliffs. They believe that the dreams they have at night are also real. Many toddlers ask how they can see those monsters if they are really asleep with their eyes really closed. Dreams are difficult to understand, even for adults.

Until toddlers can separate the real from the not real, these fears continue. They continue in us all, even into our adult life, and in many cases are no more connected with anything real than they were when we were 2 or 3 years old. Many adults are afraid of lightning and thunder, of being in a high place, of being in a crowd, of touching germs, and so forth. As we grow up, we learn that lightning almost never strikes a person, that we will not faint or fall if we stand on a balcony and look down, that a crowd is not dangerous unless a criminal is in it (and that criminals are to be found when one is on an empty street as often as in a crowd), and that germs are everywhere, our skin is covered with them and most are not dangerous. But it takes years to learn all this and to know it in our *hearts* so that we *feel* safe as well as know what is and what is not dangerous.

In the meantime, toddlers need comfort and support when feeling afraid and help in learning what is real in the world and what is not. Sometimes their fears are so unexpected that adults have a hard time taking them seriously. A common one among toddlers is fear of the bathtub. They are sometimes afraid of the toilet as well. It may be the rushing water, or the idea of a drain and all the water rushing down the drain, taking everything with it. In any case, it is *not* a good idea to force toddlers into the tub. That will only make their fear greater and make it last longer as well. Until this fear disappears on its own, toddlers can be bathed on a table or by the tub, allowing them to lean over and play in the water. Then the toddler can be encouraged to open the drain and close it. Being able to control the drain makes it much less frightening.

Patience, support, and comfort are the best medicines for the fears of toddlers, and the best cures as well. Unless toddlers are forced to confront their fears, they will pass in a short time. If forced to confront them, these fears will usually go underground and turn up later in other forms, such as fear of school, certain places, certain foods, or airplanes.

Toilet Training

In our society we believe we must train children to use the toilet. The fact is that like all of the other things toddlers are eager to learn on their own (how to feed themselves, dress themselves, and undress themselves), they would also eagerly learn to use the toilet except that adults often make it into a battle. Because this battle concerns something that comes out of children's own bodies and is felt to be part of *themselves*, they become even more protective and insistent on doing it where and when they want.

The first thing for the provider to do is discuss the question of toilet training with the parents. She should explain how important it is to: 1) agree on when; 2) have the same kind of potty; and 3) decide not to have a battle. She should explain that she has several children to care for and therefore cannot spend the day by the toilet with one of these. If the provider shows a positive and professional attitude, parents are apt to feel secure that they can rely on her. Once toilet training is begun, the provider should give the parents regular reports.

Toddlers can more easily use a potty chair than a seat on the toilet. Besides, in a family day care home where there are others who need to use the toilet putting on and taking off a seat can become a time-wasting job. A potty chair is low; toddlers can get on and off without help and it does not flush like the toilet, making the loud noise that is often frightening to toddlers.

When an older child sits on the toilet, a toddler will often go sit on the potty chair. The provider can encourage the older children to explain what they are doing on the toilet. (This may be embarrassing to them, especially if they are still at the age when toilet jokes are *very* interesting.) The toddler can practice getting in and out of his or her clothes. (When the provider and the parents have decided it is time for their child to learn to use the toilet, the parents need to understand that the toddler *must* be able to take his or her own pants off. Overalls with an elastic waist and training pants are best. The whole idea is to use their own drive for independence, to foster their own desire to "do it myself.")

Unless the toddler feels a great deal of pressure that causes a negative reaction, it is simply a matter of time for the child to be toilet trained. The provider can say to the toddler, "Did you use your potty yet?" "Tell me when you need to use it." "I think Diane just used the toilet, have you used *your* potty?" These are hints that the provider knows the toddler plans to begin using the potty. When the toddler asks for help, or if the toddler shows any interest, the provider can offer to help. Otherwise, she should not push. She should not become *too* interested, either. The whole subject should be of only minor concern. When the toddler finally does use the potty, the provider can show how pleased she is. Children this age are very eager for praise. If the provider applauds, the child will, too. As soon as the toddler figures out that this is an easy way to get praise, the training is almost done. With a little practice, there will be fewer and fewer accidents until one day the provider will realize the child is trained.

Toddler Toys

Toddlers are very interested in working on their new skills (walking, running, climbing, talking), being in close contact with their provider and parents, and studying up close all the things that they can now get their hands on. These interests should be taken into account in making daily plans.

As toddlers begin to walk, they are often content just to follow the provider from room to room, practicing the art of staying on their feet. As soon as they get their balance they want to carry things around. The larger the thing they are carrying, the better they like it. As the provider cleans up, they will happily follow her about, carrying whatever she gives them to hold. If she gives them a dust rag they will clean too.

When the day care family goes outside, toddlers should be allowed to walk. It is sad to see so many healthy toddlers and even preschool-age children riding in strollers and missing a close-up view of the world. Enough time can be allowed outside to permit toddlers to walk along, peeking into doors and windows, picking up leaves and bits of paper, touching fences and railings. These are important learning experiences.

The provider should try to find space outdoors where toddlers can safely run. It seems to be very important for toddlers to run down long halls or out in the open, over hills, along paths. They are learning about space as they practice their running. A playground with swings, seesaws, and a sandbox is a delight to a toddler. They also enjoy the large round-about on which several children can climb and ride while others push around and around. Jungle gyms, however, can be too dangerous for toddlers because they sometimes forget to hold on.

Simple toys indoors are better than fancy and expensive toys. The large cardboard blocks that look like bricks are perfect. Toddlers carry them about, stack them, and knock them down. Smaller blocks are also good. Balls of different sizes are excellent toys. Ping-pong balls are often favorites. Children's books with hard covers and pages are still the best kind. Jugs and plastic boxes of small objects are excellent. The small objects should be changed from time to time so that they do not become uninteresting. Sand, water, old containers from yogurt or cottage cheese, spoons, and plastic bottles are endlessly fascinating to toddlers and preschoolers.

Finally, large cartons or boxes from the supermarket and chairs on their sides with a cloth over them provide spaces for toddlers to climb in and out of. Space is a new discovery for toddlers. It may be that exploring all kinds of space is necessary for later learning.

TODDLERS AND OLDER CHILDREN

Although the care of toddlers is never easy or restful, it is always easier when there are others around to share the job. Providers can often engage the help of older children in keeping a toddler safe and busy. Because toddlers are amusing and eager to play, older children enjoy them, at least as long as the toddlers are not allowed to mess up the older children's games or belongings.

One of the times that older children can be helpful is during outdoor play. Toddlers are eager to practice walking and running, and since few family day care homes have enough space to run without running into things, the outdoors is the best place. When toddlers take off and run, older children are often delighted to follow to make sure the toddlers do not run into the street, or into a shopping cart in the supermarket, or into other children or adults. They can often also steer the toddlers back to the day care family. A game can be made of the running by "calling the race." As the toddler takes off, the provider can describe the first racer wearing a red shirt leaving the starting post. As the older child takes off after the toddler, she can then describe the second racer wearing green and brown, who is quickly catching up with the first racer, who is now overtaking the first racer, and so forth.

Toddlers also enjoy looking. They will stare out of the window for long periods of time. To see out, they may need to stand on a chair or couch. An older child can help keep the toddler from falling off the chair or couch. This is another ideal situation for a game between the provider and the older child. A memory game can be played as the older child names the things seen from the window. First the child names the things he or she sees outside so that the toddler can repeat the words. Then the provider repeats each thing they have said, trying to name all the things already seen. For instance, the older child points to a car and says, "car." The toddler will usually point and also say car. The provider then says, "Let's see, you have seen a *car*, a girl on a bike, a big brown cat, and so forth." Then it is the older child's turn to see how many things he or she can remember and name.

Finally, older children can be very helpful as toddlers practice new skills, such as climbing stairs. A large part of a toddler's day is spent in practicing these newly learned skills. Few providers have the time to sit on the stairs with a toddler to prevent a fall, and yet someone must be nearby at least until the toddler can climb stairs and come back down safely. For short periods of time, older children enjoy being the coach and showing the toddler how to back down, how to turn and sit without falling or missing the step, and how to look behind to tell how many steps are left.

Playing games with the older child who is toddler-watching makes that time valuable for both children. At the same time, it allows the provider to continue with whatever she needs to be doing. Even if she cannot actually see the toddler and older child, the game keeps her in close touch and lets her know that the older child is still on the job.

TODDLERS IN A FAMILY DAY CARE HOME

There is no environment for toddlers so rich in learning possibilities as a home with a family. As the provider prepares meals, talks on the phone, sorts laundry, shops, or helps the older children with their hobbies or homework, the toddler is learning all about things people do and how they do them. How the older children treat each other, treat the provider, and treat the toddler will determine how that toddler treats other people. If the toddler is treated with consideration and respect, that will be the way he or she learns to treat others. This is the age in which children learn a life-style. The example that the provider and the other children provide will determine to a large extent that style.

11

Providing for Language Development

The success or failure of nearly every effort beginning in early childhood and continuing throughout one's life depends in large part on the ability to use language. There are many examples of the power of language. Winston Churchill, Martin Luther King, John Kennedy, and Malcolm X all had something more in common than the fact that they were great men. They also used words extremely well. They had the kind of language that people listen to.

Everyone learns some language, but some people learn to speak more easily and more effectively than others. Language determines to a great degree what a person accomplishes, how a person gets along with others, how well a person does in school and on the job, how often a person is able to do what he or she wants, and how each person feels about himself or herself.

Providers have the opportunity to help the children in their care learn the kind of language that makes things possible. For this reason, this chapter is about language and how we learn it.

AN EARLY EXPERIMENT

There is an old story that has been told for hundreds of years. It is about the Emperor Frederick II who ruled the Holy Roman Empire in the 13th century. Thinking about the many languages spoken in his empire, he decided that he would find out which language humans would speak if they were not taught any particular one and learned on their own. If children never heard any language at all, how would they speak? In order to find out, he ordered his soldiers to bring him babies from all parts of the Empire. Each baby was given a nurse and the best possible care, except for one thing—the nurses were *never* to speak a word to the babies nor speak where the babies could hear. Without anyone to copy, the children would then speak whatever language is natural; they would speak like the first human beings.

Although the nurses did exactly as they were told, the experiment failed. The babies died. Even with the best care in the world, human beings cannot live without language.

CHILDREN WITHOUT LANGUAGE

When people hear such stories they immediately think of people who *do* live without a spoken language—deaf people, for instance. Deaf people, however, have a language; they have sign language. Even when they are not taught how to sign, they make up their own signs.

What about autistic children, children who do not use language to say what they think or want? These children hear and yet do not speak or even make signs. Some of them speak nonsense; they repeat commercials from television or they talk gibberish. This is a kind of illness that is difficult to understand and even more difficult to treat. There may be some physical cause of autism that we do not yet know. In any case, these children are very hard to cure. Part of their disease is to be without language, and without language it is hard to help.

HOW WE LEARN LANGUAGE

Language is one of the most difficult things human beings learn, and yet very young babies learn it. At one time, people believed that children learn language by simply listening to adults and repeating what they hear. Children do learn words that way, but words alone are not a language. They must also learn how to put words together. There is a big difference between "boy bites dog" and "dog bites boy." When children begin to put words together it becomes clear that they are not simply repeating what they have heard, they are figuring out how language works. For instance, a child will say, "Nite-nite all-gone," "Mommy bye-bye," and "Off shoe." Adults sometimes repeat this baby talk, but they never teach children to talk like this. Children do not learn to talk this way by listening to adults and copying them, and yet when children use invented words adults know what they mean. They know because even if the language is not correct, the children are beginning to learn how it works.

When children begin to speak adults make a great effort to understand. The child says, "Donnie shoe," and the adult asks, "Is that Donnie's shoe?" The child repeats, "Donnie shoe." So the adult asks, "You're giving the shoe to Donnie?" Trying to make it clearer, the child then says, "Donnie shoe." This time the adult asks "Donnie took off his shoe?" With exasperation the child says "Donnie shoe." Finally the adult understands: "You're putting on Donnie's shoe." From all these tries, understanding finally comes. The child gets the adult to understand; but more than that, the child gets new ideas about the many things words can mean.

LANGUAGE AND THOUGHT

When the child first learns the word *shoe*, it usually means just one shoe—the shoe that is in his or her hand—or on his or her foot. Soon, however, there are other shoes—the provider's shoes, the parent's shoes, the other children's shoes. Then there are many different kinds of shoes—sneakers, sandals, slippers, moccasins, loafers. All of these are different, but they are all shoes. We use words to think about groups of things, about what goes with or does not go with something else. The more words we have, the more we can think about things.

What is important to our children is not only that they learn many words but that they also learn many ways to use them. The children who do well in school and, who get along well with their friends, family, and teachers are the children who can say what they think, why they think it, and can interest other people in their thoughts. These children go on to do well as adults, both in their work and in their personal lives.

THE BEGINNING OF LANGUAGE

The provider may not have many children come to her as very young infants, but for those who do, she can provide a strong language foundation. For those who come later, she may have to fill in the foundation. At whatever age, she will be able to enrich the child's language by giving the child more words and by showing the child how to use those words to get things done.

The First Year

Although many children do not say more than a word or two in their first year, they learn a lot about language. They understand many things they hear, but more than that, they discover the joy of talking to other people and being talked to.

First Sounds In the first few weeks babies smile when they see a face, hear a voice, and watch a head move up and down. About the time that they begin smiling, they also begin to make sounds in answer to the sounds they hear. Sometimes their little faces have a very strained look, their mouths are pushed out and they frown, all from the effort of trying to make a sound. When they succeed, they may look as though they do not know where the sound came from, and indeed they do not.

<u>Key Care Ideas</u>

- When changing, dressing, bathing, or just holding infants, it is important to talk to them. If the provider's face is about a foot and a half away from the infant's and she nods as she talks and repeats some of the words, she will get some sounds in answer and some smiles as well.

Babbling At 3 to 4 months infants will "talk" with energy and concentration. They can make several different sounds, although each infant usually has a few favorites. As long as someone is there and doing her part, infants will keep on "talking." It is interesting that all children begin babbling at this age, even deaf children and the children of deaf parents who never speak to their babies. If, however, infants get no answer, they stop, missing this important step toward language.

There are several things about the babbling of 3- and 4-month old babies that is quite unlike adult conversation. The first is that when the adult starts talking, babies start talking. As long as the adult talks, they babble, *at the same time*. Then when the adult stops, they immediately stop, too.

Another thing about baby conversations is that the babies like to hear the same words repeated over and over. They babble with more energy when the adult repeats the same words over and over in a kind of singsong.

The third thing about baby conversations that changes as they grow is that the adult must keep looking into the infant's eyes. The moment he or she looks away, the babbling stops. When the adult looks into the infant's eyes again, the babbling starts up.

Finally, the sounds that infants make at this age are all vowel sounds. They say "ah-h-h-h," "eh-h-h-h," "e-e-e-e," "o-o-o," "oh-h-h-h." All of those sounds come from the throat. Later they learn to use their lips and tongue.

<u>Key Care Ideas</u>

- Conversations with infants this age are the real beginnings of language. Besides, they love it and adults do, too. Anytime an infant is face-to-face with the provider, the provider can say something like, "Wet again? Let's you and me start a laundry business." She will be rewarded with some "Ah-h-h-h's" or "o-o-o-o's" and smiles.

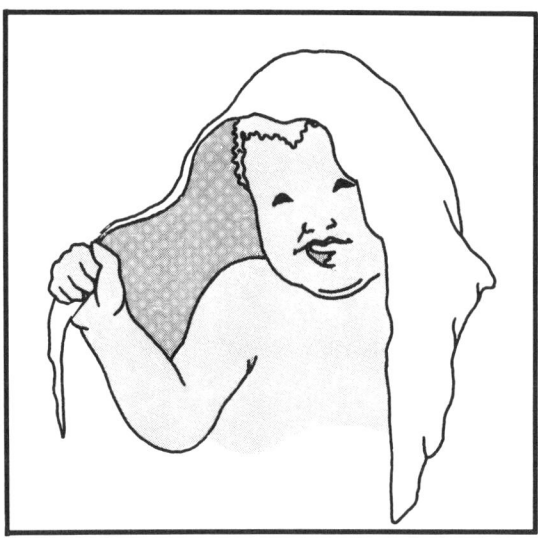
Figure 19.

Middle Infancy Somewhere between 6 and 9 months of age infants discover the sound of their own voices. Once they have, they can entertain themselves for long stretches of time making all the sounds they know, from gurgles to shouts. They can also imitate many of the sounds the provider makes.

At this time infants are also beginning to understand the meaning of many things they hear. They will even do some things they are asked to do. "Say bye-bye" will often get a raised hand. (Infants at this age cannot wave. At about one year they will open and close their hands as a way of waving.) They know what "nite-nite" and "bottle" mean. They are now ready to begin to play games.

              Key Care Ideas

- When changing or dressing an infant, the provider can put a cloth over the baby's head and say, "Where's the baby?" As the infant tries to remove the cloth, the provider can keep asking, "Where's the baby?" When the cloth is pulled off, she can say, "There she is!" Babies usually want to do these games again and again. They will try to cover their own faces with the cloth to keep the game going (see Figure 19).

- Another similar game that this age loves is "Peekaboo." This time the adult covers her face with a cloth or her hands and says, "Where's _____(her name)?" The idea of hiding and finding is very exciting to infants this age. Only the eyes need to be covered for infants to think they are completely hidden (see Figure 20).

- "Pat a Cake" is a good game because the same words are repeated:

    Pat a cake, pat a cake
    Baker's man

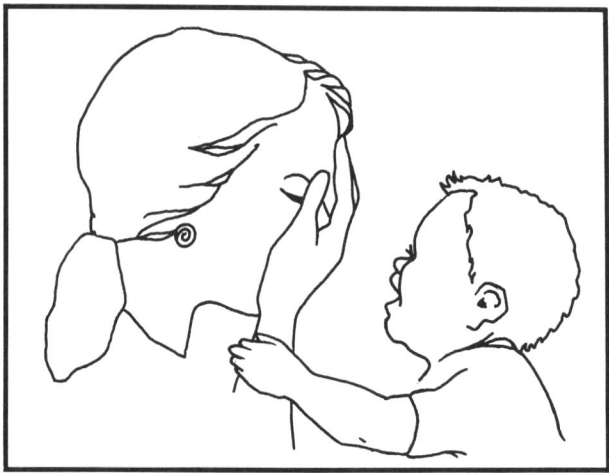

Figure 20.

> Bake me a cake as fast as you can.
> Roll it and pat it
> And mark it with B
> And put it in the oven for baby and me.

The provider holds the baby's hands and claps them together to go with the rhyme. Babies soon learn to clap their own hands as the provider claps hers (see Figure 21).

- At 7 to 9 months old, infants can learn to play "So Big." Like "Pat a Cake" they make the movements that go with the words. Again the adult takes the baby's hands in hers and asks, "How big is the baby?" Then she stretches the baby's arms up high and answers, "So-o-o-o big!" Soon babies learn to stretch their own hands up high when asked, "How big is the baby?" (see Figure 22).

End of the First Year Many infants can say a few words at one year. Most "talk" a lot, but although it may sound like real words it is mostly gibberish. They can often imitate the sounds of the voice of their favorite adults so well that it is hard to believe they are not really saying anything.

Babies learn to use their tongue and lips around 8 or 9 months, and their favorite sounds are "mum-m-m-m, mum-m-m-m," or "da-a-a, da-a-a-a." These are, of course, very pleasing to the parents who think the baby is talking to them even though the infant may direct these sounds to everyone and everything in sight. "Babababa" is another favorite noise and adults sometimes decide this means bottle. As meanings are given to babies' sounds, more conversations take place:

> Baby: Babababa
> Provider: This is no time for a bottle, here's a piece of apple to chew on.

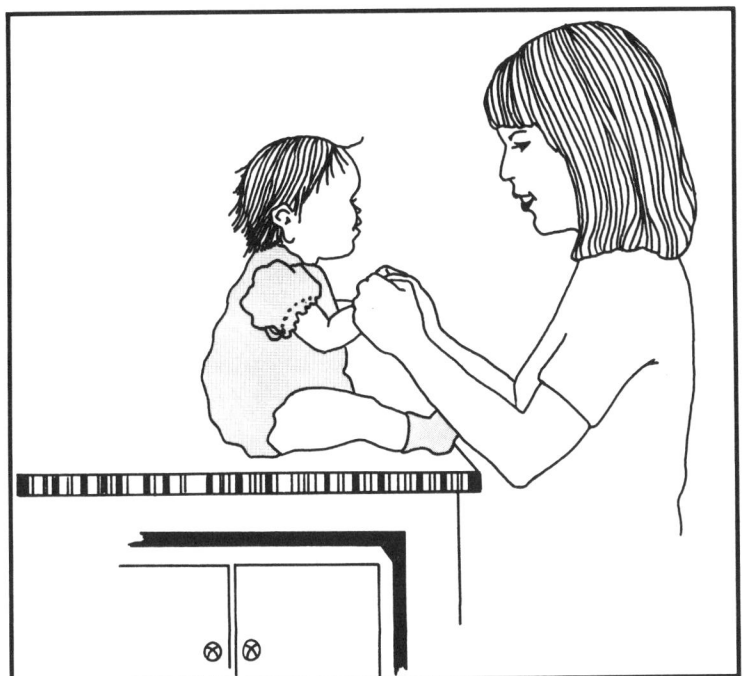

Figure 21.

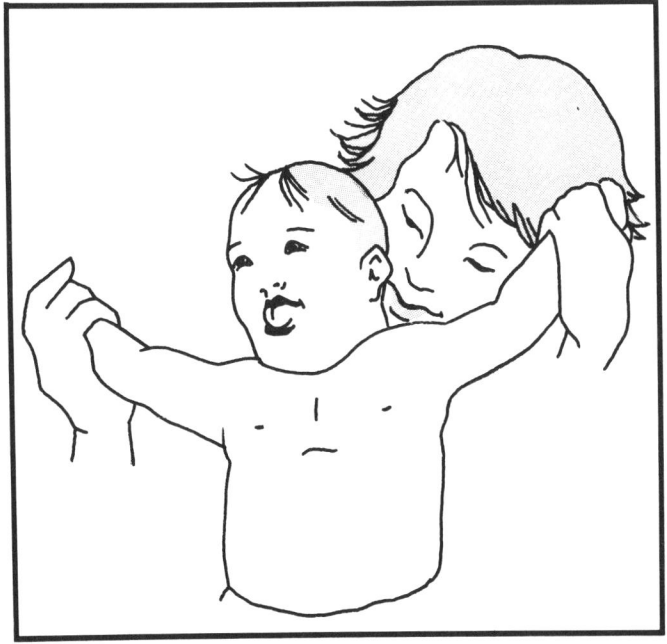

Figure 22.

Baby: Mum-mum-mum-mum.
Provider   That's good, isn't it?
Baby: Mum-mum-mum-mum.
Provider: I'll tell Mummy how much you like apple.

From these sounds babies go on to words that have a clear meaning, in fact, several meanings. One of these is "all gone." All gone means finished, I've had enough, Please stop, I want more, and any number of other things. "Num-num all-gone" can mean the plate is empty. "Nite-nite all-gone" can mean I don't want a nap. Other early words are *bye-bye, hey, hey dere,* and *no.* These are also used in many ways. By 1½, toddlers understand most, if not all, that is said to them, but they can not yet keep up their end of the conversation. By the age of 2, toddlers raised with people who talk to each other *and* to toddlers will say an amazing number of things.

Key Care Ideas

- As children begin to say two words together, the provider should answer as though they have made a perfect sentence.
    Baby: Doggie bark.
    Provider: Yes, I don't think that doggie likes people to bother him.
    Baby: Doggie big.
    Provider: That's right. He's even bigger than the doggie on our street.

- As toddlers learn more words that name things, the provider can help them with words that tell about those things. For instance, when toddlers say "ball," the provider can answer "That's a red and blue ball." Then she can show the toddler the red part and the blue part. When babies ask the name of some new thing (usually pointing and saying "guh"), the word should be given first, then after the baby seems to have the word clear, the provider can go on to talk about it a little.
    Baby: Guh.
    Provider: That's a lamp.
    Baby: Lamp.
    Provider: Right. It turns on, then on brighter, and then brighter. And that's a lamp shade.

- Toddlers enjoy looking at books and naming things or just pointing to the thing that the provider then names. Picture books of animals interest toddlers who usually learn to make the noises each animal makes before they can name the animal. Two favorite books of this type are H. A. Rey's *Where's the Baby?* and *Feed the Animals.* The pictures and rhymes in *Goodnight Moon* have delighted young children for years, and so has finding the mouse hidden on each page.

- As babies reach the end of their first year and become toddlers, the provider should make a habit of saying what she is doing or what the toddler is doing. This not only helps children add to their vocabulary, it helps them learn co-operation as well. The words make the action more acceptable. "Lunch is ready. Here you go. Up into the high chair. And here's your lunch." The conversation is so interesting to children that they are often so busy listening they do not think about objecting to the activity. Saying what is happening also makes it clear to them that there is no choice—it is time to eat or time to bathe.

- It is always preferable to make statements to toddlers, not ask questions. It is *not* helpful to give choices at this age. Questions and choices only make it harder to them to go along with what they are being asked to do. It is fine to ask questions in games such as "Where's Winnie?", "What does the doggie say?", or "How big is Benjie?" But when it comes to naptime, the provider can say "I'm going to put you down for your nap, now. You are a sleepy boy. Jamie is going to take his nap now." This helps Jamie know his provider means it and there is no use fussing.

- There are other rhyming games that babies this age enjoy. One is *This Little Piggy*, in which each line of the rhyme refers to a toe or finger. The adult takes one of the baby's toes or fingers and holds it while saying what that "piggy" did (see Figure 23).

   This little piggy went to market (one toe)
   This little piggy stayed home (another)
   This little piggy had roast beef (another)
   This little piggy had none (another)
   And this little piggy cried "Wee, wee, wee," all the way home (holding last toe).

- Another game is *Pease Porridge Hot*. The provider has to play the game alone at first, then as the baby gets the idea she can show him or her when to slap knees or hands.

Figure 23.

Providing for Language Development

Pease porridge hot (slap hands on knees)
Pease porridge cold (slap hands together)
Pease porridge in the pot (slap child's right palm with provider's right palm)
Nine days old (switch and slap baby's left palm with provider's left palm)

Toddlers

From 1 to 3 years old, children go from one- and two-word sentences to being able to carry on a real conversation. They are not only learning many new words, they are also learning about ideas. They are learning that *birthday* means cake and candles and a present, that *fall down* can mean a scraped knee, a Band-Aid, and some comforting. *Car* can mean going for a ride, or a toy, or something to look for out of the window, that there are big cars and little cars, red cars and blue, that one has to stop at the corner because of cars and that one has to go in a car to visit Granny.

As more ideas are attached to words, new words are needed. Children can now learn describing words such as fat and thin, hard and soft, long and short. They can talk about *where* things are—on the floor, in the drawer, out of town, in the air, over your head. They know what goes outside and what stays inside. They cannot understand about time yet, but they know what happens before or after certain things—dessert comes *after* lunch, a story comes *before* naptime. Two year olds can learn some colors and a few shapes, such as square, round, star, and valentine (meaning all heart shapes).

Toddlers learn the names of parts of their bodies and the names for certain feelings. They know a smile means happy and tears mean sad or hurt. They can be funny, and they can tell when someone else is being funny. Their idea of funny is often just saying something silly, but it is the beginning of humor. Adults do not usually think that putting a shoe on your head is terribly funny, but to a toddler it can be hilarious.

<u>Key Care Ideas</u>

- There are many ways to make a toddler's life rich in language, but none is more important than simply having conversations. The provider should talk about everything she does or the toddler does and include lots of words that describe. "That's a bumpy leaf. Look at the holes in it. It's all yellow except just this little green here. Can you find a leaf with no holes?"

- The conversations should not be one-way. Toddlers should be given lots of time to talk, and undivided attention when they do. Children do not listen to adults who do not listen to them.

- It is not a good idea to correct toddlers' speech. They will correct their own in time. It is best to ignore mistakes and go on talking. The only things that should be corrected are facts. "My daddy can run faster than a car." "Most cars can go faster than people can run. Like most airplanes can go faster than cars. How fast do you think a train can go?" The more toddlers practice their language, the more correct it becomes.

- The provider should use as few *no's* as possible. Instead she can say, "Use the magic marker on the paper. I'll put some newspaper under your paper so it doesn't get on the floor."
- Silly games delight toddlers. Rhymes are great fun, especially when toddlers start the game, for example, "Dog, hog, log, smog." "Last, fast, past."
- At about 2 years, children begin using language to pretend. "Me Superman, not William." "Oh, hello there Superman, maybe you would like me to make you a cape," the provider can reply. A toddler might say "I'm the Mommy and you have to go to bed now." The provider can answer, "Oh, alright, Mommy, I'll go as soon as I finish these dishes." Playing along with the pretend games lets the toddler play with ideas about what people do, how they act and why, and what kind of person he or she would like to be. The game lets the provider tell the toddler a lot about how she thinks people should act in a way that is both interesting and fun.

Preschoolers

By the time children are 3 years old, they are good talkers. Only those who live in grim situations or who have physical or mental problems are not talking at 3. Most 3 year olds want to talk about what they are doing, and by 5 they can talk about anything they have seen or done and some things they can only imagine.

A new use of language begins in the 3- to 5-year-old period. This is the time when children learn to think about what they are doing or have done or seen. They do some of their best thinking out loud, practicing language as they put ideas into words. They want to be able to say what they think and think what they say. More than that, they are beginning to think about and talk about things they *have not* seen, things they *have not* done, about what is real and what is not, what they can and cannot do, what they can have and what they cannot. For instance, they think about the moon: it is real, but is is not always there, and it rarely looks the same. People can even go there. One day, they may be able to, too. They wonder what it would be like to be on the moon.

Preschool-aged children are also learning about people. They now ask how things work, what people do, and, more often, why. Part of getting ready for school is learning to get along with people. Without language, none of this is possible. How well children do in school depends to a great extent on the language they have learned in their preschool years. Games, story telling, and story reading are almost as important as conversation.

Providing for Language Development

Key Care Ideas

- Preschool-aged children love riddles. The younger ones need very simple clues: "I'm thinking of something with fur that says meow!" As they get a little older the riddles can get harder: "I'm thinking of something you drink that's white." "I'm thinking of something that gets hot and makes toast." Soon the preschoolers can make up their own riddles. The provider should be prepared for very strange and unhelpful clues. One 5 year old said, "I'm thinking of something that moves furniture." After her family had guessed everything that they could think of, she announced, "It's a truck with a hook!" Do not correct these odd answers, the game is more important than the answers. Children do not want adults to be able to guess, they want to be able to say, "You're wrong!" That is the best part of the fun.

- When walking or playing outside, finding "look alikes" is a good game. One person says, "I see a cloud that looks like a head!" Another person says, "I see one that looks like a dog!" Clouds and shadows have shapes that look like faces, or horses, or boats, or many other things. Paper can be cut or torn into a shape of something. Guessing what shapes look like is fun and helps children see likenesses and make connections.

- There are many storybooks for young children with beautiful pictures and simple stories. These can be looked at in the library and the favorites checked out and taken home. Very young children love the books by Maurice Sendak, Robert McCloskey, and Ezra Jack Keats. *Madeleine* and *Parsley*, the *Babar* stories, *Peter Rabbit*, and *Curious George* are classics that every child should know. Preschool-age children often learn these by heart and can repeat phrases with the provider as she reads the book. Toddlers can learn many pages of *Johnny Crow's Garden*.

- Mother Goose rhymes and stories are so much a part of our culture that everyone should know them. *Rock-a-Bye Baby*, *Jack Sprat*, *The Little Red Hen*, and *This Is the House That Jack Built* are as interesting to children today as they were 100 years ago. As the provider reads them over and over, she will find that she too has learned them by heart and can recite her favorites. As she walks to the park or store with the children, they can recite together *As I Was Going to St. Ives* or *Simple Simon*. *Pease Porridge Hot* or *Polly Put the Kettle On* go with preparing snack; *Wee Willie Winkie* at naptime. *There Was an Old Woman Who Lived in a Shoe* was not a very nice provider, but is a joke all children enjoy. The rhymes of *One, Two, Buckle My Shoe* and *One Little, Two Little, Three Little Indians* are good counting games.

Sassing and Answering Back During the preschool years children begin what is called sassing or answering back. They may merely repeat what the adult says to them, imitating the words and tone of voice. The provider may say, "Pick up your things, Georgie" and Georgie may repeat it in a singsong voice or a silly voice. Some adults become very angry and think this behavior should be punished seriously. They feel it is a question of authority or treating adults "with respect." If so, they should tell the child that it upsets them when children answer back in that way, and request the child not to do it. Thereafter, unless the child is very angry with the adult and wants to show it, the problem is solved.

Some adults who are insecure or who have little confidence cannot tolerate children's questions. Those adults expect the children to accept everything they say without question or discussion. This is very unfortunate for the children. Not only do children have an innate desire to question in order to learn, but a questioning style is associated with intelligence. An intelligent person does not accept what he or she is told without thought, more information, and consideration of alternatives. Adults who are intelligent encourage children to develop inquiring minds. No one has all of the answers to all of the questions children ask, but a mature, intelligent adult can say so without fearing disrespect and can discuss with a child how an answer to a question could be found.

School-Aged Children

At 6 years children's language is no longer simply speaking and listening, they must begin to learn writing and reading as well. These new steps are discussed in Chapter 13. How easily they manage these new demands depends upon how well they can handle speaking and understanding. The first steps were taken when they were infants and learned about things by looking, touching, tasting, and recognizing them. The next step was giving the things names. Then came thinking about the things when one heard the words, even when the things were not there to see. Seeing a picture of the things then recalls both the words and what they stand for. Finally, writing the words recalls the sound of the words, the things they represent, and how they look. It takes a lot of talking and thinking to be able to put all these pieces together.

Some of the things that school-age children talk about are people, their families and friends, their feelings, what they like to do or don't like, and more abstract things like their future, death, being honest, and feeling scared. Being able to talk about what is important makes it easier to understand, to decide what to do, to know why things happen. The more at ease children are with language, the more at ease they are in the world.

Providers can help school-aged children most by talking with them about what they are doing and thinking and feeling. One big task in going to school is learning what school teachers and other children expect. The best way to learn how to get along with these new people is to talk about what happens in school. Providers must make it clear that they are interested and can be helpful and can handle children's worries and mistakes without being embarrassed or critical.

Key Care Ideas

- Pretending school at home gives preschool-aged children the chance to learn what to expect. The older children who already have school experience will eagerly join in these games. Their own feelings of importance can make the game a bit too much for the younger children unless the provider keeps an eye on them and acts as director.

- There are many word games that young children can handle and that will help them develop the skills that make for school success. If they are played for fun, if there are no winners or losers, no right or wrong answers, they will be both useful and enjoyable. In fact, once the children have caught on, they will play these games on their own. The provider can start them off by saying, "What's the biggest thing you can think of, the biggest thing in the whole world?" The children should use their imagination, even if they invent things that do not exist. The idea is to think *big*. Then the provider can ask, "What's the *softest* thing?", and then the flattest, the longest, the hardest, the sharpest, and so on.

- Another game to play is "Opposites." The provider asks the children what is the opposite of small. As they learn the easy opposites, she goes on to more difficult ones such as the opposite of narrow, inside, poor, terrible.

- As soon as the children catch on to the word games, they will want to be the one who asks. One game that is easy for young children is the "Goes With" game. It's best to begin with easy questions. "What goes with socks?" "What goes with rice?" and "What goes with sunshine?" are good ones. Again, the provider should encourage original ideas. If the children's answers seem too unrelated, the provider can ask *how* or *why* their word "Goes With." Any hint their idea is not good should be avoided.

- Another game is "Why is a _____ like a _____?" This is a favorite question on IQ tests. Playing the game gives children the chance to practice thinking of a connection between two ideas or two things. One can begin with easy ones, like "Why is a cat like a tiger?" or "Why is a pear like an apple?", always remembering that there are no wrong answers. The children can be encouraged to be creative by the provider's acceptance of their ideas and laughter with them at their efforts to be funny.

- Children love proverbs and old sayings. They find them interesting and come up with very unusual ideas about what the proverbs mean. The provider can try a few out on the children. She might ask them what people mean when they say, "A stitch in time saves nine" or "Out of sight, out of mind."

- Children of all ages enjoy riddles. Making up riddles is as much fun as guessing the answer. Once encouraged, children will make up their own and guess each other's riddles. Language games of this kind not only add to the children's storehouse of words and ideas but also sharpen their reasoning skills.

Some Bad Uses of Language

CURSE WORDS AND DIRTY WORDS When children begin school, whether nursery school, kindergarten, or first grade, they learn several uses of language that adults dislike. One of these is dirty words and curse words. In some places and among some groups these words are used frequently and no one really objects. For example, there is hardly a movie made in which these words are not said by some, if not all of the characters. Other people object to hearing and using "curse words" or "dirty words" and strongly object to hearing children use them.

The provider needs to know how the parents feel about the use of these words, and whatever their position is, she should take the same. Regardless of what language adults use, they usually find these words shocking when used by little children. If the important adults in the children's lives use curse words or dirty words, the children are bound to imitate them.

The easiest and best way to deal with this is to explain to the children that people have very strong reactions to hearing these words, and therefore they should be used with care and not around people who will object to them. Because these words are often used among children, she can say it is okay as long as the children are sure no one will hear who might be offended. Children will accept this kind of reason and respect the adult's wishes especially when the request is made by adults they love and want to please.

LANGUAGE THAT HURTS Another use of language that children are exposed to when they begin school is language that hurts. Every child at some time or another suffers the injury of being called a name or being told that he or she cannot play with the other children. Children soon learn how this is done and that they can make others suffer as they have suffered. We can spare children a great deal of pain and distress by explaining that some children are not aware of how they hurt others, and the children who are most likely to call others names or tell them they cannot play are the children who have been hurt by others. We can explain that this is the behavior of the weak, not the strong. Children are kind to others if the important adults in their lives are kind to them. When children are treated unkindly by adults, when they are laughed at, or called names, or yelled at, they will then do the same thing to those smaller and weaker than they are.

TATTLETALES One final use of language must be dealt with when children reach school age. Tattling can be learned in the home, but most often children are exposed only when they begin school. Unfortunately, many schools not only reward tattling, they may encourage it. It is not always easy for providers to combat this.

Like hurtful language, tattling is intended to do harm to someone else. Children in the family day care home can not be permitted to hurt or harm others. That they may be telling the provider something she needs to know is no excuse. A child may say to the provider, "There's a fire in the bedroom!" The child should *not* say, "Tommy was playing with matches and started a fire!" The provider is capable of finding out whatever she needs to know without encouraging tattling. Whatever excuses are offered for tattling, it is really a way of trying to look better than someone else. Because the family day care home is a place of trust and respect for others, there can be no tattling there. It is a place where children are helped to learn how to care for others and, whenever possible, to protect their friends from harm.

The Good Uses of Language Human beings use language to understand the world, to learn about things they have never seen, to get to know people and their ideas and thoughts. Because of language we can know all the things we would never be able to figure out in one lifetime. When someone asked him how he became such a genius, Issac Newton is supposed to have said, "If I have seen farther than others, it is because I stood on the shoulders of giants." Language makes it possible for all of us to stand on the shoulders of giants. If we decide we want to make an aquarium we can ask the pet store clerk or read about aquariums at the library. If we want to bake a carrot cake we can find a recipe or ask a good cook. If we want to plant some tomatoes, or make a bookshelf, or braid a rug, or fire a clay sculpture, we can find out by asking someone or reading instructions, saving the time and materials it would take to figure it out by ourselves. Language makes available to us all the world's knowledge.

Language also makes it possible for us to think about our lives and what happens to us in terms of other people's experiences and thoughts. We can listen to and read about people's reasons and choices and decide whether we agree or not. Having the successes and failures of others to guide us, we can make better decisions for ourselves. Winston Churchill said that unless we learn from history we are forced to repeat it. With language we can learn.

Language can be used to make our own lives richer and more understandable. It can also be used to do harm. The children we care for will learn the uses of language from us. They will do as we do and speak as we speak.

12

Providing for Preschoolers

Somewhere between 2½ and 3 years of age we stop calling children *toddlers* and begin calling them *preschoolers*. This label does little justice to children this age, and it is even less suitable for those who do not attend a preschool. Having no better name for this age, however, we shall also call children between 2½ and 5 years old *preschoolers*.

In some cities there are more preschoolers in family day care homes than any other age group. It may be that providers prefer children from 3 to 5. They are more independent, entertaining, and less emotionally demanding than toddlers. Children from 3 to 5 who have had a good start in their own homes or in family day care are a pleasure. They can speak well enough to say what they think, need, or want, and the things they say are often very touching and very funny. They are open about their feelings and show them freely. They are proud of what they can do and eager to learn more. They are affectionate and caring most of the time.

Of course, these good qualities of preschoolers may be missing in those who were not well cared for as infants and toddlers. Those who have had a difficult first 3 years may only speak one or two words at a time. They may be very quiet and not seem interested in toys, other children, or the provider, then they may suddenly explode into action, grabbing things and running, pushing or banging into other children and furniture. They seem to be mad or sad most of the time and are difficult to care for.

This chapter describes the average preschoolers' behavior with people—adults and children—and describes their thinking—both about the world and themselves.

BEHAVIOR WITH PEOPLE

How preschoolers act with people has a great deal to do with their experiences as infants and toddlers. The most obvious result of their early care is their trust in others. If they are eager to play, talk, do what they are asked, try out new things, they have been well cared for and probably were encouraged to be independent but were not pushed. They were helped when help was needed and left alone when they could manage. Most important, they were not laughed at or shamed or hurried unnecessarily. Naturally, all 3 year olds have moments of being babies or frustrated toddlers again. On the whole, however, they are getting ready to move outside the family, meet new people, and begin playing with other children. It is easy to see what great changes take place in these few years when we look at the difference between a 3 year old and a 5 year old.

Behavior with Adults

Most three year olds who have had a secure beginning are ready to show an interest in adults other than their parents and provider. Until this age, children are usually very attached to the people who care for them and are either not really interested in or are uncomfortable with other adults. Now, however, many children become interested in what other adults do. They ask questions about the storekeeper, the postman, the nurse in the clinic, the policeman, all of the adults they meet. During these years, they begin to pretend to be firemen, doctors, garbagemen. Children who watch television may pretend to be the heros of their favorite programs. While pretending to be Superman or the Incredible Hulk, they feel strong and powerful.

It is this interest in adults that is the means by which children learn about people and work. Between 3 and 5, most children begin to talk about what they want to be when they grow up. They see adults as powerful and capable, moving about in the world and doing things well. Because they are still small and unable to do many things, they want very much to be like these strong, able adults. For this reason, any adult who shows an interest in children and spends some time with them can have a real influence. It is important to find such adults and let the children get to know them.

Key Care Ideas

- Perhaps there are members of the provider's family who can spend some time with the children, answering their questions, taking them for walks, and talking about what they see and the many things that people do.
- Another important way that children learn about the world is by seeing people at work. This is the time when neighborhood trips are most interesting and most valuable. It is important for the children to see a variety of jobs being done by women as well as men, and for them to talk with these adults and learn something about people and their work (preparations for trips in the neighborhood are described in Chapter 5).
- After seeing some adults at work children enjoy pretending to be those adults.

They need very few props for these make-believe games. For playing store, the provider can save empty cans and cartons that can be washed and used as things to sell (making sure the cans have no sharp edges). For playing school, they will need paper and pencil and a table to serve as a desk. A make-believe restaurant needs a couple of tables (or cartons), a menu, and a few dishes. The provider can probably invent props for any of the pretend games the children want to play. For 3 year olds, who are usually only interested in playing family games pretending to be mommy, baby, and daddy, simple props are needed. By 5 or 6 years old, they play elaborate games of make-believe—make-believe library, circus, Wild West rodeo, or anything they may know about from books, television, and trips with their parents or day care family. Making props is part of the activity. These games not only help the children learn about the world but also encourage them to think about themselves as adults.

Finally, at this age children still need help with many daily tasks—tying shoes, reaching a cup, combing hair, eating soup, getting the tricycle over the curb. Learning to ask for help will make more difference in their school and home lives than almost anything else they learn. Some children already know how to get help as toddlers (see Chapter 10; more on getting help in Chapter 15).

Behavior with Other Children

Three year olds are just beginning to be interested in other children as partners and playmates. Before that age, although they like company, they are rarely able to play games that require cooperation with other children. They are more apt to show their interest by watching the others, not joining in, but sometimes playing alongside. Every now and then, they may become so interested in the other children's game that they will reach over to touch, to take, or to move something. It takes quite some time before they can understand why this upsets the other children. They are still not able to see things from another point of view.

At age 3, children may watch other children without speaking to them. If they do speak, they may merely say, "I want that," "That's mine," "Give me that," or "I want one." The art of conversation takes a lot of learning, and at this age, it often needs at least one adult present for it to happen.

Children playing side by side sometimes seem to be having a conversation when they are really talking to themselves. This is common among young preschoolers.

Child A: I'm going to put it in the water.
Child B: Mommy's gone to see Granny.
Child A: It goes down to the bottom.
Child B: Granny has a cat.
Child A: Now it's full of water.

Because they take turns speaking and may even look at each other while talking, they seem to be having a conversation, and in a way they are. It is simply that they are not always sharing the same idea or subject.

Helping Children Learn To Get Along

At home, children of different ages have to share space and materials. Since young preschoolers often want to play alongside but not with other children, they may want to be in the same room but have their own things. Even then, disputes over space and toys will arise. It is important to step in and show the children how to come to an agreement. Preschoolers, especially, do not know how to solve disputes until they are shown how, and older children may forget how when trying to protect their belongings.

<u>Key Care Ideas</u>

- The best way to put an end to these disagreements is to organize the games and space in a firm and definite way. The provider can say, "Davie and Karen, I see you two need more space for your blocks. Jenny, I'll help you put your paper and paste over here where you'll have lots of room and the blocks can't fall on you. Now the store game can have all that space over there." Setting out definite limits in a calm but firm way shows the children how to make room for each other and how to play alongside without getting into each other's way. The provider's consideration for the needs of each child shows them how to be considerate of each other.

- If there are toys that regularly cause disputes, they should be put away and only brought out when the provider is free to sit down with the children and keep an eye on things. Because young preschoolers need help in thinking of others and remembering the rules, her presence makes it easier for them to play with others and feel secure that she will see to it that everyone gets fair treatment.

- The best way to learn cooperation is to pretend to be someone who is cooperative. One reason that dress-up and make-believe games are so useful is that when children pretend to be a favorite adult, they "put on" the behavior of that adult along with the hat (or shoes, or whatever they are using in the dress-up game.) As the adult, they treat the others in the game the same way that the person they are imitating would. They use the voice, the words, the gestures, and, most of all, the character of that person.

Preschoolers like to make a game of everything. They dream up all sorts of silly ways to do things. Now that they know how things are done and can do many things for themselves, they like to pretend they have forgotten how or cannot do them anymore. They will pretend they cannot feed themselves or put on their clothes. They invent silly games like walking backwards everywhere or wearing their clothes inside out. They can become so involved in these games that they may begin to think that is the way things *should* be.

Silliness is very catching for preschoolers. They get the giggles easily and have trouble getting over them. They are also able to "catch" other moods easily. If the other children are excited, or cranky, or if a child is sad, preschoolers will suddenly become excited, or mad, or sad, too. Young preschoolers can be sympathetic, angry, or both, suddenly and without warning. They may get so carried away by these feelings that they act out their anger in ways that can hurt. They may hit, push, or poke other children without realizing that they are really hurting them. When angry, they may want to hurt others, and feel no sympathy for the tears or cries they cause. At another moment, they will pat or stroke an unhappy child, showing great tenderness and sympathy.

These are the years in which children begin to learn how to get along with others. This is the time when they find out that they are not allowed to hurt other people, that they must use words, not fists, to get what they want. They can only learn, however if *their* feelings and needs are understood and responded to. They will then be able to learn to be thoughtful and helpful with others by copying the example of the other children and the provider in the family day care home.

Children who are able to have their own way sometimes and are able to do what others want sometimes have the makings of leaders. Burton White, who has probably studied more children in their preschool years than anyone else in this country, has found that competent children are able to do two things well: they can get help when they need it from both adults and other children, and they can get their own way as well as give in sometimes to what others ask.

Key Care Ideas

- The time the provider spends showing 3 to 5 year olds how to play together or alongside peacefully will pay off in a short period of time. Once children know how to respect others and earn respect, they can solve their own disagreements. First, however, they need to know that the provider is fair, that she expects them to be fair, and that she will not go along with anyone being hurt.

- As children become older preschoolers, they are ready for real cooperation. Games such as Candyland, Parcheesi, Chutes & Ladders and card games such as Go Fish and Battle teach children to play by the rules and to wait their turn. The provider will have to play with the children until they are old enough to play among themselves (usually not before 5 or 6 years old.)

- There are other activities that require cooperation as well: turning the rope for jumping, holding the dustpan for the person who is sweeping, holding the bowl for the person using the egg beater. The provider can begin by offering to hold something or help with something the child is doing. Soon she can get one child to hold for another child while she stands by. Gradually, the children become

Providing for Preschoolers 171

ready to cooperate with each other, asking for help and giving it. It is important for the provider to show her pleasure and approval of these cooperative efforts. She can say, "Arleen, you and Stevie are doing such a good job together." "Petey, I see you helping Jeff. You are a good holder!"

THINKING ABOUT THINGS IN THE WORLD

Everything that children do requires them to think, even the simple things like dressing, eating, playing, and helping set the table. They spend a good deal of time thinking about everything they have done or seen or heard or felt. Some of this shows up in their play. They repeat what they have seen someone do or something they once did themselves in their make-believe games. Pretend games support many kinds of learning—learning about people, about themselves, and about social behavior. When children can think about what others do and imitate it, it allows them to choose to behave in one way rather than another, to learn to think about what they do before they do it. As children grow up, they take on the characteristics of the important people in their lives—the good qualities as well as the not so good ones. The ages of 3 through 5 are devoted to taking in all these qualities, trying them on for size, and keeping the ones that fit. As they get older children can fit into more and more of these borrowed behaviors, and they can borrow from more and more people—older children, teachers, even television characters. They pretend doctor and give shots, or bus driver and tell everyone to move into the back of the bus, or teacher and tell the children to sing the Good Morning Song. They also pretend to be animals at times—tigers or monkeys or dogs. This allows them to roar or bark, run and jump around, and then say that they cannot stop because tigers or dogs do not understand talking. (As children get older they give up the animal pretend games and become astronauts, construction workers, policemen, or Mohammed Ali.)

Preschoolers are also thinking about things—how they work and what they are good for. They become interested in solving puzzles and making things. At first, they are not so interested in the materials themselves, only in the things they are making. Later they become more interested in painting in many colors on many kinds of paper, in cutting paper, cloth, foil, or clay, in pasting paper, toothpicks, scraps of cloth, bits of plastic, or sparkles.

Like toddlers, preschoolers enjoy water, sand, and mud, and play for long periods of time pouring, squeezing, piling up, patting. They often talk to themselves while playing, describing the meal they are making or how the waterfall they are making will become a lake. Outdoor things like rocks, shells, leaves, acorns, nuts, seed pods, flowers, and bugs are picked up and brought home to be looked at, put in boxes, or pasted on paper. Preschool-age children often have pockets full of treasures. They need boxes to keep their things in so that they can take them out from time to time and study them. This is the beginning of an interest in natural science.

There are many ways in which the family day care home can make learning interesting and at the same time keep the children busy and contented. The following examples cover the major areas of knowledge acquired in the preschool years. It is easy to see how they are all part of children's daily lives. Most of the activities in Chapter 5 are appropriate for preschoolers.

Key Care Ideas

- **Space** There are many words we use to talk about where things are in space. During the preschool years children learn about near and far, top and bottom, high and low, front and back, up and down, in and out, here and there. In conversations with children, the provider can ask them "where" questions—if the thing they saw was close enough to touch or too far away, how it looked in front and in back, if it was right side up or upside down. As the provider unpacks groceries, she can talk about what goes in the top of the cabinet, in the bottom of the closet, and so on. This leads to more space talk, about what goes up in the sky, on the water, under the ground, on rails, and so forth.

  Children gradually learn how to get around in their neighborhood. As they walk (or ride) to the store they can tell the provider where to turn, what is on that corner, where the drugstore is. They enjoy taking turns "showing the way" and giving directions.

  By age 5 many children can tell their left from their right. Some learn it much later, and there are some adults who have never learned.

  As they build buildings with blocks and boxes or cartons, the provider can ask where one goes in, comes out, sits, or sleeps. Along with blocks and boxes, she can provide little plastic people, animals, and furniture (all available in most dime stores for very little money.) This allows children to organize their spaces and to create an imaginary world at the same time.

- **Time** Everyone has different ideas about time, although in America the general attitude is that "time is money," and "the early bird catches the worm." People who are not on time are usually considered unlikely to succeed. At this age, children begin to learn about time from the routines of every day. They wash hands before snack, nap after lunch, clean up before going home, go outside after nap. They also learn that it is *time* to go home (from the park), and that they do not have *time* to play Parcheesi now. Although they can understand that today is now, tomorrow and yesterday are difficult for the preschool-age child. Next week and last week are even harder to understand. Children love to hear about what happened "long ago" especially stories about "when you first knew me."

  Preschoolers can be encouraged to tell stories about what happened over the weekend or last night. At first, these stories are very rambling and mixed up. With practice, though, children learn to organize the story and tell what happened first, then second, then at the end.

- **Size** Children learn about size very quickly and easily. "I'm bigger than you." "I want a big piece of banana." "I only have a little bit." They also learn to see objects in the world in terms of size. They can line things up in order of size. They learn to guess the weight of an object from its size—a big block is heavier than a little block (but a golf ball is heavier than a beach ball). Talking about these everyday things helps children learn to make judgments and then check to see if their judgments are correct.

- **Goes With** In Chapter 11 the "Goes With" game is described. As children go from 3 to 5 years old, they learn that dolls go with trucks because they are both toys, meat goes with oranges because they are both food, trucks go with bicycles because they are both things with wheels that you ride. In everyday conversation they will talk about things that go with other things—this goes with the laundry, that goes in the bathroom, this goes with the other dishes. Sorting things and putting them away are part of everyday life and help children learn how to group things.

- **Matching** This is another thinking skill that preschoolers are ready to learn. Card games like Old Maid and Go Fish are matching games. Sorting laundry, finding the socks that match, setting the table so each person's place matches, are all ways in which we see things that are alike. Children often come up with their own "look alikes" such as the pattern on the cup and the pattern on a dress, or the color of a cat and the color of a carpet.

- **Same-Different** Some things do not really match but in certain ways are the same. For instance, a poodle and a police dog have the same kind of bark, ears, nose, legs, and paws, but different hair and different tails. They are the same kind of animal. A piece of paper and a blackboard do not look the same but they are used for the same thing—to write on. A paper bag and carton do not look the same but may have the same number of cookies in each. Seeing the ways in which things are the same and different is another way preschoolers think about the world. Very young children call an orange a ball, a shovel a spoon, showing that they have their own ways of seeing sameness and difference. Even little children enjoy playing with dominoes, even though they may not know all of the numbers or understand the rules of the game.

Preschool-age children are ready to use crayons, pencils, magic markers. By 5 years of age they can copy a square, a circle, and a triangle. They can copy the letters of the alphabet and many can write their names by 4 or 5. They draw people, houses, and animals. When the provider has a note for the parents, they enjoy adding a drawing or signing their names by hers. They can use old magazines and catalogs for pictures to cut out and then paste in scrapbooks of things with wheels, things to eat, toys, or people. Pictures that they especially like can be pasted on a large sheet of paper, then the children can make up a story about the picture for the provider to write under it.

THINKING ABOUT THEMSELVES

Three year olds are very interested in their bodies and continue to be for the next few years. They are eager to learn the names of body parts, what they are there for, if everyone has the same, and why some people are different. They enjoy looking in the mirror carefully studying each part of their bodies. They are curious about their backs and the back of their heads which they cannot see, even in the mirror.

They are eager to know how their bodies work, where food and liquids go in and where they come out. Having just lately become toilet trained, they are very interested in how their food and drink become feces and urine.

They are also interested in but afraid of any injury. Many children go through a stage when even a scratch is very upsetting, and even more upsetting is the sight of blood—their own or someone else's. They wonder about all that blood rushing around inside their bodies.

At this age children sometimes become so afraid of having something done to their bodies that the fear can last all their lives. One example is the fear of having a shot, of needles. There are adults who are as upset by having an injection as they were when they were children. On the other hand, having a scratch or minor cut washed, dried, and covered with a Band-aid can be very soothing and comforting.

Preschoolers are often not able to say where the pain is when they have hurt themselves or have an earache or a sore throat. They cannot yet connect the pain and the place, and the adult often has to be a detective to find the cause of the misery (see Chapter 18). By age 5, however, most children can tell where it hurts, itches, or burns. They have become more at home in their bodies.

Key Care Ideas

- Having a mirror on the bathroom door or bedroom door allows small children to look at themselves. Bathing young children together allows them to see each other's bodies. Most 3 and 4 year olds need to look at themselves a great deal to know what the body they live in is like. The provider should answer their many questions about why bodies are made the way they are, how they grow, how big they will get, how their skin can stretch. She can tell them why she gives them certain foods to make their bodies strong and healthy, why they have exercise time to make their muscles grow.

The interest that children this age have in their bodies is healthy and should be encouraged. If they feel that the provider shares their interest and is also eager to see that their bodies are well cared for and protected, they will learn to protect themselves. Children who think their bodies are valuable and are happy about themselves will not be careless or do dangerous things like get fat, take drugs or alcohol, or smoke cigarettes. During the years between 3 and 5, people learn how to care for and care about their bodies. Later on, it is much harder and may be even impossible to learn.

Exercise

At this age children need to spend a lot of time outdoors doing things that require real effort. Some providers are lucky and have yards with plenty of space. Only a little equipment is needed to provide lots of strenuous activity. For others, it is necessary to take all the children to a park or a playground, hauling the equipment or wheel toys along. This can often be made manageable by bringing ropes and balls, keeping them in a bag for carrying and for storing at home. In either case, the important issue is the exercise, and the space need only lend itself to a lot of real physical effort.

In addition to the strength and endurance that physical activity builds, important skills are acquired in outdoor play. These skills add to children's self-esteem and confidence and are admired by other children. The choice of skills depends upon the children's interests but preschoolers all learn to jump, hop, and throw and catch a ball. They learn to walk a line or a plank, climb a ladder, ride a trike then a bike, skip, play hopscotch, and by 5 years, most can rollerskate.

At home an old mattress is a wonderful place to learn tumbling—somersaults, head stands, back bends, hand stands against the wall. The provider need only lend a hand to make sure the child does not land on his or her head or on another child.

Sensitive Questions

This is the age at which most children first ask where babies come from. If the provider has not had a chance to talk to the parents about how they feel about these questions, she will now proabaly have to. In some cases the parents will need some help in understanding what these questions mean and how to answer them.

Sometime around 3 or 4 years old, children hear about someone's new baby. Although they may have heard older children say, "She has a baby in her stomach" or "She's so fat she must be going to have a baby," preschoolers cannot imagine how or really believe it. Their first questions are usually about how the baby got in the stomach (most children believe the mother ate something; some find this upsetting and get fussy about their food for a while). They do not need and cannot handle a complete description of the process of birth. When they ask, the provider should begin with a simple answer like, "The baby grows from a tiny egg the mother has in her body. It is not in her stomach, but in a special place for growing babies." When asked how the tiny egg got there, she can explain that all women have tiny eggs so that when they are grown up they can have babies. Preschoolers are not yet ready for descriptions of the father's role in making a baby.

The provider may find that some parents are not willing to talk to their children about pregnancy and birth, and do not want her to mention it either. Although preschoolers are not ready for too much knowledge, their questions should be treated seriously, they should never be laughed at, and they should be given simple but honest answers. They will ask the same question many times before they understand.

Needless to say, the provider will have to explain to the parents that she is not offering "sex education." She is merely answering the children's questions with the simplest information about how humans develop. She should report to the parents each time she is asked a question, so that they, too, become part of the educational process. She should ask how they would answer, then tell them how she answered and why. She should explain that the older children will answer these questions if she does not, and that the provider feels it is important that she give correct (and also limited) answers. If older children are present while a preschooler is asking, they may ask more direct questions and want more complete answers. She can simply tell them that she will talk with them later, that right now it is the preschooler's turn (Chapter 14 deals with older children's needs).

Another subject that comes up for the first time during the preschool years is death. Like birth, this subject is often avoided partly because parents would rather children not know about it and partly because they are not sure what to say. The provider will want to speak with the parents as soon as the subject comes up. She can explain to the parents that children only ask questions when they already know *something*, and therefore she feels that the adult has a responsibility to make sure what they know is right, not wrong. The details are not important, the simple facts are. Children do not understand that death is final. They often ask when the dead person is coming back. They also want to know when the people they love will die. Even though they may not quite understand that death is final, they begin to worry about losing the people they need and love. They also ask when *they* themselves will die. The provider needs to explain that most people live to be quite old, that their parents and provider will take good care of themselves in order to be around for a long time. She can tell the children that they have a long life ahead, and to make sure they enjoy it, they need to keep healthy and be successful in their work. She can tell them that she is there to take good care of them and to help them with their work. She can talk with them about what they want to be when they grow up and what kind of life they want to have. As she talks, the subject of death will retreat into the background. Once they are reassured that the provider will take care of them and of herself, death will begin to lose its fearfulness.

Sex Roles and Identity

This is a very sensitive subject because of the demands of today's women for fair treatment and equal opportunity. Because there are many views of what equality between men and women means, there are many different ideas and beliefs about what is fair. The provider does not really need to get involved in these questions. She does need to be clear about how she feels children should learn what being a boy or a girl means. Children 3 to 5 years old are very concerned about what being a girl or being a boy involves. To develop a strong sense of their own identity, which they will need in order to be confident, capable people, they need to feel contented about being a boy or a girl.

At one time, many parents encouraged girls to be tomboys. Now parents realize that girls really wish for the freedom that boys are given. Both sexes should be encouraged to be very active, to play games, and to acquire physical skills. Those parents also used to get upset when boys played with dolls, pretended to cook, or played at any activity that was associated with "women's work." This is no longer true. Most men have decided that caring for their children is a pleasure and a privilege and want their sons to grow up to be caring, tender, and considerate. Many men are now willing to assist in housework and cooking, especially as more and more married women are working.

For a child to know that he is a boy or she is a girl is important because to develop friendships and love relationships people have to feel good about themselves and their sex. Part of learning to be content and even pleased with one's sex involves admiring older people of the same sex. A provider can help children learn to take pleasure in their sex if she speaks well of the things women and men do well, is a good model for the girls in the family day care home, and helps the boys get to know men whom they can respect. If she talks about the things boys and girls *can* do, rather than what they cannot or should not, the children are more apt to develop good attitudes. Most of all, if the children know she is happy to be a woman and that she likes women *and* men, they will grow up to be women who enjoy being women and men who enjoy being men.

Real and Not Real

Preschoolers live in a world that is as much magical as it is real. They believe that wishing *can* make it happen, that things *should* be the way they want them to be. When they are angry they *wish* the person they are angry with was dead, and then they are afraid the person might die as a result of their wish. When they want to go to the circus, they think they *have* to, they *must*. If they want to watch a certain television program that is not on, they blame the television set. They are not yet clear about why and how things happen, and wants and wishes seem reason enough.

Part of this is their inexperience but part of it is what they are taught. After all, adults play magic games with children when they tell them about Santa Claus, the Tooth Fairy, and the Easter Bunny. We want them to believe in some things that are unreal. Even though we expect children to give up believing in Santa Claus as they also give up believing their wishes have to be granted, we do not want them to give up all of the magical unreal thoughts. We want our children to learn what is real and what is not, why things happen, and how to make them happen or not happen. As children grow up they learn more and more about the real world. They must not, however, give up all magic, all fantasy. If they do, they risk giving up the enjoyment of music, art, poetry, and being in love.

13

Providing School Readiness

When a child is ready to go off to school, the parents and provider often become aware for the first time of their role in that child's past, present, and future. It is at this moment that the parents and provider may suddenly worry about whether the child is ready, and what indeed being ready means. They suddenly think about the importance of the school experience, that first encounter with the outside world. Many people today believe that in some cases our schools are not doing a very good job, and some children are not learning as much as they could and should. Most people would probably agree that the schools are not entirely to blame. What they sometimes do not realize is that the failure of children to get from schools whatever the schools are offering or to learn what they are expected to learn will seriously affect the rest of their lives. Many adults do not know that when children do not succeed in school they are injured for life; their self-confidence never completely recovers. When they are not able to meet this first challenge and conquer it, they can never again dare so much, and thereafter they always feel a little less able, less in control of their lives. Although some children go to great efforts to overcome school failure and some become successful at things that do not require school success, they never forget that early failure, and they spend the rest of their lives trying to make up for it. Being ready for school can protect children from failure and its effects on their lives and future.

READINESS—THE PARENTS' AND PROVIDER'S ROLE

There are many responsibilities that come with the child's entrance into school that need to be considered and shared. It is wise to arrange a meeting with the parents to discuss these and decide who will be responsible for what. Some of these questions are:

1. How will the child get to school? Get to the family day care home from school?
2. If the child goes to school from the provider's home, what will the provider be responsible for? Seeing the child into the teacher's care? Picking the child up? What about bad weather?
3. Because most parents of children in family day care are working all day, some providers may have more daily contact with the school than the parents. How do the parents feel? They need to be reassured that they will receive any reports or remarks the teacher offers so that when they go for their conferences with the teacher they will feel informed about the program and their child's progress.
4. How will the demands that schools make on parents be handled? Who will be contacted if the child is hurt or becomes ill at school? Who will provide special supplies when requested by the teacher? What about bag lunches for trips? Who will attend class parties or performances?
5. Does the child need to be immunized? Most places in the country require children to be immunized against the major childhood diseases before entering school. The provider can review the immunization record of the school-aged children in the family day care home with their parents and get the necessary forms filled, signed, and ready to present to the school when the child registers. She or the parents can ask the pediatrician or well-baby clinic staff who follow the child's development how to arrange for a hearing test and an eye test. This is a time in which prevention is easy and effective. It is not possible for a child with a hearing loss or poor vision to do as well in school as a normal child; however, if the child with a hearing loss or poor vision is placed close to the teacher or objects under study, the child can often see and hear well enough to learn as well as the other children. The child's handicap is also helped by having the special attention the teacher gives to his or her needs. If handicaps such as these are not discovered and attended to, however, the child cannot avoid the experience of failure.

There are other questions, but the two key ideas to keep in mind are that close communication with the school is important to the child's success in school, and close communication between the parents and provider is important for equal and fair sharing of the many things required to make sure the child does well in school.

READINESS—WHAT IS IT?

Readiness is a word that has been given a lot of attention in the last 10 years. Programs such as Head Start are the result of the idea that readiness for school can make a difference. In many people's minds it has come to mean things like knowing the ABC's, counting to 10 or 20, naming colors and shapes, and so forth.

It is certainly true that knowing some of the same things that other children know gives children a sense of confidence, and that confidence is very important to learning, but knowing facts and figures is not readiness for school. Readiness for school has more to do with knowing about people and having confidence in oneself than with knowing how to count, write, or say the ABC's.

READINESS BEHAVIORS

What are the behaviors that assure success in school? Some of these have been learned in very early childhood and are discussed in the chapters on infants, toddlers, and preschoolers. How these behaviors help children in school, however, is the subject of this chapter.

Children begin to go to school at different ages. Being ready for preschool at 3 years old is quite different from begin ready for kindergarten at 5. The demands made on children by preschool programs are very different from those that kindergarten makes. Learning some of the behaviors described in this chapter is part of many programs for 3 and 4 year olds. How well children learn these, whether at school or at home, depends to a large degree on how much support they get from home. Children do best when the school and home work together; when the home and school have different expectations, the children are not apt to do as well in either.

Help

Children who know how to ask for assistance when they need it get more attention from the teacher and do better in school than those who try to work it out alone. Teachers usually prefer the children who ask questions and ask for help, probably because they are sure that they have these children's attention and interest.

Key Care Idea

- If a child who is about to enter school is not yet able to ask for help and get it, playing pretend school will help him or her develop this skill. The provider can pretend to be the child and let the child be the teacher. She can ask the child for all of the kinds of help she can think of—zipping up her jacket, finding the bathroom on a trip, stopping another child from bothering her, getting her a piece of paper to start a new drawing. The game can then be changed around to let the child ask for some things. The other children will want to join in the pretend game.

Friends

The importance of friends in a child's life is greater than most adults realize. It affects the child's school work as well as his or her happiness. Being able to make friends is a sign that the child has self-confidence and is both likeable and likes others. Before going to school many children will have had experience in making friends, especially in a family day care home. The provider can show the children how certain behaviors make it easy to get along with others, and how other behaviors make it difficult.

<u>Key Care Ideas</u>

- If a child is left out of a game, the provider can help that child find a way to get into the game again. When children say things like "You're not my friend," the provider can step in and help the left out child to get another friend, and at the same time let the other children know that she is not pleased with that kind of talk. A good way to handle this situation is for the provider to say to the left out child, "Who would you like to have be your friend? Go ask him or her to come help us make this terrific new snack we're having today." She can suggest that the child and "new friend" pick out a game to play, and if necessary, the provider can join in the game.

- At every age school children need the opportunity to talk about making and keeping friends. At the table or when everyone is sitting together, the provider can say, "Let's talk about friends. I'll tell you about a friend of mine, then you tell me about a friend of yours." Everyone can then say what makes a friend a *good* friend, what one expects of friends, and why certain people are friends with everyone and others have few or no friends. Just talking about friends gives children some feelings of confidence, but most of all it lets everyone learn from everyone else's experience.

- Many studies of school-aged children have shown the connection between success in school work and success in making friends. Children who are getting good grades are wanted as friends. One of the best ways to help the child who is having difficulty making friends is to help that child succeed with school work.

- Another way to encourage making friends is to let the children invite someone over in the afternoon. Many providers feel this is extra work and not part of the agreement. Each provider has to make her own decisions about this based on her own afternoon schedule, her sense of the children's needs, the cooperation and support of the children's parents, and the nature of her community.

Attention

Another critical part of school success is the ability to pay attention. Some ways to help children get involved and stay involved in play are described in the chapters on toddlers and preschoolers. Giving a little assistance and encouragement is often enough to keep children's activities going. Some children may need more help and the provider may have to play games with one particular child until that child has developed enough interest to be able to continue the game alone.

Adults make it difficult for children to learn to play alone and attentively when they interrupt their games. They sometimes do this when they feel the game is silly or annoying. Then they may offer another activity or to say it is snacktime without realizing that they are interfering with the children's ability to stick to an activity. It is much better not to interrupt any activity unless there is a good reason for it, and then the children can be told that they can leave the game where it is and come back to it later.

Key Care Ideas

- The provider can suggest activities that take some time to complete, and if necessary, sit with the children to encourage them and help them finish. If one child bothers another or tries to interfere with another child's activity, the provider will need to step in and protect the child's interest.

- For the very young, providers can begin with activities and games that require a short attention span, and gradually offer games that require longer and longer attention. They will need to stay by the children until they can play on their own, and then continue to check on them and offer encouragement from time to time.

- Choosing activities that the children enjoy is important. First, children need to be able to play with one thing for a long period. The "feeling" activities are usually the first to capture young children's attention—playing with water, sand, mud, or snow, will interest young ones for long stretches of time. Then other games can be added, such as peg boards, puzzles, blocks, cars, and other little objects to build with. Finally, games with rules, turns, and counting, such as checkers, card games and board games (see Chapter 12), engage the child's interest for longer and longer periods of time.

- A good way to find out about the children's attention span is for the provider to keep an eye on each child as she reads them a story. If the story is one the children love and know well, they will usually listen with great attention. Children who do not pay attention need help. They can be the ones to choose the story, sit nearest to the provider, turn the pages.

- The old game "Telephone" requires children to listen attentively. One person starts a "telephone message" by whispering something in another person's ear. That person then whispers it in another person's ear, and then that person whispers it to another until everyone has had the message. The last person says out loud the message that he or she heard. It is seldom the same, and usually has nothing in common with the first whispered words. Each child then says what he or she heard to trace how the message got garbled.

- "Simon Says" is another good game that teaches attentiveness. It is a copying game. One person stands in front of the others and says, "Simon says to put your hands on top of your head!" The others must all copy what the leader says and does, but only if Simon says to do it. Those who follow the instructions when the leader does not say "Simon Says" are out. When everyone is out, another person takes a turn being the leader.

Individual Styles and Interests

Even young children show different individual abilities. When these are encouraged, children's confidence and sense of who they are grows. Attentive providers are aware of each child's special qualities, and they use this awareness to help each child develop a sense of his or her own special self.

Some children love to draw and will spend long periods of time with crayons and paper. Some children show an early interest in music. When these young artists enter school, their kindergarten teachers should be told about their special interests.

Other children show a great interest in nature, and collect bugs, leaves, seeds, or rocks. Some show early athletic abilities, and are good at running, jumping rope, bike riding, catch, or activities that require strength and coordination. Some children are skilled at dealing with people. They enjoy helping other children, showing others how to do something, how to settle a disagreement, or they enjoy pretending to be a doctor, a nurse, or a teacher. All of these early interests should be recognized and encouraged. When providers tell the children's teachers about these individual qualities, they show their interest in each child in their care, and they let the teacher know that they expect the teacher to show equal interest. Teachers indeed show more interest in the children who are well cared for than in those for whom parents and providers show little interest. It is not enough for providers to *be* interested in their children, they must also make it known to the children's teachers.

Accepting Rules

When children enter school they must suddenly deal with many new rules and restrictions. Depending upon how they were cared for as toddlers, rules are either easy or difficult to accept. Children who were scolded or punished as toddlers when they refused to do things, said no to requests, or wanted to do things their own way may not have learned to accept adult direction. Children who still resist adults at age 3 or 4 are often trying to get over the natural resistance that comes with being a toddler. They have usually had too much control and too little permission to do things their way, to practice independence, and develop minds of their own.

When these children go to school, they may have real trouble accepting the demands and rules that most schools make. Before this happens, providers can usually step in and help the children get over these leftover behaviors from their toddler years.

Key Care Ideas

- The first thing to do is cut down on as many rules as possible, and only keep those that are necessary for the day care family to live together comfortably (including the adults). If there is a rule to put dishes in the sink after snack, then the child who leaves the table without keeping the rule is reminded, "Anthony, you forgot your dishes. We all put our dishes in the sink when we finish." If Anthony does not come back and get his dishes immediately, the provider must go and take his hand and lead him back to the table saying, "You see, Anthony, everyone in our home has put the dishes in the sink. Now you put yours in, too." It helps to get everyone's cooperation. The provider can ask "Joni, where are your dishes? Good for you! And yours, Albert? In the sink! Anthony, now yours are, too. Good for you!" (see Chapter 15).

- When encouraging independence, it helps to remember that all children have certain things they want to do in their own way. The provider should allow these, even if it means taking longer than it would if she did it herself. Feelings of independence and self-control are very important at this age, and children can only learn to do things for themselves quickly and well with practice.

- By age 5 children enjoy playing by rules. They often make up rules for games and for their make-believe play that are far stricter than any of the rules they have known. This is partly because of their own interest in rules and partly a way of controlling themselves and others. The provider can encourage children to talk about rules, what they are for, why they are needed, and how they make it easier for people to get along fairly. She can ask, "Why do you suppose we need a rule for this?" and "Why do you think the school has this rule?" Then she can ask them to think of reasons for the rules they live with at home and at school. It is not always easy to come up with reasons for some of the rules that schools make, but even when it is difficult, someone can think of some reason, however farfetched. Talking about these things makes accepting them easier. Telling stories about schools and the rules makes accepting them something of a game. Children especially love to hear about "olden times" and how things used to be:

  > School days, school days
  > Dear old golden rule days
  > Reading and writing and 'rithmetic
  > Taught to the tune of hickory stick

Ready for Learning

Children are ready for school when they have learned how to ask for help, how to stick with a game or other activity, and how to get along with adults and children. Once they have these skills, they should have little or no difficulty learning anything the school wants to teach.

There are no easy explanations for the fact that many American children seem to have a good deal of trouble learning to read, understanding mathematics, and acquiring the other knowledge they are expected to get in school. The natural intelligence of children has probably increased in the last century as a result of better nutrition, better disease control, and better care in general. In many poor countries around the world children with less care learn to read with little or no difficulty. Experts in education have suggested many reasons for our children's difficulties in school, and most of these have to do with feelings and behavior and not with intelligence. They agree that children must want to learn, must feel that school is a good place to be, and must think of themselves as learners. Of course, children cannot be expected to learn when they are in a school in which the other children and the adults are angry, insecure, frightened, or rebellious, and where they do not feel safe. Unfortunately, such schools do exist. If, however, children are in a reasonably well-run school and if their parents and provider have given them the preparation and support described in this chapter, they should be able to learn without difficulty.

SKILLS THAT MAKE LEARNING EASIER

Memory

A good memory is not exactly a skill, and yet it is something that can be learned with practice. Nearly everything that children are expected to learn in school requires a certain amount of memory. The way reading is taught in many schools makes a good memory absolutely necessary.

<u>Key Care Ideas</u>

- There are games for preschool and school-aged children that encourage memory, especially remembering details. The provider can make up guessing games by asking the children about something everyone saw together. For instance, she can ask, "Who remembers the lady who helped us in the library? What was the name of the book she read to us? What was her name?" Then each child can take a turn making up a memory question.
- Another good memory game requires eight small objects on a table. The provider asks the children to come and take a look. She explains that after they have a careful look, the objects will be covered and they will each get a turn to name

what they saw on the table. After the children have had a few minutes to study the objects, they are covered with a cloth that is thick enough to hide the shapes. Then each child has a turn naming all of the objects he or she can remember. The game then changes and the children are asked to turn their backs while one of the objects is removed and put out of sight. Then the children look again at the collection of objects and take turns trying to guess which one was removed. As soon as one child guesses, they turn their backs, the object is replaced and another is removed, and the game goes on. Once the children are familiar with the game, they can take turns removing the object and have the provider and other children guess. As the children develop good memories, more objects can be added to the collection.

- Using a crayon or a magic marker, the provider can draw a simple design on a sheet of paper. Depending on the age of the children, the design can be simple or more complex. For 3 or 4 year olds, it must be very simple. Here are some examples:

For 5 and 6 year olds, the design can be more complex:

The provider then shows the children one design. When they have had a good look, she puts it away, gives them a paper and crayon or marker, and asks them to draw what they saw. When they finish, they can compare their drawings with the original. The children will enjoy making a drawing for the provider to remember and copy. These games are fun if the children do not feel they are tests.

- Another good memory game is the "Trip Game." One person starts by saying, "I'm packing my suitcase and I'm going to bring my _____," and names something, for instance, bathing suit. The next person repeats the line, "I'm packing my suitcase and I'm going to bring by bathing suit and my _____," and adds something new, like flyswatter. The next person has to repeat everything so far and then add something of his or her own. When everyone has had a turn the game continues by giving each child a second and then a third turn until the list is too long to remember.

- Another "add-on" game is the storytelling game. One child starts with "Once upon a time," and then adds a beginning to the story, for example, "Once upon a time I was walking in a big city and. . . . The next child says what the first child said starting with "Once upon a time I was walking in a big city and I looked down and saw a shiny gold coin." The next child then repeats the whole story so far and adds another sentence. Each child then tells the story from the beginning, each adding some more to it. The game is played until someone comes up with an acceptable ending. Even 5 year olds can enjoy this game.

Writing

Most experts now feel that one should learn to write before learning to read. Not many schools have taken this advice, but children can still have writing experiences at home before they go to school and even after they are in school. By age 3½ many children can handle a pencil very well. This is as much a matter of practice as it is of development. As soon as the children show any interest, paper and pencils should be provided. After the children have made some drawings, they can be asked if they want to write their names on their drawings. The provider then writes the child's name, showing the child how to make each letter, naming it as she does. If the child has a long name and a nickname, she can suggest beginning with the short version. As the children learn to write and read their own and each other's names they will become familiar with the letters in each. Learning the ABC's by heart can be amusing but is no help in learning to read and write letters.

As the children learn to write a few letters with ease, they can begin to say the words they want to learn to write. The provider writes the words they request, and when they have copied them she reads their words aloud. Some children catch on to the idea and spend a lot of time copying words out of books or making up words. This is what reading is all about. When children have understood that these funny marks stand for sounds that stand for things, they have caught on to reading.

Whatever type of printing the school teaches, the provider should teach the same to avoid confusion for the children when they begin school. The manuscript letters are written like this:

abc defghijklmnopqr stuvwxyz

The manuscript capitals like this:

ABCDEFGHIJKLMNOPQRSTUVWXYZ

Mathematics

Many children can count from 1 to 20 by the age of 5. Often, however, this is a meaningless skill, similar to saying the ABC's. It has nothing to do with understanding numbers. Learning about numbers has to do with certain ideas that children acquire at home in the normal everyday activities of a family. Before mathematics has any meaning for children, they need to understand these ideas.

Key Care Ideas

- **More and less** The provider puts two small piles of buttons, raisins, or other small objects on the table. The children are asked which pile has more. After everyone gives an answer, the provider asks how they can find out for sure. Children, unless told to count, usually think of other ways to find out. (Counting has little meaning for children under 6 or 7.) The usual way is to make a row of the objects in each pile and see which row is longer. Whatever the children's suggestion or system for testing is, the provider should accept it. If the system they decide on does not really give an answer, the provider can ask what they need to do to make the two piles the same. With encouragement, they may be able to match the piles, object for object, and then add on to the smaller pile or take away from the larger pile. This game can be done with any number of objects—more or less peas on the plates, more or less blocks in two towers, more or less houses on one side of the street than on the other.

- **Bigger, smaller, taller, shorter, heavier, lighter, fuller, emptier** These are some more words that compare and help to show differences. When children are aware of these, they can begin to understand what mathematics is all about. In everyday conversations, the provider can talk about which pan is bigger, which book is heavier, which carrot is thinner, which glass is fuller, which string is longer, which building is nearer, and so on.

- **Putting things in order** Another idea that makes mathematics understandable is the idea of small to larger. On their own, children often line things up in order of size (see Chapter 12 on size games).

- **Counting things** Finally, when all of the ideas are beginning to make sense, children are ready to think of things in numbers—two socks, three paint colors, four pieces of egg, five children, five things at each person's place (plate, napkin, fork, spoon, glass). All begin to make sense as each object is touched and the number said aloud. At the table each child can check how many things are at his or her place, how many pieces of apple are on each plate, how many glasses are full, how many are empty, how many children are finished, how many grown-ups are at the table, how many girls, how many boys. Then come the trickier questions. Are there more boys or more children? Many 5 year olds cannot think of the larger group—children—in terms of the two smaller groups—boys and girls. Practice helps and questions like these are fun. Playing these games, children begin to look at the world as mathematicians do.

Science

Most children naturally have scientific minds. They are curious and full of "why" questions. The provider can encourage this by talking with them about the things they find interesting and looking for material to read to them about these interests. A child's encyclopedia is helpful, but the provider can make a list of subjects or questions that come up during the week, and on the weekly trip to the library find books that deal with these subjects.

If there are enough young scientists (one or two will do) the provider may want to encourage them to work on projects together. She can select something that matches their interests as well as what is acceptable to her. If she dislikes animals, for instance, she will not want to keep a gerbil or a hamster.

Key Care Ideas

- Young children love collections. Seeds, small rocks, leaves, shells, dead insects and flowers to press all make interesting collections. The objects can be kept in egg cartons and sorted by size, color, or any other classification. Some objects can be pasted on paper and made into books. The provider can help the children label the collection and spend time sitting with them talking about each object and why it is interesting.

- Fish are the cheapest and least demanding of pets. (Providers can suggest to the children whatever pets they find acceptable, but need not have any if they find them objectionable.) If she decides to keep a pet, a scientific approach includes learning about the best food and environment for the creature, how it lives in its natural state, how it gives birth and cares for its young, how long it lives, and what it can learn.

- If the provider decides she does not want any pets, she might not object to letting the children collect insects if they are kept in a jar with holes in the lid or a screen over the top. Providing food for insects or worms and leaves and twigs for them to crawl about on is fascinating to little children. They can make drawings of their creatures, and, with help, write the names of each and look them up in an encyclopedia or at the library.

- Other scientific experiments that children enjoy include making categories such as what sinks and what floats (all the provider needs to set up here is a pan of water; the children will think of objects to test), what dissolves and what does not (a glass of water and salt, tea, sugar, pepper, soda, flour, soap flakes, coffee, etc. to test), and what a magnet will pick up (children will find dozens of objects to test). Once the categories have been discovered, the experiment must be recorded. Children can draw pictures of all the things that float, that dissolve, and that are attracted to a magnet, and the provider can write the word under each. These can be put on the wall or taken home to the parents.

- A flashlight and a magnifying glass are fascinating to the young scientist. A mirror is also interesting. With these, children think of many experiments; the provider needs only to ask a few questions as encouragement and offer to write up the results of the children's experiments or label their drawings.

- Growing plants is another scientific activity. Seeds can be saved from the garbage—orange seeds, grapefruit seeds, avocado pits. The seeds only need to be put in soil (in paper cups or pots) and, if watered regularly, most will grow. Avocado pits need to be started in water in a glass that is small enough for half of the pit to be out of the water. If the provider does not have a glass the right size, toothpicks can be pushed into the side of the pit to hold it half out of the water, pointed end up and rounded end down. Sweet potatoes can be started this way, too. Once the roots have sprouted and are a few inches long, they can be planted in soil in pots. The tops of carrots and pineapples will grow if sliced off and placed in a dish of water.

Questioning

Children have a natural tendency to ask "why?" If they are answered, they continue to ask questions. Many of their questions have no answers, or at least no answers that we know. And yet, that is what education is all about. In 400 BC the greatest teacher of all times, Socrates, taught his students by asking them questions. He knew that asking good questions is far more important than having answers. When children ask questions, the provider can answer those for which she has answers, and for those that have no easy answers, she can ask questions about what one needs to know in order to find an answer. Good thinking is thinking of good questions. The more intelligent the person, the more questions he or she has.

Feeling Ready

Children are ready for school when they feel ready. Feeling ready has a little to do with their feelings about school and more to do with their feelings about themselves. If children feel good about themselves and their abilities, they will do well in school. If they feel insecure and not sure about themselves, they are not ready and will not do well. The provider can help the children she cares for to get ready by teaching them the skills described in this chapter. Most of all, by treating them with respect and appreciation, she can help them learn to feel confident, secure, and ready for anything that school offers.

14

Providing for School Children

Once children enter school they have entered the child's world of work. From then on, school is their work and after school is their leisure time. What they do with their work time and free time is learned by watching the adults they live with and copying their attitudes and habits. If the adults complain about their work and the people they work with and spend their leisure time sitting in front of a television set, the children will adopt the same style. They will complain about school and do as little work as possible, and then come home and waste their free time. On the other hand, if the adults talk with interest about their work and play hard in their leisure time, the children will live their own lives with the same kind of zest. As soon as they go to school and their lives become divided into two kinds of time—school time and after school time—they have taken an important step into the world of adults.

SOME OF THE WAYS ADULTS VIEW THEIR WORK AND FREE TIME

Most adults get up in the morning and go to work. Some go to factories and become one of hundreds of people alone all day with a machine. Some go out into fields, and, with a tool or a tractor, spend the day mostly alone. Some get up and spend all day in a house making life more pleasant and more attractive for themselves and for others. Some have to deal with many people, such as salespeople, clerks, office workers, nurses, and service people. These jobs are all different in the skills required and in the demands made. They all have some interesting moments, some dull and tedious times, and, occasionally, a real challenge; but the people who are doing these jobs are all very different in their feelings about their work. In the same job, there are some who enjoy going to work, who have made friends with their fellow workers, who find something interesting each day. Others hate getting up each morning, and do not find their work interesting. If they think about their jobs at all, it is to complain about the people they work with, what they are asked to do, or what they earn. For these people, there is little or no pleasure in work. The children they raise will most likely adopt these attitudes, and they may decide that there is little pleasure in *their* work, which is school.

LEISURE TIME

For most adults, as well as children, the best uses of leisure time are those that provide a complete change of pace. Those who work among many people want to be alone for a while; if their work is active, they want some quiet; if their work keeps them sitting most of the day, they crave some activity, some exercise; if their work makes physical demands, they want to do thoughtful things with their leisure time; and if their work taxes their minds, they want some time to do things that do not require thought. Because most work is a mixture of many kinds of demands, most people want many things from their leisure activities, but none that are too similar to their work tasks.

Ideally, there is always something new to learn on the job. People can only be interested in their work if their jobs occasionally offer new things to do and learn. Jobs that are the same day after day can be boring, tiring, and, unless they are very good paying, hard to stay with. For people whose jobs offer little variety and change, doing different and interesting things with their leisure time is important.

There are four main ingredients that make leisure time valuable for both adults and children. The first is *sociability*. Some leisure time is usually spent with friends—either friends that share the same interests (fishing, cards, bowling) or friends that one rarely sees (old friends from school, former neighborhoods, or former jobs). Regardless of how many people one sees at work, it is still relaxing to be with friends.

The second ingredient in good leisure time use is *emotional relaxation*. Everyone has special ways to relax emotionally. Jogging has recently become a popular form of emotional release for many people. Some people find games such as checkers, cards, and crossword puzzles relaxing. Others do things that resemble work when they are tense, like cleaning out closets, ironing, digging in the garden, carpentry. Regardless of a persons's particular preference, activities that are relaxing should be active, not passive. Watching television, for instance, is not relaxing unless the program is unusually interesting. Emotional release comes from active involvement.

A third ingredient that is often neglected is *physical activity*. Very few jobs are physically exhausting, and even those that are (such as caring for children) do not use muscles well; that is, some muscles are used constantly and others not used at all. Leisure time activities should provide a change of pace, a different kind of activity, but should not be inactive. One reason that so many people are overweight is not overeating, but a lack of exercise. Children have a great need for physical activity. Because providing time and places for physical games is often difficult, especially in large cities, many children learn to sit or stand around. The habit of doing things that require effort gets lost and in their place physical laziness sets in. As people learn to care for their bodies, however, they learn the importance of exercise, not only for children, but for adults; not only for those who are good at sports, but for those who are terrible; not only for those who are fit, but for those who have not exercised in years. Part of everyone's leisure time should be physically demanding.

The last ingredient in the good use of leisure time is *intellectual interest*. Everyone enjoys learning something new, whether it is a new crochet stitch, a new game of solitaire, a new way to refinish wood, or how to use a new kind of fishing bait. Unless one's interest is captured, there is no real enjoyment. A part of any play time must be mentally stimulating.

CHILDREN AND LEISURE TIME

The ingredients described above apply to both adults and children. The things children do with their free time may be different, but their needs are similar. Teaching children to use their after-school hours well involves more than being a good example, it involves doing things with children. One of the sad things in our country today is the separation of children and adults. Not many adults include children in their leisure activities, in fact, they often actively keep them out. Some children are not allowed in the living room when the adults have guests, or are left at home with a baby sitter when the adults go bowling, fishing, or out for pizza. When children are left out of the adult world they create a world of their own; and without the direction or supervision of adults, they are unable to learn the skills (in work and play), the values (how to tell the good from the bad), or the knowledge (about life) that adults have to offer. More than that, adults are denied the opportunity to pass on to children what they have learned, what they know, and what they enjoy.

When children come home from school, they are ready for something very different from what they have been doing all day. They also need a chance to talk a bit about their day—what happened in school and what they expect to happen the next day. Snacktime provides an energy boost as well as a comfortable time to relax and talk. If the provider plans this time she can usually have the younger children busy enough to be able to spend a little time with the school children, talking about the events of their day while they eat their snack.

Key Care Ideas

- As she reviews their day with them, the provider can ask how much and what homework they have so that she can plan time to help if needed. Homework should be put off until the children have had time to relax, play, do something that interests them, but not so long that there is no time left to do it.
- After a snack and a chance to talk over the main events of the day, children need some exercise. Most schools do not schedule enough time for physical activity and some of the afternoon should be spent playing hard.
- If there is time, the children can work on a hobby or special interest. These, of course, can be done in the evening, at home, as well.

Physical Skills

One of the things that most American schools neglect is physical activity. Some schools only have gym class two or three times a week. Periods of recess are thought of as wasted time and therefore discouraged. This is very different from other countries such as China, where children are never kept sitting more than an hour at a time. After that, they are sent outside to play games that demand a lot of effort, or they practice Wu Shu (karate in China) or acrobatics for an hour. When they return to the classroom, they are tired and glad to sit down for a while. This may explain the lower incidence of hyperactivity among children in China. If we provided our children with a balanced day of activity and quiet we might find much less hyperactivity in our country.

For the family day care provider, it may not be easy to find enough children for organized games or provide a place for intense physical activity. When the children in the family are very different ages, it is difficult to organize games that everyone can play and enjoy together.

The first thing to do is to explore the neighborhood. Scouts, Little League, and 4H Clubs all offer physical activities. The provider can discuss with the parents the need for building strength and skill in school-aged children and ask for their ideas.

Finally, if there is nothing suitable or available, the provider can start a fitness program in the home. The first step is to talk to the children about the need for physical skills. When they decide what skills they would like to develop, a program can be planned.

Figure 24.

Providing for School Children

<u>Key Care Ideas</u>

- Five to 8 year olds can jump rope, either alone or with others. Both boys and girls can jump like boxers in training, or they can play jump rope games. Jumping jacks is another exercise that athletes do to get in shape and that 6 year olds and older can also enjoy. A record of how many jumping jacks each child can do can be kept and each child's progress measured. Athletes also run in place. A stopwatch is needed to record how long each child runs in place. An exercise bar is inexpensive and fits in a doorway. Both boys and girls can do chin-ups or practice swinging their feet up, hanging by their knees, turning inside out, and so forth (see Figure 24).

- Five to 8 year olds can learn to stand on their heads and hands, do back bends, and do cartwheels. The provider can help them learn by offering a supporting hand to steady them as they practice, and to keep them from falling or hurting themselves.

- Depending upon the ages of the children, there are lots of games they can play with a ball—catch, dodge ball, and kick ball. All of these games add to their skills and their sense of confidence. They build respect for their bodies.

- Nine to 12 year olds can learn all of the skills that the younger children do and more. They especially enjoy organized sports. From time to time, the provider can ask about new possibilities in the neighborhood. Sometimes there is a new sports program at a church or a YMCA or run by the Elks, Kiwanis, or Lions Club. If not, she might see if there are other children in the neighborhood who want to join in organized games. A basketball hoop and basketball will attract players. Children need very little space to practice shooting baskets. If more space is available, they can practice batting, pitching, hitting tennis balls off the wall, or playing touch football. Girls enjoy these games just as much as boys. Along with the games, the children should continue the exercises. The younger ones can join in these and imitate the older children. The school-aged children will happily demonstrate any games or exercises they have learned at school. The children will also enjoy collecting pictures of sports figures of both sexes, all races, and all sports. None of the children in the family day care home may grow up to be a Rocky, a Dr. J., or a Chris Evert-Lloyd, but they can become strong, coordinated, and skilled.

The Arts

In recent years many schools have had to cut their budgets. One of the first things to go has been the cultural program. Often, therefore, the only place children can learn about art, music, dance, and theatre is at home or in the family day care home.

<u>Key Care Idea</u>

- Six to 12 year olds can learn about some of the arts by acting out plays. It is easiest to begin with a book or a story that has only a few characters. The provider can read the story to all of the children and then discuss with them how to act it out. Their ideas should be used whenever possible, even though the provider may have some better ones of her own. They will need help at first deciding where to have the stage and how to arrange it. A sheet or bedspread can be the curtain. Scenery can be painted on brown paper or newspaper, or old sheets can be hung as a background. Costumes often can be the dress-up clothes. For some stories (*Caps for Sale*, for instance) special items are needed, but they can be borrowed or made from paper. Often children enjoy the preparations as much or more than the performance itself. The children should be permitted to work on the production as long as they like, even though it may mean having a messy area in the home. These productions develop many skills—artistic, creative and literary—not to mention skills in cooperative play. As the children produce more and more plays, they will begin to make up their own stories. They may also make programs for their plays, listing the characters and the names of the people playing each role, or they may want to add singing parts, clowns, or dancing. The provider can help with sewing and materials. With a little encouragement and assistance, these games provide endless interest as well as the opportunity to practice many skills.

Chapter 5 on planning gives more suggestions for activities with children that are not included in this chapter, and includes details about how to introduce children to music, art, and literature. Some of these ideas can make school projects or special credit activities more interesting for the child as well as contribute something of value to share with the other children in school.

Pretend Games

Make-believe or pretend games have already been mentioned in several places. The value of these games, however, cannot be overstressed. Watching school-aged children play make-believe games often makes it possible to know what is on each child's mind, what problems each child is thinking about. As the children pretend to be different people, the provider can learn how they feel about other people and about themselves, and what, if any, difficulties they are having. Make-believe games help children work these problems out. They can often accept demands and disappointments in their lives more easily after they have played them out in pretend games. Also, while playing these games, children express their ideas and fears that they often are not able to talk about otherwise. These games relieve their worries, feelings of insecurities, and anxieties, and build up their self-confidence. They can be played with only a few dress-up clothes, and a place arranged as a pretend house, school, doctor's office, or whatever setting suits the game.

Another kind of pretend game involves building scenes with blocks or boxes, then using little plastic people, animals, cars, trucks, planes, or other small toys to play out a story or something that has happened in their lives. Shoe boxes that have been fitted with windows and doors, with walls painted or covered with paper, and furniture made of cloth and cardboard serve as doll houses in which small dolls play out scenes from the children's imagination. Games with these block buildings or shoe box houses often last for days on end and should be encouraged, in spite of the clutter and mess they may cause.

Clubs

As children reach middle childhood, they become more and more interested in the world of other children and less involved with adults. They organize secret clubs that have lots of rules about who can and cannot be in them, about what is and is not allowed, and about passwords, codes, and secret messages. These games teach children a great deal about how the world works and how to accept rules. As they make up their own rules and play by them, other people's rules become more acceptable. Devising codes and secret words are good memory games and good thinking practice as well. All that is required is a place to meet (a corner of the room with a barricade of some sort, or a sheet over a table to make a little house or, better yet, a place outdoors where a clubhouse can be arranged). With two or more children, a club is born.

Collections

Children begin collecting things even before they become school age. Preschoolers fill their pockets with "treasures"—bits of cloth, pebbles, string, a feather. By school age, however, collecting becomes more organized. Shells, baseball cards, stamps, old pennies, playing cards, and postcards are some of things that children collect, count, put in order, trade with each other, keep in boxes. These collections allow children to practice many skills, not the least of which is taking care of their belongings, keeping them in order and safe. Besides taking care of their collections, children also learn counting skills, evaluating and organizing things in categories or groups, reading, and conducting business deals as they trade. Each collector needs a secret place to keep his or her things safe—in a box, on a shelf, or in a cabinet—where no one can get to it.

Games

Board games such as Parcheesi, Scrabble, Clue, Monopoly, Boggle, Life, and those based on movies or television programs are popular with school-age children, and most provide the opportunity to practice the skills they are learning in school, such as figuring numbers, writing, and reading. The better games also require reasoning. It is a good idea to keep these board games in a closet, away from the preschool children who may play with the pieces of the games and lose them. The dining table is a good place to play because it is high enough to be out of the sight and reach of toddlers. If there are too few players, the provider can play with a preschooler, letting the preschooler pretend to play. Sometimes there is an older person in the family or a neighbor who can join in the game to add another person. Older people often enjoy these games immensely and not only add to the number of players, but to the enjoyment of all.

Crafts

Crafts are objects that are both useful and artistic. Children learn new skills working with crafts, and they develop an eye for what is attractive. Crafts are often the first things that children produce that have real value. With help, even young children can make things that are attractive enough to sell or give to someone. It requires money to get the first supplies, but if the children can then produce something attractive that they can sell, they can pay back the cost of materials and then make the money they need to buy the next batch. This is how a business works, and is as interesting to children as it is to adults.

The crafts that children can learn, of course, depend on the ages of the children. Whatever the child's age and the ability, however, the craft should be attractive and original in some way. Children need to be helped to choose useful objects to make with nice colors and pretty designs. There are many magazines and books with simple directions on how to make things. These can be used for ideas, but the provider can always make the designs more personal and more attractive. A pot holder can be made of gingham and quilted in the shape of a house, with embroidered windows and door. Christmas tree ornaments can be made of real gingerbread with icing and raisins. (see Figure 25).

Window shopping or looking at newspapers and catalogs are good ways to find ideas for things they think are attractive and fun to make. The provider will need to help the children decide what materials are needed and what they will cost. She may be able to help them think of things to use in place of an expensive item. As the children make their plans, they will be learning planning skills to use in other things they do and in their school work.

Any things that might be useful for the children's crafts and projects should be saved, sorted, and kept put away. All pieces of cloth that are left over or that are still in good shape should be kept, as well as buttons from old clothes and bits of lace. Even small pieces can be used in making patch-

Figure 25.

work quilts or appliques. It is a good idea to store these in boxes by pattern, kind of fabric, or size. Boxes of all sizes and pretty paper should be saved (wrinkles can be ironed with a warm iron). Labeling boxes of saved objects helps in finding the needed supplies. Family members, neighbors, and friends can be asked to save useful materials—ends of lace and braid, wool, buttons, sequins—for the children's crafts.

CONVERSATIONS ABOUT LIFE

The best time for adults to listen to children's thoughts about what is going on in their lives is while sharing a job or doing a project together. The job or project gives both something to do and look at while they talk. It also provides something to change the conversation to when it is time to take a break from serious talk.

These are good times to give older children, who are in school most of the day, a chance to talk alone with an adult whom they trust about their worries or concerns. The older children are, the more they need adult help and guidance. When adults think back on their own childhoods they remember all of the times they were frightened, puzzled, or upset. The notion that children are happy-go-lucky and need only a pat on the head, a good meal, and a warm bed to be content is ridiculous. We adults all remember our own childhoods too well to accept such a notion.

It is not easy to talk with children about their concerns, however; and this is probably why many adults do not. Most of the problems of childhood never really get solved, they are simply put aside. When children bring them up again, the adults remember their old discomfort and often turn away or tell the children not to worry, that the problems will work out. Adults who do talk with children can be a great help to them.

What are some of these problems? They are life's problems—getting along with others, making friends with the children who are most admired, being accepted by the respected or "in" crowd. They are problems of honesty, whether to tell on someone else, what to say when asked something that is supposed to be a secret, how to react when someone says something hurtful, untrue, or insulting to one's face or behind one's back. They are the questions about sickness (mental and physical), death, and sex. When adults refuse to talk to children about these important subjects, children have to make up their own theories. Many adults continue to live by the theories they made up in their childhoods simply because they never got any better information.

Before the provider discusses these subjects with the school-aged children in her care, however, she may need to talk with the parents. Because the parents' wishes must be respected, the provider is sometimes in the position of the school teacher. She can tell the parents what she thinks would help the child, but the final decision is the parents. Often simply telling the parents that their child seems concerned about something will help the parent to discuss it with the child. The provider can also reassure parents that these are questions all children wonder about. If she feels comfortable with the parents, she can smile and say that she is sure they remember, just as she herself remembers, how much they wondered about these questions when they were children. As described in Chapter 6, being supportive of the parents often helps them to be more supportive of their children.

USING THE PROVIDER'S INTERESTS

Every adult has a few things that he or she does well and really enjoys. Some can crochet, some bake bread, some write very good letters, some refinish furniture, some make dried flower arrangements, some make clothes, some bowl, some keep excellent household accounts, some grow houseplants or garden outdoors, and some embroider. Whatever the interest is, it should be shared with the children. As children learn the provider's skills and interests, they also have the pleasure of sharing in the adult world, and they feel competent to be able to learn a grown-up's skill. Often young children can only do a part of the job; but even then, they acquire a new skill and learn something they can be proud of. Children are thus able to share in the adult world and are less apt to want to rebel against it. They will want to protect the things they have come to value and enjoy.

Most boys no longer feel that doing something traditionally considered "women's work" will make them sissies. Children from 6 years old on, both boys and girls, can learn to sew, cook, crochet, bake, make candles, and knit, and enjoy doing them. Rosey Grier, the football player, and George VI, a King of England, have done needlework. They are not considered sissies. These skills are not only enjoyable, they are useful. There are very few things that our children are allowed to do that are really adult activities. And yet, there are places in the world in which children spend some time each day doing real work, and receive respect and appreciation for it. When children learn to make or do things that are really useful and that adults also enjoy doing, the children can take pride in what they are able to do and in themselves.

In our grandparents' and great grandparents' time, there was no separation of the generations. Old people lived with the family, children grew up among adults—their parents, often their grandparents, aunts, uncles, cousins, and sometimes even a great grandparent. They learned about life from all of these adults, and although many children in those days were not able to go to school, what they learned from the adults in their families often prepared them for the world as well or better than the schooling our children receive today. Boys grew up learning when and how to plant corn, wheat, and vegetables, care for animals, whittle wood, fish, build a barn, play the fiddle or flute, square dance, milk a cow, and repair a tractor or a Model T.

Girls learned different skills in those days, but they were just as difficult and important as those the boys learned. They learned how to make quilts, candles, soap, and herbal medicines, how to cook and bake, make clothes, weave cloth and blankets, can and preserve food, dye wool and cotton, knit, embroider, crochet, and make lace. Many learned to play the piano or the organ, to sing, dance, and recite poetry and psalms, to cure the sick, and to deliver babies—human and animal. People in those days had both knowledge and wisdom, and they passed it on to their children.

Most adults today have far fewer skills, and yet they know more than they realize. It is only when they begin to show children how to do the things they can do that they realize how much they really know; but unless they share their knowledge with children, it will be lost. There are many young adults today who do not know how to hem a dress or a pair of pants, repair a chair or a lamp, bake bread or a cake (except from a mix), play dominoes or pinochle, or bowl or swim. In most cases, their parents did and do, but for some reason have not taught their children.

As more and more parents work outside the home, often spending a half hour or more getting to and from work, they have less time to teach their children what they know. Weekends then become very valuable. The children who are in family day care are lucky; during their after school hours, they can share in the knowledge and skills of their provider.

PERSONAL KNOWLEDGE

Education is of little use unless it is remembered and made a part of our lives. It has little to do with pages of addition or lists of spelling words to memorize. Unfortunately, some schools offer little real education, and are merely places to spend the day doing tasks that have little meaning.

The provider can help the children in her home make schoolwork personal knowledge, make their education a part of their lives. To do this, however, she must take time to sit with the children to talk about their school work, look at their homework, and even read their schoolbooks so that she can have conversations with them about what they are learning and what it means to them. Sometimes it is difficult to find some personal meaning in the work that schools give to children. Often it is a matter of spelling words and memorizing tables, names, and dates. When this is the case, the best thing to do is to make it into a game involving the other children, if possible. The children can give the provider words to spell. If she makes an occasional mistake, the children will learn that making mistakes is not embarrassing and that what is important is to make the try.

If the provider spends some time each day with the school-aged children going over their homework and schoolbooks with them and talking with them about what they are doing in school, she can give their work the kind of meaning that many schools fail to give it. If the schoolwork is interesting to the provider, it will be interesting to the children regardless of its interest to their teachers or friends, and they will do their work well and take pride in it. Likewise, if the provider shows interest in their games and teaches them hobbies, crafts, and skills, they will enjoy their leisure time. A famous Viennese psychoanalyst once said that in order to enjoy life people must be able to work and to love. Perhaps something else should be added. People must also be able to play.

15

Providing Discipline

In any house in which there are several children, there are bound to be occasional cries of "That's not fair!" "That's mine!" "I had it first!" or "I want one, too!" How adults manage these protests is the basis of discipline. Teaching discipline is teaching children to be fair and just with everyone, and to live with others cooperatively and considerately. Learning discipline is learning to accept disappointment, to share, to take turns, and, every now and then, to give in to another's wishes without feeling very angry, or sad, or unloved. All of these are hard lessons, so hard that they can only be learned from someone who is loved and respected very much. They can only be learned from someone who is also disciplined.

THE BEGINNINGS OF DISCIPLINE

As soon as infants begin to crawl they can begin to bother and cause distress to the other children, who often show their feelings by pushing, yelling at, or hurting the baby. It is not uncommon for a baby to crawl over to where older children have set up a game, and with one move mess up the entire game. Depending on the age of the older children and how they have been raised, they will shove the baby away angrily, call for help, hit the baby, or pull or carry the baby away from their game. How the provider steps in and resolves the problem will teach the children a great deal about discipline. She will show them how to take care of their own problems, and how to protect the feelings of others. She will, in fact, remove the infant (who cannot know or understand why the older children's game cannot be messed up) and she will help the older children fix their game up again, telling them that she is sorry that their good game was interrupted and she knows how upset they must be.

There is a great deal of difference in how adults react when infants first do things that must be stopped. Some react to a 8 month old baby who grabs a toy that other children are playing with as though the baby meant to make them angry. They may even "teach the baby a lesson" by slapping the baby's hand. Because an infant has no idea that taking the toy upset the other children, he or she can not understand why he was slapped. Pretty soon, however, the infant will begin slapping people. Infants learn how to act by watching and copying the people who care for them. Once the older children see the adult slap the baby, they will, too, at the first excuse, and they will slap each other, as well. After all, if the grown-ups do it, it must be alright.

TODDLERS

There is probably no age at which children are so trying as when they first stand on their own two feet and begin to take on the world. The self-control of the adults who care for toddlers is put to the test. Even the most mature, responsible, and intelligent mother, father, or provider will admit to losing his or her temper occasionally. The best way to prevent embarrassing events is to be very clear about what is allowed and what is not, and what to do when a toddler does what is not allowed.

Toddlers have a combination of many new skills (walking, running, climbing) and no self-control. They are too young to be able to stop when they are told to stop. They do not have words yet to say what they want, but they *can* grab. They do not yet understand why that is not allowed. When they are told it is not allowed, they do not have the self-control to obey, nor the memory to remember the next time. They grab what they want, push others out of their way, hit at children and adults who do not give them what they want, and when things are not going their way, they throw themselves on the floor and kick and scream. With all this trying behavior, they are asking for help. Toddlers are frightened about their lack of control and need to borrow some from an understanding adult until they can develop some of their own. Adults need a great deal of self-control to be able to deal with toddlers well. If they can lend some of their own in a way that makes toddlers feel good about themselves, toddlers will soon learn to control themselves.

Testing, One, Two

This is the age at which children are busily giving words to all the things they know—words for things, feelings, actions, and rules. Chapter 10 on toddlers gives some background on the meaning of the word *no*. In terms of discipline, *no* needs one more explanation. It is a powerful word because it states independence and it usually gets a big reaction from adults. Much of the time toddlers may not even mean no, they may be merely stating their feelings. When asked if they would like to go outside, they often answer "No!" and then run to get their coat, hat, mittens, and boots—whatever they need to go out with. This is not simply contrary behavior, it is partly that words are not that real to them yet, and they are not yet sure words really mean what they seem to mean and mean it every time. Therefore, because their *no*'s do not always mean *no*, they expect the same of other peoples' *no*'s. As a result, when adults repeat *no* or get angry, it has little or no effect. The only way adults can show that *no* is serious is to back it up with action. If the *no* is about an object that the toddler must not touch, and if the toddler tries again to touch it, the adult must move the object or the toddler. It does no good to engage in battles. If the toddler returns to whatever it was, the adult must take stronger steps. She should be calm and firm and carry the child into the next room, if necessary, to make the point. The best way to deal with the many *no*'s that most toddlers declare is to ignore them, and cut down as much as possible on the *no*'s the toddler must hear. In any case, merely saying *no* rarely works with toddlers.

Some adults say that because toddlers do not understand that when an adult says "No" she means it, the only thing to do is give the toddler's hand a slap. If toddlers do not understand why they cannot have an adult's coffee cup, how on earth will they understand being hurt by that adult? And how will they understand being told later "Do not hit Julie, you hurt her!"

Tantrums

As soon as toddlers are able to move about freely and explore their surroundings, they fall in love with the world and all of the interesting things in it. It is not surprising that they cannot bear to have this interesting world or anything in it denied them. Nor is it surprising that the only way they can express their feelings is with their bodies. Their words are too new and too few to serve. Only with their bodies can they show how great their distress is when their new skills, interests, or feelings of independence are curbed.

Learning other ways of expressing disappointment and frustration comes with time and with the ability to control one's feelings and actions, but at first these feelings are too much to control. As their feelings become more easily managed, toddlers no longer need to "fall out" or scream and kick. When they are praised for their grown-up ability to put off doing something they want to do, or sharing what they had to themselves, or not playing with something that belongs to someone else, they can be more easily persuaded and they can learn to accept disappointment.

As toddlers learn more words to say what they want and feel—and *if they are listened to*—they have less need to use their bodies to show their feelings. If their parents and provider help them get ready to do something they do not want to do by saying, "I know you do not want to stop playing, but look what I have for you to take with you to nap," they can manage their feelings more easily. Toddlers who are praised for doing things well are proud of themselves and feel loved, and feeling loved and cherished is more important than having the first turn. It is the child who does not feel well loved and proud of himself or herself who can not give up the toy or game, because if he or she did, there would be nothing left.

In order to understand how hard it is to learn self-respect and self-control, one has only to notice all the people who seem to have little sense of pride or pleasure in themselves, and who are therefore still having tantrums. They are the adults who are still using their bodies to express their feelings. They are the men who start fights in bars, the women who shove their supermarket wagons ahead of others in the line at the cashier, the men who drive recklessly, the women who slap children, and the many other people who add to the violence in our society. These people are unable to help their children learn self-control because they have none themselves.

Biting

Another form of temper tantrums is biting. As long as toddlers express their feelings by biting *things*, it is not so serious. Biting people, however, *is* serious and cannot be permitted. If one child ever bites another, as soon as the provider has taken care of the bite and comforted the child who was bit, she should take the biter's face in her hands, look very hard into the child's face, and say *very* seriously, "People do not bite other people, *ever!*" Then she should wait a minute for the child to see how very serious she is, and say, "You can think about that for a few minutes, and then when you are ready, you can come back to play with the rest of us." If she treats the first bite that seriously, it may not happen again. If it should, she must repeat the process. A child will not continue to do something so very unacceptable unless: 1) he or she feels unaccepted anyway; or 2) that is the only way he or she feels able to get the provider's or someone else's attention. If the child feels good about other things he or she does and gets a good share of the provider's attention for being just himself or herself, the need to bite can be controlled.

Some children have a greater tendency to use their mouths than others. People who see and care for children often notice the great difference in children's styles, even from infancy. Some children put *everything* in their mouths and appear uncomfortable when their mouths are empty. They suck their fingers or the corner of a blanket when they are unhappy or tired. These children may also use their mouths to express anger and frustration by biting.

Providers become sensitive to each individual child's style and can often predict how each will act under stress. With biters or toddlers who are likely to become biters, it is important to prevent this destructive behavior. By being close to the children in a group, the provider can step in and resolve disputes before they become so emotional that there is a danger of biting. If the toddler is unable to accept the provider's solution to the dispute, the only recourse is to remove the child from the group, with kindness and affection, and give him or her a game or interesting activity away from the others.

When an adult bites a child to "show the child how it feels" the adult is really showing that biting *is* alright after all. The adult who bites a child is really showing that he or she is still a child, in mind if not in body. Adults who behave like children have no business caring for them and should find other ways to employ themselves.

DISCIPLINE AND PRESCHOOLERS AND SCHOOL-AGED CHILDREN

By the time children are 3, they can begin to learn the rules about how people get along, how they live together peacefully and contentedly, and the things people can and cannot do in our society. They are also speaking well enough to say clearly what they want or think and to understand what is said to them. Children who are well treated are eager to be like those adults they love and respect. If they do not always do what is expected of them, they are, after all, only just learning what it is that they can and cannot do. Each day is new and full of new events. They are not yet able to remember what is accepted in each new situation. They also want to have their own way, as does everyone, regardless of age. As far as they can see, adults *do* always have things their way, only children must give in, and very often they are right. Unless adults are able to explain why the demands are reasonable, children will simply learn that big people make little people do what the big people want them to do, and they will begin pushing the younger children around, doing just what the adults have done to them. When children behave badly to each other, it reveals a great deal about how the adults they live with behave.

At age 3 children are ready to begin learning self-control. Their brains are developing enough to remember and to think about what they are doing. Both of these require effort, and the effort is now worthwhile if it pleases the adult they love and live with. The provider's approval and affection are absolutely necessary for the 3 year old to learn self-control.

The first step in teaching discipline to 3 year olds is to decide exactly what to teach, based on the child's *very* limited abilities. Next, the provider must explain to the 3 year old that certain things are not allowed and why. "You cannot hit Laura because that hurts." Three year olds are ready to learn that hitting, biting, kicking, and pushing are not allowed. Then the provider must remember that 3 year olds are only beginning to be able to remember, and they are just learning how to stop themselves from doing something. They need gentle teaching. It helps for the provider to get down to the child's level, hold the child's hand, or put an arm around the child and say, "I know you are mad, but hollering will not help. As soon as you stop crying, I will help you find something fun to do." With 3 year olds it has to be simple. They cannot follow long explanations. A simple statement of what is *not* allowed and why and help in finding a new activity is all that is required.

DISCIPLINE AND CHILDREN

Most people use the word *discipline* to describe all of the ways adults teach children the kinds of behavior they think they should learn. Although every adult has slightly different ideas about what children should be taught, they all use discipline of some sort to teach it. Furthermore, they all believe that unless children learn certain important behaviors, they will not be able to get along in the world. This is the reason that discipline is such as emotional idea, that people get so excited when they talk about what should and should not be allowed. They are really talking about themselves, about whether they feel they have made it in the world, and about what kinds of behavior they think they should have learned and maybe did not.

DISCIPLINE IN THE FAMILY DAY CARE HOME

In the first interview with the parents, it is a good idea to bring up the question of discipline. A very general question such as "Do you have anything you would like to say about discipline?" lets the parents talk about their own ideas. Usually, they will talk about *ways* of disciplining children, rather than about the behaviors they feel should be disciplined. They will talk about punishments such as "no dessert," "go to your room," or a slap on the hand. Most people do not talk about *what* behaviors should be disciplined simply because they usually have not thought much about it. They have done more or less what their parents did or what their close friends and relatives do, and they have not thought much about the reasons. They may say that there are certain things they do not allow and name them, and they may ask about the provider's ideas about discipline.

It is at this moment that the provider needs to be very clear about what she thinks discipline is and how she handles it. A good way to begin is by saying that she has certain rules that all of the children must follow. These are:

1. We do not hurt each other.
2. We do not take each other's things without asking.
3. We do not bother each other.
4. We use good manners in what we say as well as what we do.

The parents may want to know *how* the provider teaches these rules. At this point she can say that she does *not* hit the children because of her first rule and because she believes that the best way to teach discipline is by example. She should explain to the parents that most children learn very quickly what is allowed and what is not allowed, and they behave the way the other children behave because they want to be part of the group. Finally, she should ask the parents if they have anything particular they want her to know about their child's behavior or about their own ideas about discipline. It is helpful to know the attitudes and ideas of the parents even when the provider does not agree with them. It helps her to understand the child's behavior and the child's reactions to other adults. Children who have been strictly disciplined are apt to be very cautious, secretive, or even sneaky with adults. Children who are given a lot of freedom and approval are trusting of adults and children, and are usually more open and outgoing. Whatever the parents say will help the provider understand their child. It is not necessary for her to tell them that she does or does not agree with their ideas. They will be content if she simply shows interest and listens attentively.

Teaching Children the Rules

The easiest way to teach children the rules is to talk about them together. The provider can ask for their ideas, for things that they want to add to the list of rules, for things that upset or bother them. If their suggestions are reasonable and the other children agree, they can be added to the list. The older children might like to make a sign—*House Rules*—and write the rules in their best handwriting, decorate it, and hang it somewhere.

Once these rules have been made clear and been thoroughly discussed, they serve as a guide and reminder. Even a 3 year old can understand when the provider says: "We do not hit, *ever!* Remember our first rule. We do not hurt each other. If you want something, ask for it. If someone does something you do not like, *tell* him!" It goes without saying that rules are of no use unless everyone keeps them. Children will not respect rules if they do not apply to everyone, adults included.

If the rule is *We do not take each other's things without asking*, and the provider takes the candy a child brought and puts it away out of sight, the children will know that the adult does not play by the rules. (There are times when children bring things that for one good reason or another the provider does not want them to have while in her home. In that case, how-

Providing Discipline 215

ever, she should privately ask the child who brings the unwanted thing to put whatever it is in a safe place until time to go home.)

If the rule is *We do not bother other people*, and the provider says to the children who are in the middle of a game; "Now put your things away, I need the table to fix lunch," the children will realize that not everyone plays by the rules. (Instead, she can remind the children when they set up their game that she will need the table in less than an hour. Or she can ask, "Could you move the game into the other room without messing it up too much? I will help you, if you like. I will need that table if we are to have lunch on time.")

Finally, there is no use having a rule about bad manners (which includes bad language) if adults feel they can get angry and be rude to a sales-girl, or a delivery boy, or one of the neighbors, or even talk rudely *about* someone to a friend. If children are not allowed to use curse words, and then overhear the adults they love best in the next room using some of the more select curse words in telling a story, they will know that these words are not really that shocking and that grown-ups really do not disapprove after all.

Rules for All Ages

Adults have to keep the rules they expect the children to keep. Rules have to apply to everyone, except those who are too young to understand rules. The single greatest mistake adults make about discipline is not knowing what children of different ages are able to do and remember. When adults expect more of children than the children can live up to and then punish them for not doing what they expected, the children begin to think of themselves as bad, evil, or naughty. Once we believe we *are* something, there is no longer any use in trying to be something else. When children are told they are bad, naughty, or evil their desire to be good is weakened, and may soon die out completely. On the other hand, when we show children that we believe they are *good* and will do whatever they can to live up to our expectations, the children have something to work for. There is no more powerful reward for children than the praise and approval of the adults they love and want to please.

Some Common Behaviors That Providers Need To Expect

There are many times in each day when children do things we wish they would not. Some of these can be avoided simply by planning the day carefully, by having rules that everyone understands and respects, and by knowing enough about child development to have reasonable expectations for children at every age. For instance, infants in high chairs are not given a full cup of milk or a plate full of food. They are given small amounts at a time until they learn that food is for eating. Toddlers are not given a box of crayons and left alone in a room. They are given a *large* sheet of paper, and are told that they can have more when that picture is done, and they are reminded from time to time to make sure they keep the drawing on the paper. Knowing what to expect of children at every age and planning with that in mind makes much discipline unnecessary.

There are several things that providers can do to make it easier for the children to learn self-control. The first is preparation. As she understands each child's strengths, weaknesses, interests, abilities, and his or her struggles to learn something new, she can plan her day to give each child the best opportunity to do something to feel successful, satisfied, and good humored. Each child has certain activities that he or she enjoys and does with concentration. Time should be allotted to these and space to avoid interference or distraction by others.

Group learning is also part of children's experience. At snacktime or mealtime the provider can discuss with the children any changes in the day's routine or any special requests that she has. Changes in the rules are confusing to children. From time to time she needs to ask the children's opinions and views, to make sure they understand the rules, and to help them assume responsibility for keeping them. Later, when a rule is broken, as is bound to happen at some time or other, the provider can say, "I know you forgot about that rule. I will remind you every now and then so you can remember next time. It is important for all of us to keep our rules, *all* of the time."

During group discussions the provider can remind the group to be careful about certain things that need attention. For example, if the children go to the store with the provider, there is the inevitable problem of requests for gum, candy, cookies, or other items that supermarkets display at the cashiers just to catch childrens' attention while they wait to check out. If, however, it has been clearly explained and the children understand in advance that there is no use asking, the provider will only need to remind them saying, "Remember that we do not buy candy or gum or anything else that is not on our list. Does everybody remember?"

Hitting, Grabbing, Pushing With even the most skillful care there is sure to be a certain amount of pushing, hitting, grabbing, and shoving. As with biting, these hurting behaviors have to be stopped immediately. It is not necessary to ask whose fault it is or how the problem started. First, the child who is hurting another must be removed. The provider can then say to the child calmly and firmly, "We do not hurt others. You can sit here until you are able to *talk* to us about what you want." She will need to remain close to the scene until the child is able to talk and explain, and the problem can be resolved. In the meantime, she should not give the child who has been removed from the scene any attention. In a couple of minutes, she can ask if the child wants to tell her about it. The provider must then listen and offer whatever solution seems fair. She can say to the child, "As soon as you feel like you are ready, you can play with the others." It is not wise to let the time the child is sitting outside the group last long. The sooner the child is allowed back with the others, the less punished he or she will feel. Punishment is *not* the intent, teaching self-control is. People studying child development have discovered that harsh punishment makes children *less* self-controlled than children who are talked to and reasoned with. Adults must remember that they are not trying to get even with the children, they are trying to educate them.

Not Telling the Truth All children say things that are not true, just as all adults do. Little children are as uncertain about what is real and not real as they are about the meaning of *no*. For some time they believe what they say, as though saying it made it real. Little children often say things they *wish* were true, such as, "The glass fell off the table all by itself." Much of what adults say to each other is also meant to "put a good face on it," or "put things in their proper light." Successful adults have, among other skills, the ability to persuade others to see things *their* way, or convince others that what they themselves did was for the best. That is basically no different from the child who says "I didn't take it, I just put it in my pocket so it wouldn't get lost."

In dealing with lying there are a couple of things to keep in mind. The first is that everyone tells lies. Therefore, to tell children they must *never* lie is ridiculous, especially because they will hear the adult tell someone she cannot meet them today because a repairman is coming, or some other excuse that the children know is untrue. These social lies are meant to spare other people's feelings and make things easier for oneself, and everyone tells them. For this reason, adults who say to children, "You must not ever tell lies," are not telling the truth.

Another thing to remember is that many lies are told to cover up something the person is ashamed of. To feel ashamed one must know what is right and wrong and know that what one has done was wrong. Lying is meant to cover up the shame. Therefore, it makes little sense for adults to punish or scold children for lying. Lying is a symptom, not a disease. The disease is feeling bad about oneself. Children can be helped to feel good about themselves, they can be praised for how well they do things, how nicely they help others, how understanding they are, how smart they are. The more they learn to respect themselves, the more they will want to live up to their own ideas of what they think is right, and the less they will need to lie. Being told they should not lie only makes them feel worse about themselves, and as the disease gets worse, the symptoms do, too. When the provider says, "I know you felt bad about that, and I'm sure you won't do it again. We all make mistakes, and that's how we learn," it shows she has faith in the child's own good sense and good intentions. The child will then try hard to keep the faith.

Taking What Belongs to Someone Else Like lying, stealing is something all children do at one time or another. The best cure is to make as little as possible of the event while making sure that the object is returned. Requiring a public confession or anything else that embarrasses the child is not helpful, it is even harmful. Simply requiring that the object be returned quietly will make the point without damaging the child's self-esteem. In the end, what we do or do not do is a matter of what kind of person we think we are. People who think well of themselves do not do dishonest things because dishonesty does not go with being the kind of person they know they are.

With several children in the home, the provider is sure to have an occasional incident of stealing to deal with. Children who take things often feel needy and are trying to "get something" to fill this need. Because there is often no one thing they really need, the provider can only give them some special attention. Extra love and concern will usually cure their need to take something. In the meantime, she must say, "I think this belongs in my top drawer. Put it in there for me, please." "Is this Carry's purse? Go put it in her box so she will have it when she goes home."

DISCIPLINE AND CONTROL

Discipline is the means to an end. The end, or goal, is control. Most of the unhappiness, fear, anger, and frustration that people feel comes from feeling that they have lost control. It is at these times that people do things they would not ordinarily do, things that they later regret. In many cases people react to feeling out of control by attacking others. By lashing out at others, they are really trying to protect themselves. It is for this reason that violence is actually *not* a show of strength, but of weakness. People are violent when they feel cornered, unprotected, weak, and out of control.

Therefore, adults who are severe and strict with children are really trying to get things under control. In this case, the things are the children, and themselves. Strict disciplinarians are people who are *not* strong or secure, but who feel that things will easily fall apart if they are not very careful.

There are adults who believe it is good for children to accept discipline without a word, who believe in "respecting authority." There have been times in the history of man when whole societies were built on "authority"—the dukes ruled the peasants in the Middle Ages, the slave owners ruled the slaves in pre-Civil War days. Both the peasants and the slaves had to do what they were told and not answer back!

In today's world, however, learning to obey and to accept discipline is no longer useful or practical. It is, in fact, poor training for success in life. Children must learn instead to be responsible for themselves, to think and decide what to do, to have *self*-discipline, not because they will be punished if they do not, but because they will not be successful in life if they do not. They need to learn what will happen as a result of what they do and say. They cannot learn to think for themselves if they are always told what to do.

This is not to say that children do not need rules, or that everyone should do what he or she wants. In every home children must learn how to live with others, they must learn what is permitted and not permitted, what they can and cannot do. As long as these rules are based on reason and not on authority, they are both useful and helpful. When the children participate in making the rules, they learn how to think about others, about the results of actions—their own and other people's—and about being responsible. They learn self-discipline and self-control.

Fairness

Children often say "That's not fair," and they are very often right. There is much in the world that is unfair. Some adults use this as an excuse for unfairness in the home. They say that their children have to learn to take it, to accept unfairness because that is the way the world is. That is like saying that because there is much hunger in the world, children should learn to go hungry to bed. This is unreasonable, but more than that, it is irresponsible. It is the responsibility of adults to help children learn to think for themselves, to treat other people with consideration and respect, and to do what they believe is right, not because they will get caught, but because they believe themselves to be decent people. These things are never learned by being disciplined. They are learned by being cared for by loving, respectful, thoughtful adults.

What children consider fair and what adults consider fair are often very different. Children's views of most things are different from those of adults because their knowledge is limited and their beliefs are based on their own particular experience. They cannot simply accept adult views without understanding *why*. Fairness needs to be discussed so that everyone can give an opinion and an agreement can be reached.

When one child declares, "That's not fair!" the provider can take a moment to talk about it. It usually means the child feels another is getting special favors. If this is true, the provider needs to know about it, and she may need to change the rules. Perhaps one child does get to play longer or gets an extra turn or does not help with cleaning up. If this is the case, the provider can simply say, "I didn't realize. You are right. We will change that right now!" Letting children voice their opinions not only shows the provider's commitment to fairness, but also encourages the children to be fair to each other.

Teaching discipline is hard work. It forces adults to look at their own behavior and beliefs, and most of all, it requires them to have the self-discipline and self-control they expect the children to learn.

16

Providing Care for the Sick Child

One of the important roles the family day care provider plays is the role of nurse. Even if her contract with the parents states that children who are sick must not be brought to the provider, there will be times when a child becomes suddenly ill during the day or has mild symptoms which suddenly become serious. Recognizing the signs of illness, deciding what to do about the illness, and carrying out the decisions or treatment requires knowledge and experience. This chapter presents the knowledge required; the profession of child care will provide the experience.

Before accepting a child into the family day care home, the provider must be sure to discuss the question of illness with the parents. To do this she needs to have a policy about sick children and a definition of what she and the parents consider sick. She has to know what kinds of care she is permitted to give. If a child has a cold, for example (and young children have frequent colds), she will have to decide in advance how bad the cold is based on the time required to care for a sick child and the risk of contagion for the other children. Children with mild colds can develop sudden high fevers that need immediate care. If the provider accepts children with mild illnesses such as colds and mild diarrhea, she must have the parents' permission *in writing* to give the child any medication prescribed by the doctor. She will also need full instructions in the event of sudden serious illness—fever, vomiting, diarrhea, sore throat, or difficulty breathing. She also needs the name of the doctor or clinic where the child is known and where his or her records are kept, the telephone number of a parent at work, and two friends or neighbors who will come and look after the other children while the provider takes the sick child to the doctor or clinic. The signed permission forms must be notarized in some states. Once they are in order, they are kept in the child's file, and the telephone numbers are posted on the wall by the telephone.

Infants will not have completed their immunizations when placed in family day care. Toddlers will usually have completed their first set, and will need only boosters. It is necessary for *all* children in family day care to have *all* the immunizations available.

Schedule of Immunizations

Age	Immunization
2 months	First combined diptheria, tetanus, whooping cough First polio
4 months	Second combined diptheria, tetanus, whooping cough Second polio
6 months	Third combined diptheria, tetanus, whooping cough Third polio (now only given in risk areas)
12 months	Tuberculin test
15 months	Measles, rubella, mumps
18 months	Combined diptheria, tetanus, whooping cough booster
4 to 6 years	Another combined diptheria, tetanus, whooping cough booster Polio booster
14 to 16 years	Last combined diptheria, tetanus, and whooping cough booster

RECOGNIZING ILLNESS

One problem about describing the sick child is defining how sick sick is. People have very different views about illness, and their views determine what they do about it. For some people, a child with a runny nose is not well and should be kept at home, kept warm, given lots of liquids, and not allowed to run about. For others, a child with a moderate fever is not really sick and is allowed to play as usual, go outside, and eat whatever he or she pleases. To everyone, the idea of illness is a little frightening. Some people react by protecting the body at even the slightest sign of illness, doing as much as possible to cure the symptoms "before they become worse." Other people react to signs of illness by pretending they do not exist, ignoring the symptoms in the hope of "building up resistance," and not allowing the child to become a weakling. Somewhere between these two extremes the provider will find the happy medium for her profession. Children learn to value and protect themselves by being cared for by adults who know how to give good care. By being sensitive to the body needs of the children in her care, the provider teaches the children to care for their own bodies, to be sensitive to needs (their own and others'), to respect good health as basic to a good life, and to use their good sense when they are not well to treat themselves in such a way that they can get well again quickly.

A QUIET PLACE AWAY FROM THE OTHER CHILDREN

There are two very good reasons why the provider needs a quiet place for a sick child. The first is for the child's care, the second is to protect the other children. Most childhood illnesses, from an upset stomach to chicken pox, are passed from child to child. Although it is impossible to keep the children in a family day care home from spreading some germs, the amount of spreading can be reduced. The most important way is to have a separate place for the child who is carrying a lot of germs around.

Furthermore, children who are not well need a quiet place to rest. Their bodies have to fight off the germs that make them sick, and often it is a tough fight. While the fight is going on, their bodies are the weapons, and they cannot win the battle if the weapons are not in good shape.

Some children are unhappy in a quiet place away from the other children. They often feel left out or punished. There must be a clear difference between the quiet place for children who are not well and the place children go when their behavior is out of control and they need to get themselves together again before rejoining the group.

The quiet place needs two kinds of equipment. The first is medical—a bed, a cot, or a comfortable couch with blankets or a quilt, pillows to be propped up, and a lamp to read by, do puzzles, or play activity book games, a thermometer, petroleum jelly, an ice bag, medication to control fever (used only with the doctor's and parents' permission), and a small pan.

The second kind of equipment has to do with morale, an important part of any care. Unless a child is very ill, the quiet place will have to provide special entertainment. Otherwise, no child will remain quiet and alone contentedly. A small television set or radio, very special games (such as coloring books, activity books, small puzzles or other games for one person that are easy to manage in bed), magic markers or special crayons reserved for use in the quiet place, picture books, construction paper, scissors, paste, and old magazines to cut up all help make the quiet place a special and pleasant place to be. For toddlers, special toys are needed that are kept for the sick child and not used at any other time (beads and strings or a box of buttons, nesting boxes with little secret objects in each, a jack in the box, or any other games that are interesting to the particular toddlers or young preschoolers in the home).

Finally, the provider needs a small tray and special dishes for serving liquids, soft foods, or whatever is the proper diet for the sick child. A special glass (a Star Wars or Miss Piggy glass or cup) and a bowl for soup make taking liquids more interesting. A flower, a sour ball (if the child is not nauseated), or a card made by the other children makes the tray a treat, regardless of what is being served on it. Little treats make it easier for the sick child to accept being kept separated. An unhappy child is more difficult to care for and slower to get well.

GENERAL CARE

We are living in what we call modern times, and yet many people do things to the sick (and to themselves when they are sick) that may be dangerous. People still give castor oil or an enema to a child with a stomach ache. They stuff food into a child with a heavy cold or croup. They feed eggs to a nauseated child. All are done to make the child (or themselves) better and all make the child (or themselves) worse. Mostly these treatments are old wives' tales or treatments that the parents or grandparents practiced and taught their children. Castor oil can be very dangerous, as in the case of appendicitis, and should *never* be taken when not prescribed by a doctor. This is true of all practices learned from one's parents or grandparents. Unless recommended by a doctor, home remedies should not be used.

ILLNESSES OF INFANTS

Colic

This is not strictly speaking an illness, although colic does make many infants uncomfortable for the first 3 months of life. There is no cure; it is outgrown as the infant's digestive system grows up and can handle taking in milk and digesting it.

Symptoms Infants cry soon or immediately after being fed. They pull their knees up and appear to have cramps in their stomachs. They often want to suck on their fingers, hands, a blanket, or anything they can get their hands on.

Treatment for Colic Feeding the infant smaller amounts more often sometimes helps. The infant must *not* be overfed, however. To avoid this, an exact record of the number of ounces and times the infant is fed must be kept. As the day advances, the provider can add the number of ounces the infant is taking, check the number against the recommended total number of ounces to be offered in a 24-hour period, and that way avoid overfeeding the infant. A pacifier is sometimes comforting. The provider will have to hold it at first until the infant learns to keep it in his or her mouth. When an infant is crying hard and seems to be having cramps, the provider can hold the child against her chest or face down on her lap, gently patting the infant's back. The warmth of the provider's body will often soothe the distressed baby. Comfort is really the only thing one can offer a colicky baby. Happily, it is all over in about 3 months.

Teething

Like colic, teething is not strictly an illness. Some babies seem to suffer with each tooth, often for weeks before the tooth appears. Other babies take teething in stride. Some people think teething causes all sorts of illnesses. This is not true—teething does not cause illness. Like colic, teething is a problem that goes away on its own and making the baby comfortable is therefore the main treatment.

Symptoms The baby's gums look swollen and it is often possible to feel a small lump under the gum where the tooth is. Babies like to have their gums gently rubbed. They begin to drool when teething and continue drooling until most of their teeth are in.

Treatment for Teething There are many teething devices on the market. The ones that can be put in the refrigerator and made cool are sometimes more comforting. These have to be held for young infants. Older babies can hold them themselves. Most babies chew on their pacifiers when teething and prefer them to other teething toys.

Colds

Very young infants usually do not catch colds because they do not come in contact with many colds. It is a good idea to keep an older child with a cold away from an infant because when an infant does catch a cold, he or she is more miserable than an older child. Because young infants spend most of their time lying down, it is harder for them to clear their noses enough to breathe.

Symptoms The main symptoms are a stuffed-up or runny nose and sneezing.

Treatment for Colds The infant should be kept in the quiet room with the vaporizer going. The room should be warm so that the baby does not get chilled when being changed. Drug stores sell a nose syringe that makes it easy to clear the infant's nose of mucus. Be sure to squeeze the bulb *before* putting syringe in the infant's nose. It can be very difficult and frustrating for the infant to suck. It may help the infant breathe to prop up the head end of the mattress a little, raising the infant's head so that some of the mucus can drain. *Take the infant's temperature. Report any fever over 101°F to the doctor. Report a cough to the doctor.*

Vomiting and Diarrhea

If vomiting or diarrhea continue for more than 6 hours, call the doctor. If there is any blood in the child's vomitus or diarrhea, call the doctor. If there is any fever with the vomiting or diarrhea, call the doctor.

Diarrhea Symptoms Diarrhea refers to more than loose or soft stools. When babies or young children have colds, they may have loose stools. Diarrhea means watery stools, often greenish, with a distinct odor.

Treatment for Diarrhea Consult the doctor. Diarrhea is very dangerous to infants. While waiting to see the doctor, give the infant water instead of the usual formula or milk.

Treatment for Vomiting Any vomiting that lasts more than a few hours must be reported to the doctor. Even if the infant only vomits once, do not give the child anything to drink or eat. Keep the infant quiet. After 2 hours, give plain water. If the child is very thirsty or hungry give water for the first 2 or 3 hours, then give the usual formula or milk diluted half with water. If there is no more vomiting, return to the usual formula.

Rashes

A rash on an infant's body can be caused by a number of things—heat, diaper rash, eczema, or an allergy. *Consult a doctor to find out what kind of rash it is.* If it is a heat rash or a diaper rash, it can be treated at home.

Treatment for Heat Rash This is also called prickly heat. This rash usually starts in the baby's neck and on the shoulders when the weather gets warm. The rash begins with pimples and then sometimes develops blisters. The first thing to do is to make sure the infant is not overdressed. Then the rash can be kept powdered with cornstarch. A tablespoonful of bicarbonate of soda in the baby's bath is also very soothing.

Treatment for Diaper Rash Some babies' skin is more sensitive to urine than others'. Diaper rash begins with red, rough skin, then may develop pimples, and then raw sore spots appear. It is important to make sure all soap is rinsed off in the bath. After the baby is dried carefully, zinc ointment can be put on the diaper area. Powder, oil, and lotion are often not enough protection. If frequent washing and zinc ointment on the carefully dried area are not enough to clear up the rash, consult the doctor. As infants grow older, their skin sometimes becomes more sensitive to urine.

ILLNESSES OF CHILDREN

Colds

The most common illness of children is the common cold, and along with it all the illnesses that often occur with colds, such as sore throats and earaches. In a family day care home, it is difficult to keep a child with a cold separate from the other children. If the provider does not, however, it is likely that the other children will catch the cold. Because a child can give his or her cold to another child even before the cold symptoms have been noticed, it is even more difficult not to pass the cold around. Once the symptoms appear it will make life easier for the provider if she can keep the child with the cold away from the other children. This is where the quiet place becomes very important. The provider will have to wash her hands frequently when caring for children with colds or any other illness, in order to avoid passing the germs.

Symptoms   Report any of these to the doctor immediately:

Fever over 101°F
Weakness
Vomiting
Headache or earache (holding the ear or pulling at it)
Severe coughing
Hard or fast breathing

These are all signs that the child has something more serious than a cold and needs treatment by a doctor immediately.

Treatment for Colds   Same as for infants.

Fever

A fever is not an illness. It is a sign of illness, a sign that the body is fighting off an illness. Children can also be sick, even very sick, without running a fever. Usually, however, fever tells the story of the illness, and gives a report of the progress of the body in the battle against the illness.

Always report a fever of 101°F or more to a doctor.

Treatment for Fever   See Chapter 17, p. 251.

Convulsions

Children can have convulsions from a high fever or from other causes.

Treatment for Convulsions See Chapter 17, p. 251.

Strep Throat

Any time a child has a sore throat with fever there is the possibility of a strep throat, although not all sore throats are caused by strep infections. The child must see a doctor. Strep throats are very contagious. Keep the child with a sore throat in the quiet place away from the other children.

Symptoms Sore throat. Fever. Sometimes nausea and vomiting.

Treatment for Strep Throat *See the doctor.* Treatment with correct antibiotic is important. Keep the child in bed in the quiet place. Give something to drink every hour—Juices, clear soups such as beef bouillon and chicken broth, Jell-O, and sherbet. *Check the child's fever every 3 or 4 hours.* Report any fever over 101°F to the doctor. See section on Fever in Chapter 17 for treatment of fever over 103°F. If the child vomits, do not give the child anything to eat or drink for a few hours. Then give a very little water. If there is no more vomiting, give a very little bit of ginger ale or cola. If the soda is allowed to sit until it becomes flat, it is easier to digest. If there is no more vomiting the child can again have some juice.

Scarlet Fever

Scarlet fever is a strep throat with a rash. *If a rash appears, see the doctor.* The treatment is the same as for strep throat.

Digestive Upsets—Upset Stomach or Diarrhea

Besides colds and all the illnesses that affect the child's nose, throat, and chest, the next most common illnesses are those that affect the child's stomach and intestines. *Remember that any vomiting or diarrhea that lasts more than a few hours must be reported to the doctor. Any trace of blood or any fever with the vomiting and diarrhea must also be reported.*

Symptoms Vomiting, or diarrhea, or both.

Treatment for Digestive Upsets Do not give the child any food or any medicine. Keep the child quiet and in bed. After the vomiting stops, give a very little bit of water. If there is no more vomiting and the child wants something, give a very little bit of flat cola or ginger ale. After a few hours, if there is no vomiting, give clear soup such as chicken broth or beef bouillon (making sure there is no fat in it). If there is no more vomiting or diarrhea, give soft foods with *no fat*. Jell-O, baked potato (no butter or sour cream), rice, cream of wheat, or grits. If the child has diarrhea and no vomiting, it is important to replace the liquid that the child is losing. Apple juice and yogurt are good. Skim milk is alright, but not whole milk. Tea with a little sugar is fine.

Flu, Virus, Influenza

This is a very contagious disease, by whatever name it is called. It is easy to spread and hard to cure. The child who might have flu should be kept separate from the rest of the children, in the quiet place. The child's dishes should be washed separately. Adults caring for children with flu need to wash their hands often so that they do not carry the germs to the other children.

Symptoms Chills, weakness, sleepy, and tired. Headache, aching joints, sore throat. No appetite, may feel dizzy or nauseated. Sudden high fever.

Treatment for Flu, Virus, Influenza See a doctor. In the meantime keep the child quiet, in the quiet place. Give plenty of liquids—juice, broth, and soda.

Chicken Pox

One of the last of the childhood diseases for which there is no vaccine is chicken pox. It is very contagious until all blisters have scabs and no new ones appear. If the provider suspects chicken pox, she should keep the child away from the other children in the quiet place.

Symptoms Chicken pox begins with a fever and itching. The child will be very uncomfortable. The spots begin on the chest, stomach, and back. They look like pimples, then like blisters. These then get a crust on top, like scabs.

Treatment for Chicken Pox See the doctor. The most important treatment is rest. Calamine lotion can be put on the spots to help the itching. The skin should be kept clean with soap and water. The child's fingernails should be cut so that he or she will not scratch the tops off the blisters. The spots can leave a scar if they are scratched enough to make a real scab. Aspirin should not be given to children with chicken pox because it can cause complications.

Roseola

There are no vaccines to prevent roseola. It affects very young children, usually between 6 months and 3 years old.

Symptoms Roseola begins with a sudden high fever that lasts 3 to 5 days. After the fever is gone, a rash shows up on the chest, stomach, or back and then spreads to the rest of the body.

Treatment for Roseola See the doctor. The most important treatment is rest. Medicine to control fever must be used with great care.

Allergies

Some children develop sensitivities to foods, plants, pollen in the air, and other irritants, such as dust, feathers, automobile exhaust, animal fur, or certain medicines. These are called allergies. A few, such as allergy to certain seafoods, can last a lifetime. Because the symptoms are severe, it is not a good idea to try to see if a child is still allergic.

Symptoms Food allergies usually show up as a rash. Eczema in children is often considered a food allergy. A more serious allergy to food will cause hives, which look like raised welts. Certain plants cause reactions that are not strictly allergies. Poison ivy, poison sumac, and poison oak cause blisters. Some fibers such as wool can also cause a skin rash. Animal fur can cause itching skin as well as sneezing and difficulty breathing. Pollen, dust, feathers, and other irritants in the air can cause sneezing, watery eyes, runny nose, coughing, and wheezing. Drugs such as penicillin and the sulfa drugs can cause very serious allergies that can be fatal. (See Figure 26 for common causes of allergies.)

Treatment for Allergies Any shortness of breath is an emergency that needs immediate medical care. Infants, toddlers, and young children are usually given only one new food at a time. If there is any reaction, it is easy to figure out which new food caused it. Infants are no longer given solid food before 6 months, which removes a major cause of food allergies. Occasionally, an infant will be allergic to milk and will come in to family day care on a special formula. Babies with celiac disease are not able to digest any fats or starches before the age of 2 years. The provider will have instructions to continue special diets for such children from the pediatrician in charge. She need only keep in touch with the doctor to learn what changes should be made and when. Food allergies are treated by not giving those foods to the child. These allergies should be made known to the school when the child begins to have lunch or snack at school. Allergies to fabric and other things that irritate the skin are treated the same way—by avoiding them.

Figure 26.

In winter, a long-sleeved shirt can protect the child's skin from the touch of wool. If the allergy is severe, no wool clothing or blankets should be used. *For poison ivy, poison oak, and poison sumac, see a doctor.* All clothes that might have touched the plants must be removed. The child is then washed with soap and water. Any parts of the child's body that touched the plant with rubbing alcohol are wiped and covered with calamine lotion to treat the itching. *Drug allergies* are very severe. If a child in family day care has a drug allergy, he or she should wear a medical alert bracelet or a medal around the neck.

Other Childhood Diseases

There are many severe illnesses that affect children as well as adults, such as pneumonia, meningitis, and severe bronchitis. An alert adult notices signs of illness in children and acts quickly. An infant who cries more than usual or appears to be ill, a child who has a fever, seems weak and tired, or otherwise appears ill, needs to see a doctor to discover what is wrong. At times doctors may need to be convinced that the child is really ill, especially if there is no high fever. The provider must explain how she can tell that the child is ill. By describing the difference between the child's usual behavior and the behavior that suggests illness, she can convince the doctor to take a careful look. Some illnesses, like meningitis, are difficult to diagnose. Doctors need the help of the persons who know the child best to understand the difference between the child's behavior when ill and when well.

As the provider cares for the sick children in her home, she is doing more than merely helping them recover from their illnesses, she is teaching them (and often their parents) how one cares for the sick. Many people never learn basic home nursing, and as a result take longer to recover from illnesses. They often do things to themselves—use home remedies or follow old wives' tales or advice—that not only make the illness worse, but weaken their bodies in the process. The human body has amazing powers to make itself well. When people recognize the body's signals and respect them, when they learn how to care for the sick, they and the children they care for benefit in sickness and in health.

17

Providing in an Emergency

There are two ways to deal with emergencies. The first is *prevention* and the second is *preparation*. Even the best of both will not prevent all emergencies, but prevention can cut down on the number of emergencies and preparation can reduce their seriousness. Anyone who takes care of children should know everything in this chapter by heart. When there is an emergency, there is *no* time to go read and find out what to do. The time lost in looking up the first aid for a particular emergency can actually mean life or death to the person in trouble. There are a few skills that require practice, such as artificial respiration, and the rest is simply good sense. Unfortunately, the first thing that people are apt to lose in an emergency is good sense. People often react with fear and distress, and only when the emergency is over realize what they should have done. Going over this chapter with a friend or member of the family will make it easy to learn what to do in every kind of emergency. Older children can ask questions about each page and also learn all of the first aid in this chapter. In emergency care what one does not know *can* hurt, and in fact, can do permanent damage.

PREVENTION

Chapter 4 describes how the provider can make her home a safe place. It is not possible to say too much about prevention and precaution. More children die from accidents than from illnesses. Doctors can cure many more illnesses today than they could a generation ago; but parents and other adults who care for children have not learned as much about preventing accidents and injuries. Nor have we taught children enough about how to take care of themselves.

WHAT IS SAFE

One of the hardest jobs adults face in caring for children is deciding what is safe and what is not. One reason for this is that there are no rules to follow. What is safe for a child changes every couple of months, depending on the child's age, abilities, and understanding. At every age each child is different; what is safe for one is not for another.

Infants

This is the time of least danger. Young infants are unable to get into much trouble; however, any plastic bag or plastic paper of any kind can suffocate a baby and must be kept away from cribs or any other place where young children can get to them.

Small objects are also a major cause of infant death or near death. Toys that have parts that come off or can break off are not safe. Button eyes on stuffed animals often come off, as do buttons on clothes. Pins left within reach can be swallowed.

A baby's bottle should never be propped. Aside from the fact that infants can choke and suffocate, they miss an important experience if they are not held while being fed. If it is ever impossible to hold the infant, the feeding can be delayed a few minutes until there is time to hold the baby or an older child can be asked to feed the baby.

Infants cannot be left on the changing table, the bed, the couch, in a crib with one side down, or any other place from which they can fall. Even 1-month-old babies can travel from one end of a crib to the other. Falls probably injure more infants and toddlers than any other accident.

Toddlers

Waxed floors and spills cause many a toddler to fall. Children this age are still insecure on their feet, and a slippery floor or scatter rugs can make walking dangerous.

Gates are needed at the top and bottom of any stairs. Balconies and porches must have strong railings. Windows, of course, need screens or guards.

A harness should be kept in the carriage, high chair, and stroller. Toddlers are eager climbers and are too young to understand about falling. "No, no" at this age may stop a particular behavior at a particular time, but toddlers' brains are not well developed enough for their memory to work reliably. They cannot be counted on not to climb on the table or couch a second time. They are only safe from falls when an adult (or older child) has an eye on them.

Toddlers are more apt to have accidents when they are tired or hungry. Adults are more apt to forget to keep an eye out when *they* are tired. The provider should try to pace the children's day and her own to avoid periods when everyone is frazzled or exhausted.

Preschoolers and Older

In Chapter 4 each room in the house is reviewed for possible dangers. Poisons should *never* be kept anywhere children can find them. Most poisoning accidents occur before mealtimes, when children are hungry and more apt to eat aspirins, detergents, paint, birth control pills, plant leaves, or whatever they find.

Certain places should be kept locked, especially closets where medicines, cleaning supplies, paints, insecticides, cosmetics, plant and yard care equipment, are kept. Any cluttered closet should be locked. A child can reach for something and pull down a whole pile of things on her or his head.

Unused refrigerators often are the cause of suffocation. The doors of any trunk, freezer, refrigerator, or other appliance not in use should be removed.

Children should not roughhouse in the house—rough play is fine outdoors but not indoors. If children are getting enough exercise they will be content to play quiet games indoors.

Children need to learn to pick up their toys, boots, or other belongings so they do not remain on the floor to trip over. Nothing should ever be left on the stairs. Appliances that are not in use should be unplugged. Extension cords should not be plugged into the wall when not in use.

Many houseplants are poisonous. As long as there are young children in the house, it is sensible not to have any plants that could poison a child if eaten.

SAFETY OUTDOORS

Almost as many accidents happen outdoors as indoors. As the provider goes for walks with the children she should go over the rules for crossing streets. She can talk about the danger of approaching animals one doesn't know. She can explain why it is not a good idea to accept rides from strangers.

The Provider's Own Yard

The yard must be checked for any dangers. Holes that children can fall into or twist an ankle in should be filled and leveled. If there is no fence around the yard the provider can walk with the children around the boundaries of the space to show them where they are allowed to play.

Equipment that is simple and can be used in many different ways is the best. A swing from a tree branch made of rope and a tire or a wooden seat, a wagon, an old tire filled with sand, a place to dig, a place to plant flowers or vegetables, and a tub for water in summer, is enough equipment. From time to time, these need to be checked for safety. Sand should be covered at night to keep dogs and cats out.

Playground

If the provider lives in the city and uses public playgrounds, she needs some rules to protect the children from accidents. These include:

Do not kneel or stand on swings.
Do not get off the swing or seesaw until it is still or until the other person is ready.
Do not try to climb up the slide backwards.
One child slides down the slide at a time.
No children under 5 are allowed on the jungle gym.

The provider should look over the playground equipment when she takes the children in. Is the sand in the sandbox reasonably clean? Can she spot any children in the wading pool who have skin problems? Is the drinking fountain clean, with no garbage in it?

When children are taught to check for safety at home and outdoors in the park or playground, they enjoy the grown-up job and at the same time learn how to check for safety themselves.

PREPARATION FOR EMERGENCIES

The following emergencies are arranged by symptom so that it is easy to look up a particular injury or emergency. The provider must not wait for one to happen, however. She needs to know the basic emergency treatments so well that she only has to check for the details after she has acted swiftly and correctly. Hippocrates, the father of medicine, who lived in ancient Greece some 400 years before Christ, said, "First, do no harm." Many people make the injury worse by doing the wrong thing. For instance, a child is hit by a car. Someone runs up, picks up the child, and carries the child to a nearby house or store to call for help. By picking up the child that person has caused severe internal bleeding and injury to the child's spine. Another example: A child is burned by tipping over a pot of hot water. Someone immediately puts butter or margarine or some other grease all over the burn, making it much more difficult for the doctor to clean and treat and allowing the burn to get worse in the meantime. The rest of this chapter should be read with someone who can question the provider until she knows by heart what to do in all of the emergencies described. Then she will be prepared to "do no harm."

SOMEONE TO CALL IN AN EMERGENCY

When a child has to be taken to the hospital, the provider has to consider what she can do with the other children. The ideal situation is to have someone stay at home with them while she takes the injured child to the emergency room. If there are adult members of the provider's family living with her who are at home during the day, she has someone available no matter when an emergency occurs. If an accident should happen in the park or playground, she can telephone this person to come immediately and get the other children while she goes to the hospital with the hurt child.

Failing an adult member of the family, the provider can have one or two close neighbors or friends she can call on. In this case, the provider needs to know in advance when the neighbor is at home and away, and have the other neighbor or friend cover for her. This friend could also meet a child due to arrive from school at the family day care home while the provider is taking the hurt child to the hospital. Telephone numbers of neighbors and friends who are available should be posted with the other emergency numbers by the telephone.

Some providers belong to agencies that have procedures to follow in an emergency. In some agencies, the first call the provider must make is to the agency director who then sees to the care of the other children and notifies the parent.

Someone must have the task of calling the injured child's parent and telling him or her to meet the child and provider at the hospital. It is better if someone other than the provider can take on this job, simply because time is precious and the provider cannot delay taking the child who is hurt to the emergency room.

Finally, should the provider be on a trip when an emergency occurs and there is no other adult along, she has no choice but to take all of the children with her to the hospital. The older ones will keep an eye on the younger ones in the waiting room of the emergency room. It is wise to do some preparation for such an event. In family conversations during mealtimes or snacktimes, the provider can bring up the question of how the children would manage if she had to take all of them to the hospital for one child to be treated. Discussions of what kind of behavior is appropriate in a hospital waiting room, of some of the things they might do to pass the time, and of how each would feel about it will help to prepare the children in case of need. Older children can assume a responsible role in an emergency, especially if they have an idea of what to expect. They can remain calm and reassure the younger ones while they wait to return home with the provider and the wounded child.

FIRST AID SUPPLIES

To be able to do the right thing one needs the right equipment. A box supplied with the proper first aid necessities should be kept in an easy-to-reach place. The following list can be used to stock up on supplies (or to check off the items in a ready-made first aid kit). The list can then be pasted inside the top of the box to make sure that anything that is used is replaced and nothing is missing when needed:

Absorbent cotton
Adhesive strip bandages, assorted sizes
Adhesive tape, ½ to 1 inch wide
Butterfly bandages
Cotton-tipped swabs
Large triangular bandages
Sterile eye pads
Sterile gauze bandages, assorted sizes
Sterile gauze pads
Tourniquet (a short strong stick and clean cloth, 2 inches wide and 20 inches long)
Ammonia inhalant

Calamine lotion
Hydrogen peroxide
Petroleum jelly
Rubbing alcohol
Salt or salt tablets (for heat exhaustion)
Drinking cups (paper or plastic)
Measuring cup
Measuring spoons
Safety pins
Sharp needles (to remove splinters)
Sharp scissors with rounded ends
Tongue depressors
Tweezers (to remove splinters)

In addition to the regular first aid kit there are two special kits. One is for accidental poisoning. It contains syrup of ipecac (to make the child vomit) and activated charcoal (to absorb the poison). *These medicines are only used when directed by the Poison Control Center or a doctor.*

The second special kit is a snake bite kit. It contains a band to tie around the part of the body affected, sterile blades, and a suction device. If the provider lives in the city, she is not likely to need this kit.

The provider also needs a rectal thermometer, hot water bottle, and ice bag for treating minor illnesses in the home. All of these things need to be kept handy, but carefully locked in a closet so that the children cannot get to them.

TELEPHONE NUMBERS

Over the telephone in the house, the provider needs a list of the following numbers written in clear large print.

```
POLICE _____  FIRE _____
RESCUE SQUAD OR EMERGENCY AMBULANCE _____
POISON CONTROL CENTER _____
HOSPITAL EMERGENCY _____
A NEIGHBOR OR FRIEND _____
A SECOND NEIGHBOR OR FRIEND _____
TAXI _____  DRUG STORE THAT DELIVERS _____
ELECTRIC COMPANY _____  GAS COMPANY _____
OIL COMPANY _____  WATER DEPARTMENT _____
```

Under those numbers *each* child's name and the following information is written:

```
CHILD'S NAME _____
   MOTHER AT WORK _____
   FATHER AT WORK _____
   DOCTOR _____  DENTIST _____
   CLINIC _____
```

FIRST THINGS TO DO IN AN EMERGENCY

There are certain things the provider must know when emergency treatment needs to be given. If a child is hurt, the following things are looked at in this order:

1. **Pulse** Put your fingers against the large artery in the child's neck and feel for the heartbeat. For infants, put the fingers under the child's left nipple to feel the heartbeat. This takes practice, so do it with well children until you can find the pulse easily.
2. **Breathing** Check the child's breathing. Put your ear close to the child's mouth and nose in order to feel and hear any air coming out.
3. **Bleeding** Look the child over quickly, but *do not move the child*. Gently check underneath the child's body using your hand or looking at the clothes the child is lying on, all without moving the child. Any serious bleeding must be taken care of immediately.
4. **Poisoning** Look at the child's mouth to see if there are any stains or burns that show the child swallowed something. If there are, treat for poisoning.
5. **Shock** If the child is badly hurt, treat for shock.
6. **Broken bones** If there are any signs that the child has broken a bone, treat for broken bones.
7. **Burns** If child is burned, check the body carefully for all areas that might be burned. Treat for burns.
8. **Cold exposure and frostbite** If the weather is cold and the child has been out in the cold, treat for cold exposure and frostbite.
9. **Heat exhaustion and sunstroke** If the weather is hot, check for heat exhaustion and sunstroke.

In all of the above, *send for the parents* and *get medical help immediately*.

Pulse

If there is no pulse, have someone call for an ambulance immediately.

Place the child on his or her back on a hard surface. Place the heel of your hand on the child's chest (Figure 27).

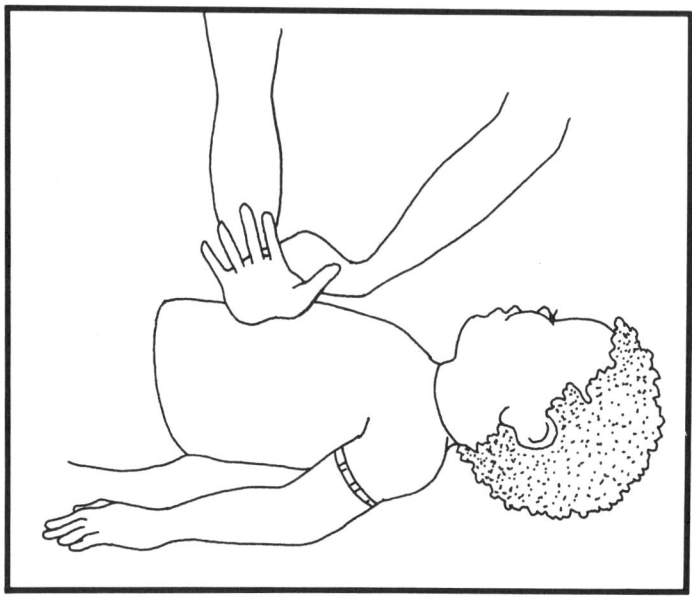

Figure 27.

Make short quick pushes down, pressing the child's chest in about ½ inch with each push. Time these so that there are about 80 per minute.

If the child is not breathing, combine this treatment with *artificial respiration*. Every five pushes, breathe into the child's mouth. See instructions in *Breathing, Artificial Respiration*.

When the heartbeat starts again, stop the treatment but continue artificial respiration until the child is breathing again. For infants, instead of using the heel of the hand against the child's chest, press the chest down with the three middle fingers (Figure 28). Place one hand under the infant's

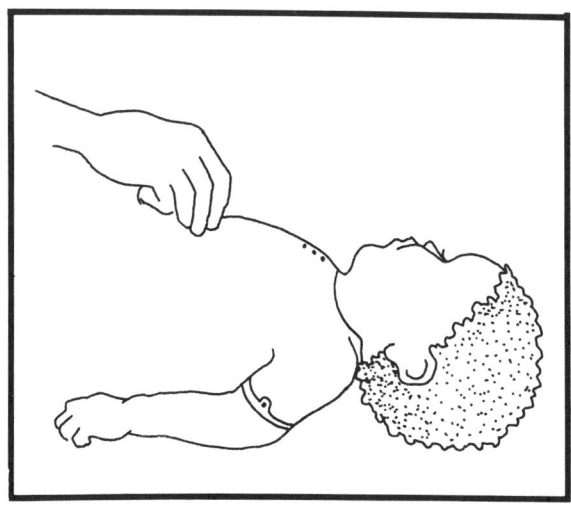

Figure 28.

back and press in the spot shown below, about 100 times a minute. After every five pushes, breathe into the infant's mouth, just as your fingers come up, letting the air go into the child's lungs. Use short, gentle puffs of air.

Breathing

If the child is not breathing, give artificial respiration.

Artificial Respiration Put the child on his or her back with the neck straight (Figure 29). Check that there is nothing in the child's mouth. Check the child's pulse. If there is none, see *Pulse* section (p. 239). If the child is *very young*, cover the child's mouth *and* nose with your mouth. Give four quick puffs of air into the child's mouth. If you are doing it right, the child's chest will expand with each puff. Then give a puff every 20 seconds until the child is breathing again. If no air comes out of the child's mouth after each puff, treat for *choking*. If the child is older, pinch the child's nose and place your mouth over the child's mouth.

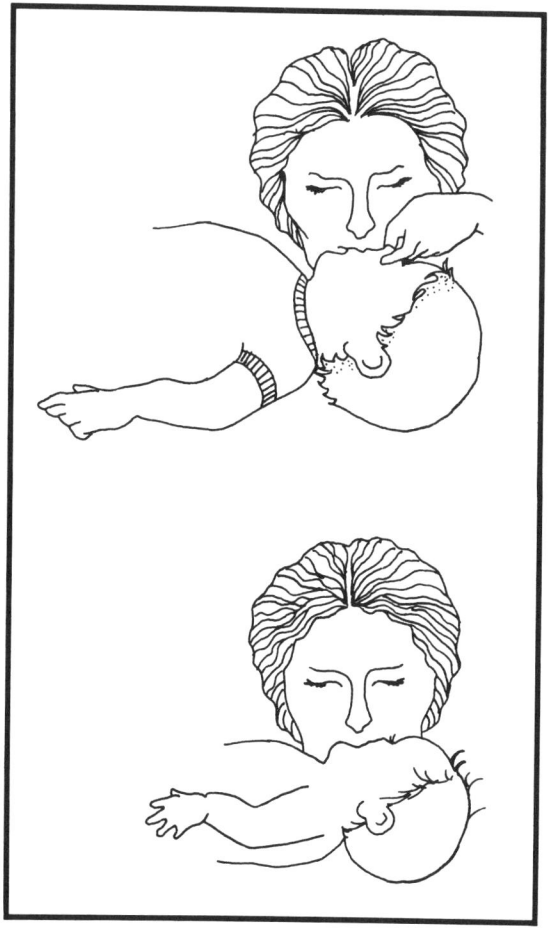

Figure 29.

Providing in an Emergency

Figure 30.

As soon as the child's breathing starts again treat for *shock* and *get medical help immediately.*

Choking If the child can cough or speak, do not do anything.

If the child cannot breathe, speak, or cough, do the following and have someone send for an ambulance.

Hold the child against your body, the child's back against your chest. Place your fist under the child's ribs, in the middle. Then with your other hand over your fist, pull in sharply, pushing up a bit as you do so.

Infants and toddlers can also be held against your body the same way with the infant's back against your chest (Figure 30). Be sure that as you pull in sharply, you adjust for the infant's small size. The air in the child's lungs should force out whatever is causing the child to choke.

Bleeding

Practice pressing on the pressure points until it is easy to find them on all of the children (Figure 31).

Using a Tourniquet Only use a tourniquet when it is *not* possible to control the bleeding by pressing on the pressure points. Tourniquets can be made if the injury is on the arms, legs, hands, or feet.

Put the band of cloth around the child's arm or leg above the cut and between the cut and the child's heart. Make a single knot in the band, then place the stick on the knot and tie the other half of the knot over the stick. Turn the stick until the bleeding stops. Tie the ends of the band around the arm or leg to keep the stick in place (Figure 32).

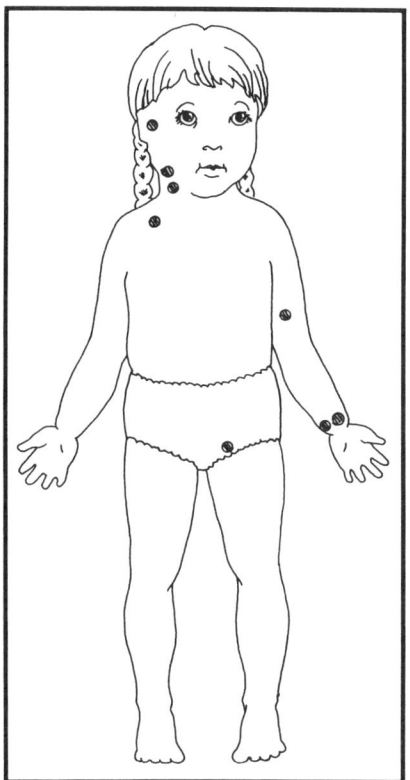

Figure 31.

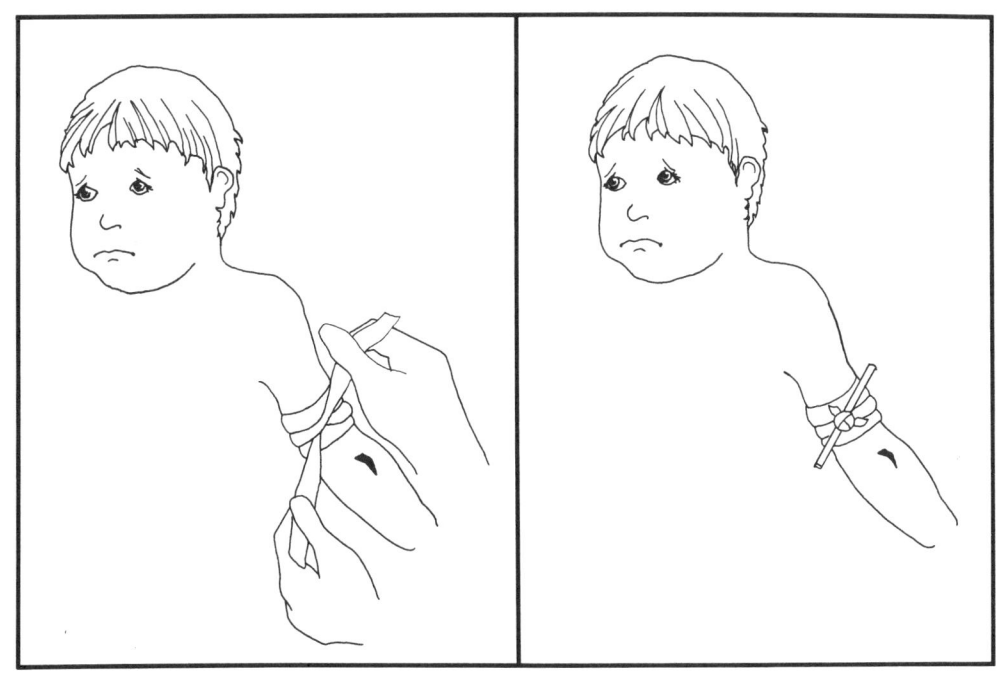

Figure 32.

Providing in an Emergency 243

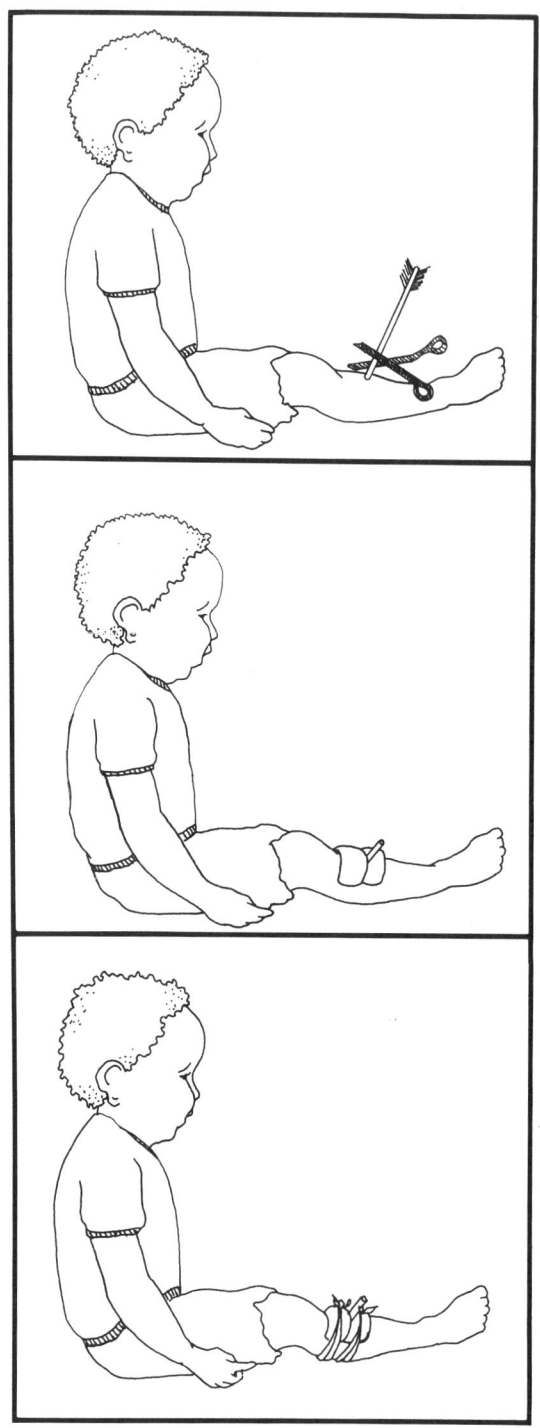

Figure 33.

Loosen it every 10 minutes for a few seconds.

Place adhesive tape on the child's forehead and write on it the exact time that the tourniquet was applied.

Get medical help immediately.

When bleeding can be controlled by pressing on the pressure points, continue to press as you take the child immediately to the hospital.

When bleeding is less serious, place a gauze pad on the cut, then hold the pad tightly against the cut until the bleeding stops or at least lessens.

If possible, raise the cut part of the body above the level of the child's heart.

As soon as the bleeding lessens, bandage the gauze to the cut.

Check the child's pulse from time to time to make sure the bandage has not cut off all circulation.

If a finger or toe or any part of the child body is cut off, wrap it in wet sterile gauze, put it in a plastic bag, put the bag in a pan of ice and take it with you to the hospital.

If something is stuck into the child, do not try to pull it out. Treat for bleeding by pressing on the pressure points if necessary, and *get medical help* (Figure 33).

For bleeding in the child's ear, nose, mouth, or on the head, use pressure on a gauze pad over the cut and *get medical help.*

For bleeding from a cut in the child's chest or belly, cover the opening with plastic or aluminum foil, tape it down, and *go immediately to the hospital.*

Poisoning

> CALL THE LOCAL POISON CONTROL CENTER IMMEDIATELY.
> SAVE WHATEVER THE POISON WAS IN AND A SAMPLE OF THE VOMIT.
> WATCH BREATHING CAREFULLY.
> GIVE ARTIFICIAL RESPIRATION IF NECESSARY.
> DO NOT GIVE ANYTHING TO DRINK IF THE CHILD IS UNCONSCIOUS
> ALWAYS GET MEDICAL HELP AFTER CARRYING OUT POISON CONTROL CENTER INSTRUCTION.

If the Poison Control Center instructs you to make the child vomit, give 1 tablespoon of syrup of ipecac. If the child does not vomit in 15 minutes, give another tablespoon. *Do not* give a third.

Hold the child's head between his or her knees while he or she is vomiting. When the vomiting is finished, give 5 or 6 teaspoons of activated charcoal in a glass of water.

Get medical help.

Poisons Breathed but not Swallowed

> GET MEDICAL HELP AND OXYGEN IMMEDIATELY.
> CALL THE POISON CONTROL CENTER.
> WATCH BREATHING CAREFULLY.
> GIVE ARTIFICIAL RESPIRATION IF NECESSARY.

Remove child from the place where the poison fumes are. Loosen tight clothing and treat for shock. Do not let the child become chilled. If the child's skin is burned, treat for burns.

Shock

> ALWAYS TREAT FOR SHOCK IF THE CHILD IS SERIOUSLY HURT.
> DO NOT GIVE ANYTHING TO DRINK.
> DO NOT OVERHEAT.
> GET MEDICAL HELP IMMEDIATELY.

The symptoms of shock are:

Paleness
Cold, clammy skin
Weak or irregular breathing
Nausea
Weakness

Place the child lying down and cover with a blanket. If the child is cold or damp, place a blanket under him or her.

If the child's head is injured and he or she is having trouble breathing, raise the neck and shoulders a little.

Otherwise, raise the legs about 8 to 12 inches with a pillow or folded blanket. If this causes pain, *do not do it.*

Keep the child covered (Figure 34).

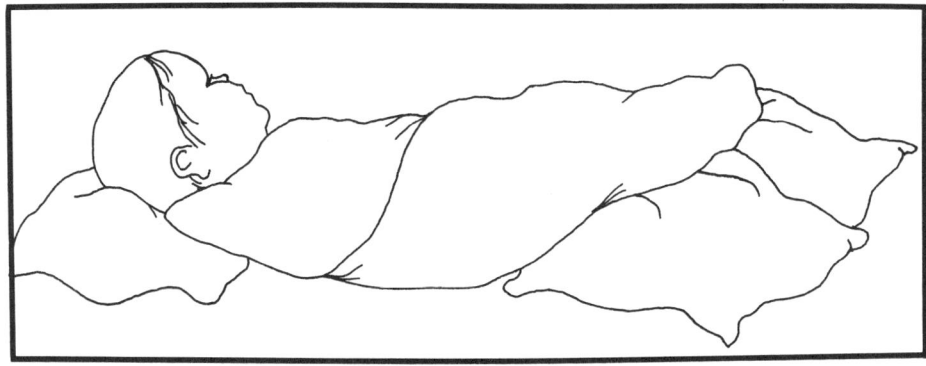

Figure 34.

Broken Bones

If you suspect that the child might have broken a bone, the main thing is to keep that part of the body absolutely still until you get to the hospital.

If you are not sure whether the bone is broken or not, *always* treat it as if it was broken (Figure 35).

If a piece of bone is sticking out of the skin, treat for bleeding.

Always treat for shock.

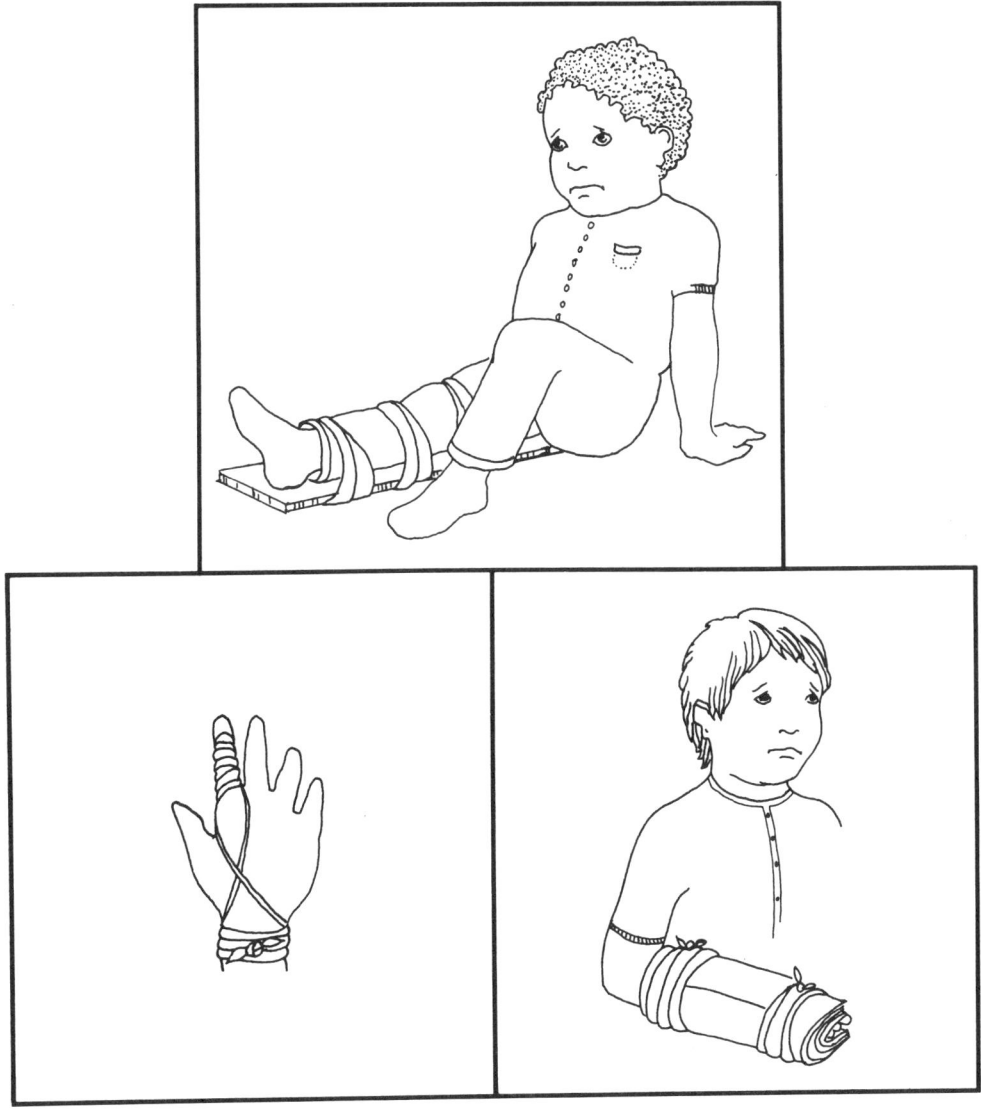

Figure 35.

Burns

NEVER PUT ANY KIND OF GREASE OR MEDICINE ON A BURN.
NEVER PULL THE SKIN OFF THE BLISTERS.
PUT THE BURNED AREA UNDER COLD WATER (Figure 36).
SOAK CLOTHS IN ICE WATER AND PLACE ON THE BURN.
GET MEDICAL HELP.

Figure 36.

Chemical Burns

PUT CHILD UNDER A COOL SHOWER, OR
USE A GARDEN HOSE (Figure 37), OR
POUR WATER OVER THE CHILD WITH A BUCKET.
THEN COVER THE BURNS WITH COLD CLOTHS AND GET TO THE
  HOSPITAL.

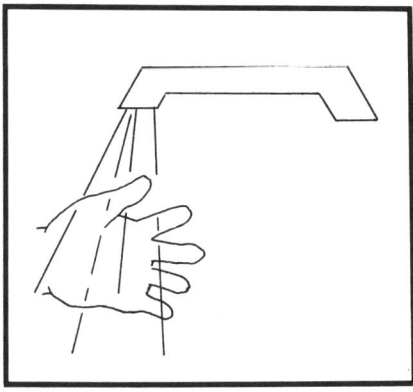

Figure 37.

Cold Exposure and Frostbite

Cold Exposure When child has been out in extreme cold or has fallen into very cold water:

> REMOVE PROMPTLY TO A WARM PLACE.
> UNDRESS AND PLACE IN A BATHTUB OF WARM, NOT HOT, WATER.
> PLACE TOWELS ON A RADIATOR OR IN A LOW OVEN TO WARM.
> GENTLY DRY CHILD WITH WARM, NOT HOT, TOWELS.
> WRAP IN WARM TOWELS OR A BLANKET AND GO IMMEDIATELY TO THE HOSPITAL (Figure 38).

Figure 38.

Frostbite
Treat frostbite the same way that you treat cold exposure:

> DO NOT RUB OR MASSAGE THE SKIN.
> DO NOT USE HOT WATER OR HOT WATER BOTTLES.
> DO NOT GIVE ANYTHING ALCOHOLIC TO DRINK.
> TREAT FROSTBITE THE SAME WAY THAT YOU TREAT COLD EXPOSURE:
> PLACE IN A BATHTUB OF WARM, NOT HOT, WATER.
> TOWEL DRY WITH WARM TOWELS.

When the parts of the child's body that were frostbitten begin to get pink take out of the warm tub and dry carefully. Raise and lower these parts of the body (arm or leg) to help circulation.

Go to the hospital.

Providing in an Emergency

Heat Exhaustion and Sunstroke

The most important thing to do is *lower the child's body temperature.*

PLACE THE CHILD IN A TUB WITH LUKEWARM WATER, OR
WRAP IN WET LUKEWARM SHEETS UNTIL THE TEMPERATURE COMES
   DOWN (Figure 39).
TAKE THE CHILD TO THE HOSPITAL.

Figure 39.

Fever

For any fever, *get medical advise*. Do not use medication, enemas, or alcohol or ice water baths unless advised to do so by a doctor. If the child's fever goes to 103°F, the following treatment should be given while waiting for the doctor or parent to arrive:

UNDRESS THE CHILD, AVOIDING DRAFTS THAT WILL CAUSE A CHILL.
PUT THE CHILD IN A TUB WITH A LITTLE LUKEWARM WATER SO THAT THE CHILD'S BODY IS MORE OUT THAN IN THE WATER.
WITH A SPONGE OR WASHCLOTH, RINSE OFF THE CHILD'S BODY FOR 15 TO 20 MINUTES.
TAKE THE CHILD OUT OF THE WATER AND RUB DRY GENTLY.

Convulsions

Always report a convulsion to the doctor immediately. Do not give the child anything to drink. Make sure the child can't be hurt by anything nearby, such as a toy. Try to loosen the child's clothing. *Do not* try to hold the child still. As soon as the convulsion stops, turn the child on his or her left side. Watch the child's breathing. If the child stops breathing, give artificial respiration.

18

Providing for Special Children

One of the many skills a good provider has is the ability to notice a problem or the beginning of a problem when it occurs in any of the children she cares for. This skill comes from knowing how to look at children, finding clues when something is amiss, making careful notes to study, and, when necessary, sharing these with the parents and perhaps a specialist. Because many behaviors are normal at certain ages and not at others, she needs to have some knowledge about child development. Of course, the provider is not expected to be a pediatrician, psychiatrist, or any other kind of specialist, but she does need to know when to ask for help. First, however, she must notice the problem, make regular notes about what she is noticing, talk with the parents, and then, if needed, get some professional help.

Many years ago, when a child did not seem to be developing quite right, parents and other relatives shook their heads and decided that the child would probably outgrow the problem or else would grow up to be just like Uncle Louis or Aunt Jewel, and be a little strange. And because they did nothing about the problem, that is more or less what happened. The reason is easy to understand. People did nothing for the child who was not developing well because they did not know what to do, and very often, there was no one who could tell them what to do. Child development is a very young science, and only a couple of generations ago no one had ever heard of studying how children develop. Even today many pediatricians have had no training in how children learn, in the psychology of childhood, in how their emotions affect their lives, or in how to notice problems other than illness. They often fail to notice certain problems of development, or even physical handicaps such as deafness, until the parent points them out. When parents ask about a child who is slow or seems to be having trouble, pediatricians often say something like: "All children develop at different rates, slow in some things and quicker in others. I wouldn't worry; it all works out in the end." It does not, of course. Even if adults are not able to notice anything, other children often do, and they can make the problem worse by making fun of the child, by keeping her or him out of their group or games, and by making the child feel different or "not quite right."

Every child runs into some sort of difficulty growing up. Therefore, when parents and providers talk about the children there are two things they want to think about: 1) is there a problem that requires help? (Can this help be found at home, in the family day care home, or from a specialist?); and 2) how can parents and provider (and perhaps a specialist) best work together to bring about the quickest and easiest solution possible?

TALKING ABOUT PROBLEMS WITH PARENTS

When a child seems to be having trouble of some kind, the provider needs to consider how she will present the problem to the parents. Chapters 6 and 7 give some suggestions. The first thing for the provider to do is to make careful notes on the problem—when it occurs, how it appears, what the child does, how often, and finally, what seems to help. She can then ask for a meeting with the parents in order to share these notes, ask if the child has the same difficulty when at home, and make suggestions about what she thinks should be done for the child. Parents find it easier to accept a problem concerning their child if they are helped to decide how to handle it.

CHILDREN'S WAYS OF DEALING WITH PROBLEMS

Some children are better at finding ways to manage their difficulties than others, just as some children have abilities like drawing or singing that others do not have. Looking at how the child who lacks certain skills manages without them, we can understand better not only the child's difficulty, but the child's strengths as well. Often a child will make up for a problem or difficulty so well that it remains hidden. There are children who find clever ways to cover up a problem by adding something they *can* do to an activity or game, by being especially helpful to an adult or other child, or by showing off. Without realizing it, providers and parents also help these children by pointing out something they do very well, or by finding ways to make it easier for them. Because helping children is a natural instinct of adults who care for children, they are sometimes so busy helping that they do not notice the problem. Keeping notes makes it easier to pick up on something that might otherwise be overlooked.

CARING FOR SPECIAL CHILDREN

The provider must decide how she feels about having a child in her day care home who needs special care. Because family day care is very personal at-home care, it is often the best place for children with difficulties or handicaps. The provider can give more personal care on an individual basis than a teacher or a caregiver in a day care center. On the other hand, not every provider can accept every kind of problem. Each provider must know her own strengths and abilities. She can then decide what kinds of problems or handicaps she will take on and what kinds she must refuse.

INFANTS

The provider can refer to Chapter 9 on infants as a reminder when to expect the well-known infant behaviors—rolling over, sitting alone, crawling, babbling, reaching for and grasping a toy, standing, and walking. If an infant in the family day care home is delayed in learning any of these, it should first be called to the parent's attention, and after talking it over with the parent the provider can suggest talking to the pediatrician or the well-baby clinic doctor. This chapter considers some of the problems that are hard to notice and that are not part of the development of the average child.

Hearing

For some reason, hearing problems often go unnoticed. One good way to make sure that an infant has average hearing is to make the following test. The baby (even when only a few days old) is held in the adult's hands so that the baby is facing the adult. Someone else comes quietly from behind, stands on one side of the baby and speaks softly, about 2 feet away from the infant's head. If the infant does not turn his or her head toward the voice, the provider should make a note of it in her book, record the date, and try again in a day or so.

If the infant still does not respond, the test should be repeated. A variation on this test can be done with a small bell. When the infant is in the crib, awake but not crying, the bell is rung softly a couple of feet away from one side of the infant's head (Figure 40). If the infant turns to the sound, there is no need to worry. A note should be made in the Baby Book recording the infant's successful performance. If the infant does not turn to the sound, the test needs to be tried again. Each time the provider does the test, she makes a note in the book and puts the date next to her notes. After two or three tries, if the child does not appear to hear the bell, the provider should make a date with the parents to talk about it.

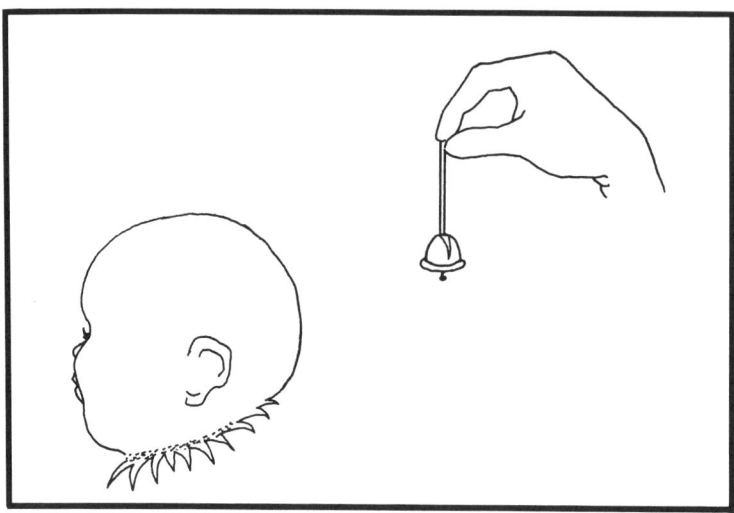

Figure 40.

Most pediatricians give hearing tests to infants at about one year. If the pediatrician the parents are using does not, the provider should ask for it. It is possible for children to have a small hearing loss without being deaf, but it takes a professional test to discover it.

Seeing

Loss of sight is usually noticed even in very young infants. Because babies do a lot of looking—at adult's faces, at bright color, at their own hands—it is very easy to notice that something is wrong when an infant does not look at things attentively.

To check a small infant's vision, dangle a ball of red yarn or some other colorful object about 14 feet from the infant's face. As soon as the baby is looking at it, gently move it to one side, slowly, and then to the other (Figure 41). Even very young infants a couple of weeks old will follow the object with their eyes. Notes of the infant's behavior should be made in the record book or in the Baby Book.

While the provider feeds and changes an infant, she should take advantage of the opportunity for a conversation, and talk, smile, and nod to the infant. If there is no response, if the infant does not stare into the provider's eyes and return her smile, it can mean a loss of vision or a problem in responding to people. Either way, the provider needs to tell the parents and get a professional opinion. Her notes will be useful when the provider talks with the parents and again when she talks to the doctor.

Reaching

A child can have normal vision but be very slow at grabbing and holding something held out to him or her. By 4 or 5 months infants have no

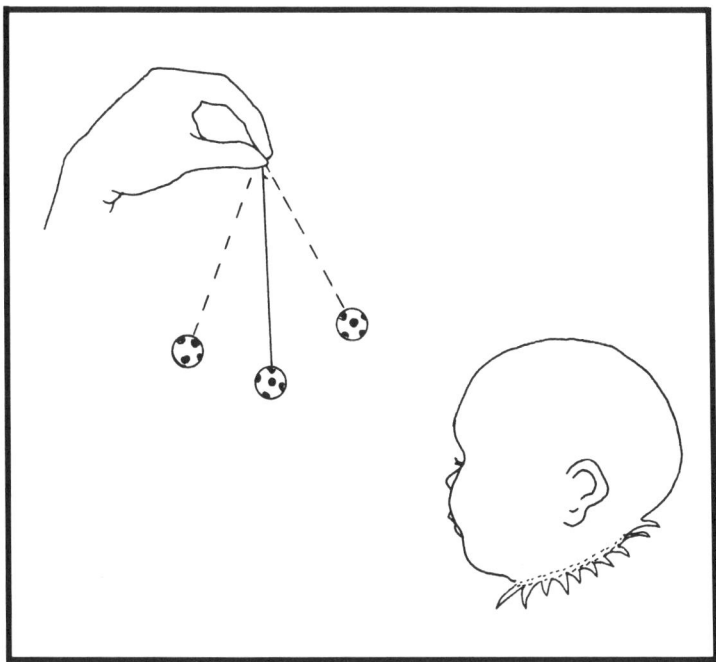

Figure 41.

trouble grabbing and holding anything within reach that catches their interest. If a baby in the family day care home does not reach or grab at things, the provider will want to make a note of it. If by 5 months the infant cannot grasp a toy within reach, the provider needs to talk to the parents and then to a pediatrician.

Babbling

Early language is described in the chapters on infants (Chapter 9), on toddlers (Chapter 10), and on language (Chapter 11). Any delay of more than 1 or 2 months in a child's language development, beginning with babbling at 3 months, needs to be discussed with a pediatrician. If there is no hearing problem, and if the child is getting plenty of attention, it could mean some sort of trouble responding to people.

Crying, Startling, Nervousness

Some infants are very sensitive to noise, bright lights, being played with, or the activity of other children around them. They may cry hard and long when upset, and be very hard to comfort. These infants also jump, even when the noise they hear is not very loud, and they react to bright lights or loud voices with crying or trembling. All infants have different ways of reacting to people and things, but those who are easily upset and hard to comfort may have a serious problem. The provider should keep a record of any unusual distress and long or hard crying. If her efforts to protect the infant from noise, confusion, and upset do not work, she should talk to the parents about it. One of the early signs of certain kinds of learning or emotional problems can be this kind of sensitivity.

Head Banging and Crib Rocking

Beginning in infancy or sometimes later, babies may bang their heads on the mattress or headboard of the crib, or sometimes they get up on their knees and rock the crib, banging it against the wall. This seems to be an attempt to shut out the world in babies who have trouble getting to sleep. This behavior should be recorded in the Baby Book when it occurs, and notes made about how long it continues. It needs to be discussed with the parents.

Quiet, Withdrawn Behavior

The opposite of the baby who is very nervous, jumpy, cries easily, and is hard to comfort is the baby who shows little or no emotion, who looks away when picked up or spoken to, and who does not cry or smile much, even when held by the parent or provider. This is just as serious a problem as high-strung behavior. It needs to be talked over with the parents, then with a pediatrician.

TODDLERS

By the time infants become toddlers, poor hearing and poor eyesight usually have been noticed. Some of the other problems that occur when infants become toddlers are harder to notice, and to know what to do about.

Problems with People

Early signs of trouble in relating to people include not looking at people's faces and crying when held and comforted by a familiar adult. Children with no real attachment to anyone are in trouble. They may not babble or they may repeat sounds or words. Sometimes they make the same sounds over and over as if talking to themselves. Unusual behaviors of this kind should be noted in the record book, and if the provider is not able to get the child to become attached to her, respond to her, or laugh and play games with her, it should be discussed with the parents and then with a doctor.

Clumsiness

Toddlers are all clumsy; learning to walk and run is difficult. Some toddlers fall all the time, bang into furniture, and seem to have no idea how to go around things. If this continues, however, to the age of 2 or 2½, it is serious enough to be discussed with the parents and a doctor. Before doing so, however, the provider will want to make notes in her book for a few weeks describing the child's falls or other clumsy behavior.

Emotional Problems

Toddlers are highly emotional and, as described in Chapter 10, often difficult to manage because of their strong feelings. At the same time they are often fearful, and unless given help and support, may find harmful ways of dealing with their fears and emotions. Some of these harmful ways are physical. They may develop asthma, eczema, or tics as a result of emotional distress. A tic may begin as a little twitch, blink, or shrug of one or both shoulders. When children are nervous, frightened, or upset in any way, these tics are more obvious. If any of these physical problems appear, the first step is to offer the child a lot of affection and tenderness. Demands on the toddler to learn certain things should be dropped for the moment, including any efforts at toilet training that might be going on. Comforting, calming, and fewer demands are often enough to cure these problems. In any case, the provider should make notes about the symptoms or fears or very strong feelings and about her methods for relieving them. If they do not go away, she should talk with the parents and then see a doctor.

Speech Problems

The chapters on toddlers and on language describe the beginnings of speech. "Baby talk" is normal, and in some children continues longer than in others, especially if the parents and provider make a game of it. Stuttering may appear at this age, and is best dealt with by listening calmly to the child and by *not* correcting the child's speech in any way. It should be made very clear to the other children that they are not to interrupt the child who stutters, nor are they allowed to correct or help the child finish a sentence. The less attention paid to stuttering, the sooner it will go away. The child who is given time and patience should soon get over stuttering.

Other Signs of Possible Trouble

Some new skills that toddlers learn are noticed only when they are absent. Toddlers learn to drink from a cup, stack blocks, hold a spoon and eat from it, pull off their shoes and socks, climb on and off chairs, and other furniture. They carry things around and put them in piles. Whenever a toddler is unable to or uninterested in doing these things it could be a sign that something is not right. On the other hand, if only one of these skills is missing, and the toddler is developing well in other ways, the provider should simply make a note of the unusual behavior or missing skill, and keep it in mind. If there is a real problem, other skills will be missing as well.

PRESCHOOLERS

As children get older, the chance that a big problem will go unnoticed becomes smaller. Still, there are small problems that can occur, and although harder to notice and to cure, they can make a big difference in a child's life.

Hyperactivity

In the last 10 years or so hyperactivity has become a common diagnosis. It is connected with some learning problems and with some emotional problems. It is often used as a way of describing behaviors and problems that are not understood and that are hard to treat.

Children at age 3 or 4 are usually active at certain times of the day and at other times are quiet. They have moments when they cuddle up and sit quietly to hear a favorite story. They will stand very still to watch something interesting in the street. They will play quietly and attentively lining up little cars and trucks between buildings of small blocks. Hyperactive children cannot do these things because they cannot be still and attentive for long enough. Even in the middle of something they enjoy, they wiggle and squirm, and then jump up and move about.

There is also something out of control about the way they move. They knock things over, push things too far or too hard, run into things instead of moving around them, drop things, squeeze things too hard, or just run around for no reason. They are never still, never relaxed for more than a few moments at a time. When asked to please sit still, they cannot.

Because hyperactive children do poorly in school, it is important to get help for them before they begin school. The provider should keep notes on any hyperactivity she notices in the children in her care, then talk to the parents about getting some help for the child before he or she begins school and has to face the problems that come when a child cannot do what the school expects, which in most cases is to spend a lot of time sitting still and paying attention.

Sensitivity

There are other behaviors that often go with hyperactivity. Some children who are hyperactive are also very sensitive, they get upset very easily, cry easily or get angry and throw things, or scream at the other children. Often these moods pass quickly and they are sorry for what they have done, and want to hug and kiss and make up. All preschoolers are busy learning how to play with and share with other children, and often find it difficult or upsetting. There is a difference, however, between the preschooler who has trouble sharing a favorite toy or taking turns doing something he or she loves to do and the child who goes to pieces *everytime* he or she is asked to share or wait, and has rages or screams several times each day.

Here again the provider should keep a record of the number of times a very sensitive child gets upset in a day. Then she will be able to compare this child's behavior with that of the other children, in both frequency and intensity, and have actual numbers to discuss with the parents. If the child continues to go to pieces, even when separated from the other children, and given special times to be alone and to play without interruption, the child is sure to have trouble in school and should have some attention before starting.

Language

By the end of the preschool years, 3- to 5-year-old children should be able to speak and understand without difficulty. There are still words that preschoolers pronounce wrong and times when they mix up what they are saying, but on the whole, they can say whatever they want clearly and easily.

Some children, on the other hand, at 5 or 6 are still saying "He gotted it first," or "Why you not have it?" This kind of mixed-up language is a sign of trouble at this age. They may also say things that are silly or impossible and seem to say them seriously. The difference is clear between children who are making jokes (preschoolers love making jokes and being silly) and children who say they will be Superman tomorrow and *believe* it. Their language shows they are not sure what is real and what is pretend. Any fantastic things the children say should be recorded exactly as they are said. These will be useful when going for help.

Hearing and Seeing

By the time children are 4 or 5 years old, any serious hearing problem or really poor eye sight will have been noticed. Often, however, children who have many sore throats with fever (tonsillitis) or earaches will have some hearing loss. To make sure the loss is not enough to make school difficult for the child, it is wise to have a hearing test done before the child enters first grade. Likewise, the children's eyes should be tested before entering kindergarten. Often children are able to see well enough to manage at home but are not able to see the blackboard in school clearly.

Finally, the provider will want to review the chapter on preschoolers (Chapter 12) and on getting ready for school (Chapter 13). Children who cannot do the games of sorting or organizing things that go together, of lining things up by size, and of seeing what things are alike and what are different may need more practice or some special help.

SCHOOL-AGED CHILDREN

By the time children are school age, most problems of a physical nature are already obvious. Even learning disabilities can usually be discovered by 5 or 6 years of age. Although the provider still needs to keep an eye out for any problems that may occur, a child who has been developing well and who has the skills expected at that age is likely to continue to do well.

The kinds of problems that begin in school-aged children or seem serious for the first time are usually emotional problems. Some of the fears, worries, or feelings of pressure or of not being able to do what is expected only show up during these years. Some of these begin with physical symptoms. The child's voice may show the strain by being too loud or by being quiet and expressionless. Some children develop skin problems such as eczema. Some show signs of nervousness such as yawning a lot, of swallowing air and belching. Some even begin vomiting before school in the morning, or begin having to leave the class to urinate many times during the day. Other signs of nervousness or emotional distress are asthma, hay fever, and tics. Some children begin masturbating often and when in the company of others.

A word here about masturbation: All children masturbate occasionally. It is part of discovering one's own body and how it works. At different times in a child's life, there will be more or less interest in masturbating. During the years between six and the beginning of adolescence, children are interested in team games, sports, muscle building, and often masturbate less than at other ages. With the beginning of adolescence, the hormones produced by the developing sex glands cause new feelings and an interest in masturbation. Children usually realize when still quite young that adults are made uncomfortable or even angry by seeing children masturbate, and so they rarely do it in public. Some worried or frightened children will masturbate in school, in public, or with the family, even though they realize that it is disapproved. At this point, parents and providers need to be concerned about the child's fear, insecurities, and worries, not the masturbation.

Another way that children's fears and worries show up is in sleep problems. Some children have trouble falling asleep, others have nightmares and are afraid to go back to sleep for fear of having the same nightmare again. In conversations with the parents, the provider can ask about their children's sleep habits. If the parents report sleep problems, she can look for other signs of nervousness and worry. Sometimes children's fears only appear as sleep problems without any daytime symptoms, although this is unusual.

It may be possible to relieve the worries, fears, and insecurities of childhood without professional help. Sometimes giving more affection and attention, helping with homework, taking time to sit alone and talk about what goes on in school or with the other children in the class is all that is needed to make the child feel safe, loved, and competent, and the symptoms may go away of their own accord. If the parents are very demanding, the provider might suggest they give the child more freedom and more support. Most often these fears begin at home, not at school, and require the parents to be more accepting and less demanding of their children. Family day care offers children a safe, supportive, affectionate place to grow strong and secure. Even if the parents' own insecurities cause them to be very strict and punishing, the family day care home can be reassuring, comforting, and give the child a sense of his or her own worth and competence. The provider's care is not a substitute for professional advice, but it can make professional help unnecessary sometimes. And even when a specialist is needed, that advice and guidance is useless unless carried out by adults who care for children with attentiveness, tenderness, and consideration.

19

Providing Food for Growth and Strength

Children who are well fed are healthy looking, strong, and bright-eyed, and have few colds or other illnesses. They are also alert, attentive, and energetic. Children who are *not* well fed may have dry skin, dry hair, runny noses, and scratches and scrapes that take a long time to heal. They are often tired. They may be thin or fat, but they do not have good, strong bodies. They are often sick. Food plays an important part in making children healthy or unhealthy, strong or weak. In Mexico doctors have even found a connection between a baby's intelligence and the mother having had enough good food during her pregnancy. Eating enough good food can also make a difference between birth and 5 years old when a child's brain doubles in size. Finally, the right kind of food can help to prevent health problems such as high blood pressure, diabetes, heart disease, and anemia.

Because food is so important, why do so many people eat food that is junk? Partly because they do not realize how important good food is, and partly because they have learned to enjoy eating these things and find it difficult to change their habits. Mostly, however, it is a matter of not knowing how very important it is to eat well.

The human body is changing all the time. It is made up of trillions of tiny cells—blood cells, bone cells, muscle cells, and nerve cells. Every cell has to be fed so that it can do the job it is designed to do. These cells are constantly dying and new ones are being made. For instance, the cells on our skin are either dying or being worn or scraped off. If our skin did not make new cells, we would quickly wear holes in our bodies. Cuts, broken bones, and burns all heal because we can make new cells.

The inside of our body is also made of cells—our lungs, stomachs, hearts, and all of our organs are made of millions of tiny cells. They are like machines that need fuel in order to work and that fuel is food. Good food helps all parts of the body work well. Poor food and junk food can cause bad teeth, constipation, fatigue, nervousness, and even serious illnesses.

The food we eat is made up of about 50 different chemicals, all of which are needed by the body to work well and to make new cells. Some of these are vitamins, some minerals, some proteins, some starches, and some fats. Because these chemicals can only do certain jobs, we need different kinds of food in order to get enough of all the different chemicals. When we do not get certain ones, we become unhealthy. When we get too much of certain ones, we also become unhealthy (for instance, we get fat if we eat too much protein, fat, starch, or sugar).

The kinds of food and the amounts we need can be measured in calories. A calorie is the measure of energy our food provides. Because most of us do not exercise very much, we do not use up all of the energy our food gives us. The leftovers are stored as fat. Everytime we eat 3,500 calories more than we need, we add a pound of fat. If over a few days we eat a cup of peanuts, a piece of pie with ice cream, and a milk shake in addition to our usual meals, we add a pound of fat. If we throw in some potato chips and cookies, we have added more than a pound. This extra food is filled with "empty calories."

To be healthy we must avoid empty calories. This chapter contains the general rules about food and what foods are rich in the fuel our bodies need, what foods have empty calories and should not be eaten, what foods should be eaten with what, and, finally, how to eat well for less money.

Americans in general are interested in food and in losing weight. We buy thousands of books and magazines about dieting and try every diet suggested, many of them fad diets. Diet and health food stores have sprung up all over the country; some of them offer food that is very expensive and often not even healthy. People buy it, however, because these foods and the fad diets promise health and, at the same time, weight control.

It is certainly true that Americans are overweight, in fact, one in every three is. More people in America are dangerously fat than in any country in the world. At the same time, many Americans are undernourished, that is, not well fed. We are fat and yet starving for the very kind of food we need to be healthy.

The reason is clear: we do not know enough about the importance of food. More than that, many of us have poor eating habits. Children in family day care can learn good habits if the provider knows four things: 1) the food that makes people healthy; 2) how to buy it as cheaply as possible; 3) how to prepare delicious meals and snacks from the good and cheap food; and 4) how to do all this without spending too much time.

FOODS THAT MAKE PEOPLE HEALTHY

Children generally need the same kinds of foods that adults need to be healthy. Infants need a special diet (for the first months, just milk, then a little orange or apple juice, and then some soft solid food). Children and adolescents need more energy food than the average adult (who gets little or no exercise). Good food habits begin in early childhood and can last a lifetime. Bad food habits also begin in early childhood, and they can also last a lifetime. One needs only to look at the people one passes in the street to see the results of bad food habits.

The Four Kinds of Food

The four kinds of food we need to get the 50 necessary chemicals are:

1. Vegetables and fruits
2. Breads and cereals
3. Milk, cheese, and other dairy products
4. Meat, fish, poultry, eggs, dried beans and peas, nuts, and seeds

There are some other foods that do not fit into any one of these four groups, such as fats (butter, oil, margarine, the fat in bacon, sausage, and other meats) and sweets (cakes, pies, cookies, puddings, soda pop, jam, honey, icings, sugar). We eat far too much of these, which is one reason why we are the fattest people in the world. Jean Mayer, who is one of the most respected experts on food and nutrition in the country, says the average American eats 105 pounds of sugar in a year. No wonder so many are fat. He also says that if we would do without sugar altogether we would be much healthier.

We need some of each of the four main kinds of food each day. We do not need fats and sweets. When planning meals the provider can think about the four groups and have some of each kind of food at every meal. Little children only need small servings, but they should have the same complete menu that older children and adults have. The older children and adults simply take larger servings.

A sample meal plan for the children in family day care follows. If the provider does not serve breakfast to the children, she has only three meals to plan—two snacks and lunch. Next to each food in the meal plan is a number that indicates which food group it comes from. This helps the provider make sure that all four food groups are included.

Breakfast	Morning Snack
Apple (1)	Orange juice (1)
Cream of Wheat (2)	Bread (2)
Milk (3)	Peanut butter (4)

Providing Food for Growth and Strength

Lunch	Afternoon Snack
Meat loaf (4)	Raisins (1)
Noodles (2)	Apple juice (1)
Sliced tomatoes (1)	Graham crackers (2)
Banana (1)	
Milk (3)	

There are more foods from group 1 in the sample plan than from any other group. These foods are rich in vitamins and minerals, are good energy foods, are not fattening, and are not very expensive. Children do not ask for potato chips, cakes, and other empty calorie snack foods unless they are used as treats or bribes. Snacks of raisins, grapes, quarters of apple, orange (or any other fruit in season), carrot and celery sticks, cubes of cheese (such as Swiss, Cheddar, or Muenster), nuts, seeds, hard-boiled eggs, fruit juices, and homemade milk shakes are fun to eat, delicious, and full of nutrition.

The most expensive food group is group 4, the meat group. There are many substitutes for meat, however. Eggs, cheese, fish, dried peas and beans (if served with rice), and even peanut butter provide the same nutrition. Dried peas and beans and peanut butter are not high quality protein and need supplements of some milk, cheese, eggs, or grain food to increase the quality of protein. On a day when rice and beans are served at lunch the provider can serve hard-boiled eggs in quarters for afternoon snack or cubes of cheese with whole wheat crackers. She can even cook the beans with a little ham or pork. With just a little meat the beans (black-eyed peas, chick peas, or lentils) become a perfectly good meat substitute.

Children 9 years and older need more than two glasses of milk a day. If they do not drink that much, they can instead eat yogurt (plain or with fresh or canned fruit or a *little* honey) or any kind of cheese.

Choosing Foods in Each Group

To make it easier for the provider to choose from all four groups when planning her menus, here are some common foods in each group:

Group 1: Vegetables and fruits

Beets	Green peas	Apples	Peaches
Broccoli	Mustard greens	Apricots	Pears
Brussel sprouts	Peppers	Bananas	Strawberries
Cabbage	Potatoes	Cantaloupe	Tangerines
Carrots	Spinach	Grapefruit	Watermelon
Collards	Sweet potatoes	Honeydew melon	
Corn	Tomatoes	Lemons	

Group 2: Breads and cereals (use whole wheat or enriched products)
Cooked cereals like oatmeal, Cream of Wheat, Wheatina
Sugarless dry cereals
Rice

Group 2: *Cont.*

Cornmeal
Grits
Spaghetti, noodles, macaroni, and other pasta
Rolls, muffins, pancakes, waffles, saltless pretzels, bagels, oatmeal, raisin and peanut butter cookies, whole wheat crackers

Group 3: Milk, cheese, and other dairy products
Milk, all kinds, including skim, buttermilk, dry milk
Cheese, all kinds, including cottage cheese, cream cheese, hard cheeses
Yogurt

Group 4: Meat, fish, poultry, eggs, dried beans and peas, and nuts and seeds

Beef	Lamb	Eggs
Veal	Poultry	Fish
Pork	Liver	Dried beans and peas
	Kidneys	Nuts
		Peanuts and peanut butter
		Lentils
		Soy beans
		Seeds

FEEDING INFANTS AND TODDLERS

Feeding infants and toddlers in a family day care home need not give the provider more work or more expense. Pediatricians generally agree that solid foods should not be given before about 6 months. All of the strained foods that used to be given to infants of only a few weeks or months in order for them to sleep through the night are no longer recommended. In fact, they are blamed for many of the allergies that children develop. Because infants' bodies do not yet produce the enzymes necessary to digest many foods, these foods often irritate their intestines, sometimes causing serious allergies.

The American Academy of Pediatrics now recommends that babies be given their first solid foods at about 6 months. These can include baby cereals mixed with enough milk to be thin and soupy, mashed fruits mixed with a little plain yogurt, or fruits put through a blender with a little orange juice and cottage cheese so that they become a smooth, easy-to-swallow mixture.

At 9 months foods with lumps can be added. These can include mashed table foods (the food that the rest of the children are eating). By the end of the first year babies should be eating most of the same foods the rest of the family is served.

A blender is very helpful in making table foods into baby foods. A much cheaper machine, usually called a baby food grinder, sells for less than

$10 and is just as good. The point is to avoid baby foods in jars. They contain much too much sugar, salt, and empty calories. Furthermore, they are very expensive. The food the provider prepares for the other children can be put in the baby food grinder or blender, and for a small fraction of the cost of the baby food in jars, the infant has a much healthier meal.

Because toddlers enjoy feeding themselves, foods they can pick up are perfect. Little bits served in small dishes or on cupcake papers encourage them to eat rather than play with the food. They can be given more when the food they have is finished. Because this is not the age to teach elegant table manners, the more the toddler can eat with his or her fingers, the better. Children this age can often manage dishes of cooked cereal or thick vegetable soup with a spoon. Small amounts of milk at a time in a cup with two handles or with a no-spill top make it easy for the toddler to drink. Again, refills can be offered as soon as the cup is empty.

One more word of caution is in order. Adults often feel that toddlers are not eating enough "to keep a bird alive." This is rarely if ever true. Healthy children will eat as much of what is offered as they need. The danger of overfeeding infants and toddlers is far greater than that of underfeeding. Providers need only offer a selection of the four food groups and toddlers will eat as much as they need.

GETTING CHILDREN TO ENJOY GOOD FOOD

One way to make sure children enjoy nutritious food is to let them help prepare the food. While preparing treats with the children, the provider can talk to them about how their bodies use these good foods to become and stay strong and healthy. Another way to make sure children enjoy good food is to let them help plan menus. At first the provider will have to suggest most of the meals. On the day the meals for the next week are planned, the provider can sit down with the children and have a "food conference." If the children make a good suggestion, it should be used, or if not, the provider can make a note and say she will use their ideas somewhere else in the week. She can give the children a choice, and they can choose what they want. The children can also suggest snacks. The provider may have to give choices for the children to select from, such as banana milk shake, juice with club soda, Bran Chex, pretzels and nuts in a mixed bag, yogurt shake with fruit, hot apple juice with raisins and orange slices, hot cocoa, and oatmeal cookies.

If the provider keeps her favorite recipes on 3" × 5" cards in a box, she can let the children help her go through them for ideas. They can also pull out a favorite recipe to prepare by themselves under her watchful eye. Instead of putting the cards in strict alphabetical order, they can be grouped as *Snacks, Mixed Dishes* (including meat substitutes such as macaroni and cheese or rice and peas), *Vegetable Dishes, Desserts, Salads* (children can prepare lots of salads by themselves), *Breads,* and so forth.

Once or twice a week, the provider can let the children help bake muffins or sweet bread to use as snack and as dessert. Children enjoy these projects, they can measure, stir, and learn to use the beater. They can grease the loaf pan or put papers in muffin tins. They can also help prepare cut-up fruit, baked apples, sliced bananas, or any number of other simple dishes and snacks.

LEARNING IN THE KITCHEN

When the provider is cooking, she can take the time to teach children about washing their hands carefully before working with any food, using a clean fork or spoon to mix food, and not putting the spoon used to taste food back into the food they are preparing. Once they have learned these rules, they can do many useful tasks in the kitchen and in the process learn a great deal.

Children will admire the star pattern they find when an apple is cut in half across the middle. They will see how much peanut butter it takes to spread on eight crackers or six slices of bread. They will count the seeds in a slice of watermelon or in an orange. They will learn that a hard-boiled egg cut in four pieces has four quarters, and that after one is eaten there are three quarters left. After two quarters are eaten, half of the egg is gone.

When apples are cheaper (in the fall) they should be used often. Besides eating them raw, the provider can make applesauce, apple pudding, apple bread, and baked apples. Each of these apple dishes takes a different kind of preparation, and children can learn common recipe words such as scrape, peel, sift, stir, beat, mash, strain, measure, and stuff.

City children often have no way of knowing where foods come from and how they get to the supermarket. Country children usually know how the foods that are native to their area get to the table. Still, not many children ever see a cow milked, a fish caught in a net, a whole lamb cut up by a butcher, an apple picked, a potato dug, corn ground, or apricots and grapes spread out to dry. As the provider prepares meals with the children, she can invent games to play that will give them some of this useful information. She can say, "I'm thinking of something made from milk that has holes in it" or "I'm thinking of something that comes from a hog and is long and skinny." The children will soon be making up their own riddles for the provider to guess.

Children learn from many other activities that are part of food preparation. They learn to set the table, to put away food in its proper place, to clean up after meals, and to estimate how much of certain foods are needed, for instance, how many biscuits or muffins the day care family will eat or how much milk is needed to fill everyone's glass. Children should be encouraged to help in all of these jobs.

On rainy days when everyone has to stay indoors, the provider might suggest that the children make afternoon snacktime into a restaurant game. They can make restaurant menus with all of the fancy dishes they can think of and then decorate them. They can take turns being waiters and waitresses, taking the orders and writing them on a pad of paper (or pretending to) and bringing the food on trays. The waiters and waitresses will serve carefully from the guest's left side, unless the guest is left-handed, then from the right side. The waiter can announce the specialities of the day or suggest one of the chef's famous dishes. These games are not only fun for the children, but they are also good practice in social skills.

SHOPPING ECONOMICALLY

One of the biggest budget items for every family is food. Everytime there is a television news report on the cost of living, food prices have gone up. Although food is expensive, healthy food is actually less expensive than junk food. A family can eat very well for less money by knowing how to choose food carefully.

Making Lists To Go with Menus

It is important to have a strict list for shopping. Otherwise, it is easy to be carried away and spend money on things that are not really needed. On the other hand, for certain foods such as vegetables and fruits it is best to wait to decide until in the store. The prices of cauliflower or broccoli can vary as much as 50 cents in a week. One should take advantage of the foods that are in season, not only because they cost less, but because they are fresher and better tasting.

Most supermarkets have specials. The provider should check these out each week and, when possible, take advantage of the sales. She may want to make changes in her menus and shopping list when she finds that chicken is on sale, and substitute roast chicken for meat loaf or whatever other meat dish she had planned to have. If there is a special on canned peaches, she can take advantage of it and have peaches and yogurt instead of bananas and graham crackers as planned.

Buying Store Brands

Some supermarket chains have their own brand name foods. For example, the A & P has both A & P brand and a cheaper brand called Ann Page. These cost less than name brands and are just as good. Some supermarket chains also sell foods that have no brand names, called no-frills generic products, and these are even cheaper. The bag or can or box has a plain white and black label that simply says "salt" or "rice" or "peanuts" on it to identify the item.

Unit Pricing

Unit pricing lets the provider compare prices regardless of the size of the package. On the shelf that holds apple juice there will be a small sticker that says what a quart of Mott's apple juice costs and also the price of the particular can on that shelf. Next to it will be the cost of a quart of Red Cheek apple juice and the cost of *that* size can. The provider can look at these stickers and find out which size and which brand provides the cheapest quart of apple juice. Usually the largest can of the store brand or generic brand will have the smallest unit price. Having a day care family allows the provider to take advantage of these large sizes.

Fillers, Mixes, Coatings

Every month or two there is a new mix on the market to add to hamburger to make it go further or to coat on chicken or pork chops to make them tender or juicy. The ridiculous thing is that these often cost more than the food they are supposed to help. In other words, the mixture that "helps" hamburger go further costs more than more hamburger. Worse than that, these mixtures are not good food. There are many good foods one can add to make certain foods go further, such as egg and breadcrumbs, mashed vegetables, or rice.

The same is true of mixes. The main difference between making a cake from a mix or from "scratch" is the money and the time spent. The mix costs much more and has less food value, but saves time. One good thing about a house full of children is that there are a lot of helpers. They can save the provider time by doing the measuring, and not only learn a lot in the process, but produce a better and a cheaper cake. They can also help with the clean up.

In general, it is a good idea not to buy any of these "time savers." They do not save that much time, they cost more, and they all contain things that are not real food. The provider can get more food value for her money by making her own coatings, helpers, and mixes instead of buying the ready-mades.

She can also use dry milk in recipes that call for milk. Once mixed with water according to instructions on the package, this milk works just as well as whole milk and is much cheaper.

There are ready-made cupcakes and other desserts or cakes in the supermarket that some parents buy to avoid having to make dessert. These are empty-calorie foods and have the least amount of food value for the most money.

Here are some ways to tell high empty calorie foods from good low calorie foods:

Empty high-calorie foods are:	Low calorie foods are:
Thick, oily, greasy-crisp (like french fries)	Bulky, crisp (like apples, dry roasted peanuts)
Gooey, smooth, slick (like candy, banana splits)	Watery, watery crisp (like carrots, celery, grapes, and oranges)
Sweet, sticky (like cakes, cookies)	

PREPARING GOOD MEALS AND SNACKS

In every part of the country there are different food tastes, likes, and dislikes based on the kinds of food grown or raised or caught there and on the habits and choices of the people who have lived there and handed down their favorite recipes. For instance, there are Tex-Mex, Boston baked beans, and Soul Food. Each of these has its own way of providing all of the necessary nutrients that the body needs for health. All providers have to do is keep in mind the four food groups that make up a balanced diet. This may take a lot of thinking at first, but it quickly becomes a habit. Then when she thinks of snacks, the provider thinks of cubes of cheese with carrot and celery sticks (instead of sweet punches, potato chips, or Danish pastries, which are poor in food value and high in calories and price). Instead of buying soda pop or fruit-flavored drinks (like Kool-Aid or Hawaiian Punch), she buys real fruit juices and mixes them herself with club soda to have twice as much food and half as many calories, and she saves money in the process.

On rainy days preparing the afternoon snack is a great cooking activity. The children can decide what they want to cook (carrot cake, oatmeal raisin cookies, cut-up fruits, apple pudding) based on what ingredients are on hand. They can make enough for each child to give a piece to his or her parent. If the provider has cupcake papers on hand, it is easy to make an extra treat for each child's parent by baking a small cake in a muffin cup for each. The parents will be happy to know that the food their children are being given to eat and drink is carefully chosen and cooked to provide all the nutrients that their bodies need to be strong and healthy. The little treats the provider shares with them will also encourage them to think about whether the food in the meals and snacks they prepare at home include the nutrients that they need. She must not let the parents feel that she is being critical of their food habits, however. Instead she can ask them for recipes of dishes that their children especially like, and if she feels these dishes have enough good food for the money and time spent, she can add them to her file of recipes. If not, she does not have to use them, nor say anything to the parent.

Sometimes a recipe can be improved by changing a couple of the ingredients. For instance, Jello desserts contain nothing but sugar, and are simply empty calories. To make a good dessert out of a package of Jell-O the provider can make the following recipe:

Creamy Fruit Gelatin

¼ cup fruit flavored gelatin (Jell-O)
½ cup orange or apple juice
1 can fruit, drained (8 ounce can)
2 tablespoons lemon juice
⅔ cup evaporated milk

1. Bring fruit juice to a boil and add to gelatin. Stir in lemon juice.
2. When cooled, stir in evaporated milk.
3. Chill in refrigerator until mixture begins to set.
4. Beat mixture with an egg beater until it is light and fluffy.
5. Fold in the fruit. Chill again until set.
6. To unmold, dip bowl or mold in a pan of warm water for a few seconds.

With the milk and fruit added, the dessert includes food from both groups 1 and 3. (This recipe is from a cookbook called *A Cookbook for Day Care Parents and Family Day Care Providers for Everyday Use and Special Occasions*, published by the Day Care Council of New York, Inc.)

SPECIAL FOOD NEEDS

School-aged children need about the same amounts of foods from the four food groups as adults. They especially need a good breakfast before going to school in order to be alert, attentive, and able to work. In the morning the provider can put peanut butter, whole wheat bread, milk, and fruit out on the table so that her school-aged children can have something more than they may have had at home. Or she can offer them one of the unsweetened dry cereals with milk and fruit.

Afternoon snacks are also important for school children. They can join in the planning of the next weeks' snack menus and choose the snacks that they will enjoy.

Allergies

The provider may have to plan with extra care to provide a child who has allergies to some foods with substitutes that will make up a complete menu. Once she has thought up good substitutes, the provider may find it easier to feed the substitutes to everyone, and only serve the foods that the allergic child cannot eat on the days when he or she is absent. Some very common foods such as tomatoes or eggs can cause allergies in certain children. In this case, it does not make sense to leave these foods out of everyone's diet. As long as the substitute is one the allergic child really enjoys, the difference in the foods served will not make him or her unhappy or feel left out.

Posting the Menus

After the children and provider have completed their menus for the next week and made their shopping list, the children can decorate the menu with crayon drawings or whatever they choose, and then put it on the wall or bulletin board for their parents to see when they bring and pick up the children. The children's special choices can be labeled, so that each can show his or her parents what dish will be served or prepared especially for him or her.

The Provider's Own Family's Meals

Depending on the size of her own family, the provider may find it easier to cook for both her own and her day care family at the same time, or she may have someone in her family who will take on the job of preparing the family dinner. In any case, cooking two meat loaves is not much more work than cooking one, and means that the provider has something already prepared either for her family's dinner or for her day care family's lunch the next day. The important thing to remember is to keep the business accounts separate. When shopping, the provider needs two lists, one for her business and one for her own family. She can then make estimates of the cost of the day care share when she prepares a dish for both the family's dinner and the day care children's lunch.

SITTING DOWN TOGETHER TO EAT AND TALK

All through history mealtimes have been important social events. In ancient Rome people spent half their lives at their meals. The rich Romans lay down on couches to eat. In the Middle Ages both peasants and rich people spent many of their nonworking hours seated at the table, eating and exchanging news or religious or other views. In the early days of America, the farm workers came to the table and everyone sat down to talk over the day's work and plan for the next.

Today people in a family often snack in between meals instead of sitting down to eat. Or the members of a family have different schedules and therefore rarely eat together. Sometimes the children are fed separately and do not eat with their parents. When mealtimes are no longer a time for everyone to sit together and talk about their interests, activities, each other's views, and the news of the world, or make plans together, an important social experience is lost, and children are denied the chance to learn about and from each other. In times past even infants were included in the mealtime gathering. people took turns holding the infant while they ate.

The family day care home can bring back this valuable experience and make it an important event of the day. Little children then naturally learn from the older children and adults at the table, and do not need training in how to behave properly at the dinner table. When the attention is on the conversation and not on how much of each food everyone eats or on table manners, children learn to enjoy the food and talk, and they look forward to mealtimes.

There is no place in good child care for saying to a child, "You cannot have any dessert if you do not eat your vegetables." One reason some children stuff themselves with sweets is to make up for all those desserts they could not have. When there is no discussion about who eats what and all table conversation is about what everyone is doing and thinking, there are no eating problems. All children have certain foods they like better than others, but these likes and dislikes can be taken care of in the menu planning time, *not* at the table. When children help themselves from serving dishes and are not ordered to "finish this" or "eat that," they learn to eat what the other children and adults eat and to enjoy mealtimes and snacktimes for the food and the company. When people sit around a table and talk and eat together, they are carrying on one of the oldest traditions of civilization.

20

The Family Day Care Provider—A Summing Up

By now there should be no doubt left that the job of family day care provider constantly presents new problems to be solved, new skills to master, and new knowledge to be acquired. Sometimes the work can become so absorbing that it is difficult to look at objectively. From time to time however, the provider needs to do just that—she needs to examine every detail of her job to make sure it is satisfactory. Once she has done her review, she can look with pride at all the things she is doing well, and she can make a list of all the things she may want to work on or change in the future.

Although every job needs to be reviewed from time to time, it is especially important for those who are self-employed. People who have no supervisor or boss to say "Well done!" or "You need to work on that" are left with the task of judging their own work. They are their own bosses, and therefore their own supervisors. Self-examination becomes one more job that providers must do.

It is a very rewarding job, however. It may be the only time providers think about how very complex child care is and how many things they do, and do well. Looking carefully and objectively at everything they do each day reassures providers that they are doing a difficult job well and also allows them to notice any little things they might otherwise overlook, some of which may need some attention.

This chapter contains a checklist of all the things the provider does. It is meant to be used as a review. It also gives the provider a chance to realize how much she is learning each day, and has already learned, as well as any things she might want to find out more about.

LIVING AND LEARNING

There is an old saying that we learn something new every day. Certainly the ability to learn does not end when we finish school. Adults learn many things more easily and more quickly than children do. Besides, adults are often free to learn the things they want to learn, not what they *have* to learn. Just as with children, the more self-confidence adults have, the more open they are to learning new things. The adult who seems to be uninterested in new things, unwilling to hear other people's ideas or opinions, or unable to try something new, is probably a person who was discouraged as a child and lost faith in his or her ability to learn. Most people, happily, continue to learn throughout their lives. They learn from their friends and family, from books, from neighbors, from the service people they deal with, from programs on television, from newspapers, and from magazines. They set goals for themselves and then go about realizing these goals.

People who deal with children have much to learn. This is true for two reasons: 1) because we know so little about child development; and 2) because even if we manage to learn all there is to know, each child remains an individual and can only be understood as one example of how human beings develop. Although we know more and more about what children need in order to do well, deciding what each particular child's needs are at any particular time becomes the task of the person who cares for that child. As the provider decides how to meet each child's needs each day, she is learning more about that child, about child development, and about the job of child care.

REVIEWING THE SITUATION

There are some parts of the provider's job that need to be reviewed often and some others that need review less often. The first section of this chapter deals with those that need to be considered about once every 3 months. They are the organization of space, activities, and time—how the provider has organized her home into a workplace, the activities she has planned for the children, and how she has planned her own and the children's use of time. These three have a lot to do with how the day goes, whether it is easy and smooth or rushed and irritating. Sometimes a small change in how the room is arranged, in the time allowed for outdoor play, or in planning something interesting for the young children to do while the provider spends some time with the school-aged children can make a big difference in everyone's day. Each section asks a few key questions, then ends with a summary statement to be used as a self-evaluation.

Organization

1. Space Does the arrangement of space suit the present number of children and their current ages? Is there space for the youngest to play safely and out of the way of the older children? Can the older children work on their projects or homework safely away from the younger children? Can the provider do her own work and keep an eye on the children at the same time? Has she arranged her work space to make things as easy as possible for her to do what she has to do? Are things also arranged so that the children can do as much for themselves as they are able? Put away their things? Wash up? Help at meal times? Are there quiet places for the children to be alone? Are there little places where children can go to look at a book, play with a toy, or just sit undisturbed and think?

Is the space arranged for everyone's convenience?
☐ yes ☐ needs some attention

2. Activities Are the planned activities interesting to the children at their present ages? Has the provider planned something that interests each child each day? Are there activities that continue over a period of days? Are the children 4 years and older able to get what they need (games, materials, whatever) by themselves and set up their own activities?

Is there some ongoing subject of interest that everyone (except infants and toddlers, of course) can share? When a second grader explains about the dinosaurs he or she is studying, does the provider find ways for all the children to get interested in some dinosaur activity? Are trips planned to encourage the children's current interests? Does the provider read books aloud or provide materials for art activities around a current interest? Is she careful to pick up on each child's suggestions or ideas and not let a few, or one or two, do all the suggesting?

Does the provider listen carefully to the children's conversation for clues to what might be a good activity for their interests of the moment? Does she plan to take advantage of current events such as a fair, a parade, a show at a museum or library, or a special program on television? Does she plan other activities that are related to current events so that she makes the most of the children's attention? Do her plans also reflect the time of year, the seasons and holidays, such as walks in the woods (or botanical gardens) to collect leaves in the fall, trips to look in store windows before Christmas, trips to the zoo or a farm to see the baby animals in the spring? Does she discuss with the children the major news events in our country, in her city, in the world?

Are the activities she plans interesting to the children and do they make good use of local resources?
☐ yes ☐ needs some attention

3. Time Are the days planned so that everyone knows the routine (when lunch is, or naps, baths, snacks, and clean-up)? Is there enough time to do what is needed each day without feeling rushed and bothered? Do the children's needs fit comfortably into the schedule? Are they able to finish their activities, or at least the part they want to finish in the time allowed? Do the older children have time to get some exercise as well as do some of their homework? Are the younger children's activities planned so that the provider is free to spend some time with the older children when they are free?

Are rest times balanced with very active times? Are the children relaxed enough indoors so that the provider knows they are getting enough exercise? Are mealtimes comfortable and easy, with time for lots of talk about what everyone's interests are? Are clean-up times accepted as part of the day's work? Are nap and rest times part of the routine so that everyone gets ready as much by himself or herself as age and practice allow? Does the provider arrange extra time when a particular activity, project, or trip is planned so that the usual routine gets adjusted to a special need? Does she schedule a quiet time at the end of the day so that everyone has time to get his or her things together and then sit quietly with the provider before going home, either to hear a story, to talk about the day, or to plan for the next? Docs she then have time for a few quiet words with each parent as he or she arrives in both the morning and evening?

Does her day allow her to spend some time with each child alone, giving the child the opportunity to talk over what is going on in his or her life, and giving the provider the opportunity to notice carefully how the child is doing, what progress is being made, and what needs attention?

Is the day planned so that everyone has time to do what needs to be done with ease and satisfaction?
  ☐ yes   ☐ needs some attention

Business

Once every quarter (3 months) the provider needs to go over her books to see how the business is doing. It is easy to do this quarterly because she probably has payments (for example, estimated tax) that demand her attention every 3 months. When she is taking care of these she can look over her books and check on the business.

She should look at her expenses first. Does her income cover all of her business-related expenses? How much is left over? Is she making at least a minimum wage as a professional child care person?

If she is, what are some of the expenses she can plan for in the future? (fence the yard, buy a larger refrigerator or dishwasher, trade in her car for a station wagon?) How soon can she realistically plan these and how much can she take on each month as added expenses?

If she is not making a minimum wage, what can she do to increase her income?

Looking over the expenses, do they appear to be constant over time? Are there big differences from month to month? What accounts for the differences? If there are repairs on equipment or appliances does the provider need to replace any of these? Are her major expenses planned for?

Should she give some thought to where she might cut expenses? Is she shopping where she gets the best value for her money? Is she taking advantage of sales and specials? Is she using neighborhood resources as much as possible? Does she know the local storekeepers and do they know her? Has she explained to them what her work is and asked for their contributions when they have samples or specials, large cartons, packaging materials, wood scraps, or day old bread? Has she already taken advantage of the fact that most people respond to children and to the person who cares for them by offering to help in some way?

Is the business doing well enough for the provider to plan for the future and make some money now?
☐ yes   ☐ needs some attention

The Children

The next and the most important check she needs to make every 3 months is the progress each child is making. If she has been making notes in her daily book, now is the time to look them over, to summarize them, and to think about a program for each child. The following guide will help her to look carefully at the development of each child in her family day care home, beginning with the toddlers. For infants, she should refer to the chapters on infants and on language in order to make sure that they are developing well in every way. After she has completed these quarterly reviews on each child, she should make an appointment to share them with the parents. The following checklist is a useful format with which to plan a meeting with the parents to talk about the child's progress, special abilities, special needs, and plans for the future. The parents will be reassured to know that the provider plans in a professional way and has goals for the children. They will be encouraged and more apt to cooperate with her if she feels the child needs some attention or consultation, and they will respect and appreciate her care and concern.

1. Feelings of Self-worth Does the child show pride and pleasure in himself or herself as well as in what he or she can do? Is the child pleased with a job well done or something made even before the provider shows her approval? Can the child do an activity with concentration and without frequent reassurance? Is the child's confidence such that he or she can try something new without too much fear or hesitation? Does the child feel secure enough not to need attention or special consideration constantly? Does the child feel free to express fears, unhappiness, and anger, as well as happiness and contentment? Can the child ask for help when needed, as well as sometimes try new things alone?

Does the child show confidence and pleasure in himself or herself?
☐ yes   ☐ needs some attention

2. Social Skills Does the child know how to ask for help? Can he or she take turns most of the time? If the child does not want to share, can he or she persuade others to wait? Will the child say what he or she wants, rather than grab or hit another child? Does the child have enough self-control to abide by the rule *We do not hurt others*?

Do other children play with and include the child in their games? Can the child join in an activity with other children and with the provider and be welcome even if the child is really too young to help or play? Can the child accept instruction or assistance from the provider as well as from the other children?

Does the child have friends among the children in the day care family or at school? Does the child show sympathy and understanding, and when it is appropriate, anger and disappointment? Can the child accept and talk with adults and children he or she does not know?

Does the child have good social skills for his or her age?
☐ yes   ☐ needs some attention

3. Discovery Skills Is the child interested in the world around him or her—the things, the people, how they work, what they do? Does the child show interest in new and unknown things? When the provider calls attention to something, does the child respond with interest? Is the child interested in how things work and why they happen? Does the child watch with interest what goes on at home and outside? Does the child suggest ideas and ways to try to find out how things work, or why they do the things they do?

Is the child interested in discovering more and more about things and people?
☐ yes   ☐ needs some attention

4. Awareness of What Goes On in the Immediate Environment Does the child notice what happens around him or her? When the daily routine is changed slightly, does the child pick up on it? Does the child notice something new—a bowl of flowers on the table or a new color tablecloth or paper napkin?

Does the child notice the results of his or her actions? Does he or she then adjust for these results (the block that makes the tower fall? the ice cube that makes the water spill out of the glass? the sleeve that is inside out)?

Does the child notice other people's feelings and moods? Is he or she alert to other children's interests and activities?

Is the child attentive to people and things in the immediate environment?
   ☐ yes   ☐ needs some attention

5. Interest in Events Large and Small   Is the child interested in the day-to-day events that happen—the delivery of mail or of oil, the neighbor's new kittens or fence, the arrival of someone's grandmother for a visit, the planning of a birthday celebration? Does the child ask questions, make comments, and listen to discussion of these events with interest?

Does the school-age child show interest in the world outside, in the names of other children's teachers, in their class projects as well as his or her own, in the sports teams at school and nationally, in major events such as an election, the invasion of some country in the world, the launching of a space satellite? Is he or she eager to hear more and talk about such events?

Is the child aware of and interested in events in the world?
   ☐ yes   ☐ needs some attention

6. Problem Solving Skills   Does the child try to figure things out or how things work by himself or herself? Does the child take things apart and try to put them together again? Does the child use things in ways that are different from what they are meant for? Does the child find something to replace what ever is broken or lost or used up? When something does not work out the way it was supposed to, does the child have another idea or suggestion? Does the child show interest in how things work, in the home and out?

Is the child able to figure out ways to solve problems?
   ☐ yes   ☐ needs some attention

7. Creativity and Imagination   Does the child enjoy creative activities (painting, drawing, story telling, acting out stories, making up dances, songs)? Can the child express his or her own ideas, rather than copy those of other children? Does the child prefer creating an original drawing or painting to copying someone else's? Does the child engage in imaginative play, pretending to be someone in a story or a character in a movie or on television? Does the child use dolls and toys to create scenes? Does the child enjoy inventing stories or games to play with the other children? Can the child join in a pretend game that an adult starts or that other children are playing?

Does the child enjoy creative and imaginative play?
   ☐ yes   ☐ needs some attention

A Summing Up   285

8. Flexibility Does the child try other ways of doing what he or she wants if the first fails? Does the child accept changes in the routine if the reason is explained? When asked how else something might be done, does the child offer suggestions? When asked why someone did something, can the child offer ideas? Can the child suggest more than one possible result of an action or an event? When an adult offers another way of doing something, can the child accept it? Does the child offer other ideas if the first effort fails or the plans have to be changed?

Does the child show flexibility in play, at home, and in school?
☐ yes ☐ needs some attention

9. School Readiness All of the above skills are part of school readiness. Others are listed in Chapter 13 on getting ready for school. These can be used to evaluate the readiness of children who are 4 and 5 years old. The provider is probably already aware of the strengths and weaknesses of those children who are beginning school or are in second and third grade. By the time children are 9 or 10 years old, their academic abilities are obvious to the provider, to the parents, and to their teachers, so that together they are able to cooperate in making plans to support each child's achievement and progress.

Is the child able to do the schoolwork that is expected?
☐ yes ☐ needs some attention

10. Self-care and Safety Toddlers begin to show interest in doing things for themselves, such as brushing their teeth, washing their hands, and using the toilet. They also begin to learn about safety—not touching things that are hot or that will tip over and stopping at corners. As children grow older their sense of safety and of taking care of themselves grows, and they know not to climb too high in a tree or not to stand close to the train track. Part of children's growing sense of self-care comes from having been well cared for, another part comes from having talked about safety, of how accidents happen, and how to prevent them.

Does the child care for himself or herself as well as can be expected for the age? Does the child know the safety rules appropriate for that age? Does the child brush teeth, wash hands and face, and use a napkin or a tissue without having to be told? Is the child able to dress himself or herself as well as other children the same age? Does the child take pride in himself or herself and enjoy being complimented on having a clean face, brushed hair, and bright smile? Is the child able to say "no" to other children who suggest a dangerous activity?

Does the child have the self-care and safety skills expected of the age?
☐ yes ☐ needs some attention

11. Discipline and Self-control Chapter 15 describes the development of self-control. Accepting rules and learning self-control begins in toddlerhood and continues throughout life. What is expected of young children is different from that of the middle years of childhood and different from that of adolescents. Does the child have the consideration of others that is expected at his or her age? Can the child use enough control not to hurt others when angry or disappointed?

Does the child have the self-control expected of the age and can he or she accept reasonable rules?
☐ yes   ☐ needs some attention

12. Language Skills Chapter 11 describes the development of language. In a group of children it is sometimes necessary to observe each child's language ability closely because frequently one or two children speak for the others. When an adult asks what the children would like for snack next week, or if the children would like to stay outside a little longer, or who brought the apples, one or two children may answer for the group. Unless the adult asks the particular response of the quieter children she may not know how well they can or cannot express themselves. Checking out each child's language skills allows the adult to notice which child needs more encouragement to speak out.

Does the child have the language skills expected for that age?
☐ yes   ☐ needs some attention

13. General Physical Health Every 3 months it is a good idea to look at each child's general physical condition. How many days has that child been sick? What is the child's status on immunizations? What is the child's energy level, appetite, and alertness? Does the child awake from naps refreshed and full of energy? Is the child's skin and hair healthy? Are the dental check-ups good? Is the child as strong and as coordinated as others the same age?

Is the child in good physical condition?
☐ yes   ☐ needs some attention

The Provider

Having been reassured about the children's development, the provider needs to look at her own growth and satisfaction. This includes her feelings about the job of family day care and herself as a provider. To be satisfied with the job, she needs to feel first of all that she is doing a good job according to her own standards, according to the parents' satisfaction, and according to the children's contentment and progress. Second, she needs to feel that she is being properly rewarded for her work, both in the appreciation of those she renders service to and in the money she is making. Third, she must feel that she is growing and learning, that each day she understands more and more about children's development, behaviors, needs, and abilities. She must be able to take the time to read articles about child care, education, child psychology, special needs of special children, dealing with other adults, or whatever interests her most. She must be able to see her own growth in terms of her ability to cope with crises, to spend long and active days with children without being completely exhausted, and to feel at the end of the day that it was a good day for everyone. She must feel increasing confidence in her ability to deal with the parents, and secure in their trust and cooperation. She must feel, finally, that family day care is a challenging and worthwhile occupation, one that she is proud to perform.

As the provider evaluates the children in her care, she is also evaluating herself. As she finds the areas of strength and weakness in the children, she is finding out what she does easily and well and what she needs to work on. Evaluating the children not only tells the provider what *their* needs are, it also gives her a chance to examine her own performance and decide what she should spend some time on, pay some attention to, give some extra help with. It helps her to evaluate her own development.

MORE FREQUENT REVIEWS: EVERY MONTH, EVERY WEEK, AND EVERY DAY

Every month as the provider pays her bills and looks at her income and expenses, she is evaluating her business. At this time, she can think about where she might spend less money and where she might want to spend more. If she is saving for a special purchase, she can check on her progress.

She can also look over her inventory and decide what she needs to stock up on and what she may have overstocked. As the children grow, their activities change and the materials required for these activities change. When a new infant comes into the family day care home, the materials needed change again. As the interests of her children change from month to month and season to season, the provider should look over the supplies she has on hand and decide what she wants to get.

Every week as the provider sits down with her children to plan the next week's menus she asks about any special school activities or projects the children are working on. She also asks for suggestions of things the children might want to do during the coming week. She then makes notes about the plans for the week to come as she writes out her menus and shopping list. She takes this opportunity to review the week past and ask for the children's comments on what happened, what they did, what they especially enjoyed or what was disappointing. Asking for suggestions about how to do things differently next time allows the children to take on some responsibility for planning and organizing. When children participate in planning activities they are apt to participate in the activity with more enthusiasm and they learn more from the experience. When it is *their* activity they are more cooperative, more responsible, and more involved. They can look back at the activity later and say how they might do it differently next time. They are learning how to make good judgments.

Every day the provider evaluates her work as she thinks about the day just ended. As she sits and rests she thinks about how the day went, whether it was easy or tiring, busy or boring, fun or irritating. She thinks about each child's day, how many smiles, laughs, and tears. She remembers the arrival of the parents at the end of the day, what she was able to tell each about his or her child's day, the achievements she was able to report, and the amusing and touching moments she could describe. She also considers the concerns she has about each child and reviews in her mind what she has done about them and what she may need to do next. She thinks about which concerns she may need to share with the parents in the near future and how she will go about it. She may make a note about something she wants to remember to do or find out about the next day.

Priorities

The purpose of this kind of examination is to look at the work in progress. It has already been said that the work the family day care provider does includes many different jobs, all of which involve human beings who are constantly changing. The goals of the job change as the children change. Furthermore, because there are many people involved, there are many different goals. The provider has goals for the children, for their parents, and for herself. The parents have their own goals for their children and for themselves, and even the children want certain things for themselves. The provider considers all of these and determines which ones need attention and which will come in good time. She thinks about these goals in terms of her checklist on each child and considers the progress she and they are making. As she shares her review of each child's progress with that child's parents, she shares her goals for the child and she learns more about how close her goals are to those of the child's parents.

Perhaps the most useful result of this periodic review is that it forces the provider to look at children as changing beings. It makes her think about how they were only a few months ago, how much they have learned, grown, and changed, and how much they will learn and change in the next few months. It makes her realize that child care is not working with something that *is*, but with something that is *becoming*, that is changing before her very eyes. More than that, she realizes that what she does has an effect on that change. Although it is never possible to know exactly *what* effect or how *much* (because child development is such an inexact science), she knows that everything she does for the children is in some way absorbed and becomes a part of what they are and will be. It makes the little things she does each day important. It makes the work of child care both serious and significant.

As the family day care provider watches the children in her care grow and develop into independent, competent people, she thinks about all of the changes she has watched them go through, and she wonders about the little ones and how they, too, will grow and change over time.

More than that, she knows that it is not only the children who will change, but the world as well in ways we never expected. We cannot predict what the world will be like when the children of today are grown any more than we can predict what the children will be like.

Whatever the world is like when they are grown, however, one thing is sure: the children of today will have to be strong, confident, and thoughtful people to meet the demands of tomorrow. The family day care provider who is caring for children today can help them become the kind of people who will do more than meet the demands of tomorrow. She can help them become people who will demand that tomorrow's world be a better place for themselves and for others. She can even give them the strength to help make that happen.

Index

Accident records, 18
Accidents, *see* Emergency care
Accountant, provider as, 4
   see *also* Business, of family day care
Active play, 63
Activities, 62–64
   active, 63
   art, 66–67
   attention learned through, 185
   child's needs influencing, 63–64
   evaluation of, 74, 75, 281–282
   indoor, 62, 70–74
   learning about the community, 65–66
   library visits, 66
   literature, 70–71
   music, 67–68
   outdoor, 62–70
   physical exercise, 64–65
   quiet, 62–63
   records of, 21–22
   self-care skills, 73–74
   social skills, 72–73
   trips, 68–70
   see *also* Games; Planning
Advertising, getting clients by, 16, 17
Agencies
   child abuse and, 79
   emergency procedures indicated by, 237
   recruiting children through, 16
Agencies, provisions offered by, 12–14
   equipment and supplies, 12–13, 15
   fees paid of children referred, 13
   food allowances, 13
   insurance, 12
   lending library of toys and books, 13
   medical and dental benefits for the provider, 13
   referral, 13
   training and educational programs for the provider, 14
Aggression, 91
Alcohol abuse of parents, 79, 80, 109
Allergies
   to fabrics, 230, 232
   to food, 230, 269, 275–276
   treating child with, 230–232
Answering back, 90–91, 162–163
Appendicitis, 224
Architect, provider as, 4
   see *also* Home of provider
Art
   activities relating to, 66–67
   agency supplying materials for, 12
   kitchen as place for activities relating to, 49, 51
   for school-aged children, 203–204
Artificial respiration
   for cessation of breathing, 241–242
   for lack of pulse, 240–241
Asthma, 262
Attendance records, 18, 21
Attention, school readiness indicated by, 185–186

Babbling, 119, 125, 154
   problems with, 257
Babies, preschoolers questioning where they come from, 176–177
   see *also* Infants
Baby Book, 112
   feeding records in, 114
   for middle infancy, 123, 124, 127, 128, 129
Bath
   in early infancy, 115
   in middle infancy, 124, 128
   toddler's fear of, 145–146
Bathroom
   burns prevented in, 47
   cuts prevented in, 46
   efficient arrangement for infants and toddlers, 49, 50–51
   equipment needed for, 15
   independence fostered in, 50–51
   poisons in, removed from children's reach, 46

Battered women, provider's role
  concerning, 80
Bedroom
  equipment needed for, 15
  independence fostered by routines in, 50
  as quiet area, 49, 50
  see also Naps; Sleep
Beds, 15, 48
  see also Cribs; Sleep
Beginnings in family day care
  infants, 38
  parents remaining with child in, 37, 39
  preschoolers, 41
  second visit, 37
  toddlers, 38–41
  tour of home of provider, 37
  see also First interview
Behavior problems
  in school, 98
  spoiled behavior, 132–133
  working out with parent, 83, 84
  see also Discipline
Birth, preschoolers' questions about,
  176–177
Birthdays of children, planning for, 60
Biting people, by toddlers, 212–213
Bleeding, checking for in an emergency,
  239, 242–245
Block area, of living room, 52
Board games, for school-aged children,
  202–203
Bodies, preschoolers' interest in their,
  175–176
Books, see Literature; Reading
Bottles, toddlers and, 141
  weaning from, 89, 131
Breads and cereals, 267, 268–269
  see also Food
Breakfast, 275
Breathing, checking for in an emergency,
  239, 241–242
Broken bones, emergency care for, 239, 247
Burns
  emergency care for, 239, 248
  prevented in home of provider, 46–47
Burping, in early infancy, 114
Business, family day care as a, 3–4
  advertising, 16, 17
  equipment and supplies for, 15
  evaluation of, 282–283, 288
  expenses, 21, 22, 23–27, 282–283
  food stamp program, 27
  getting clients, 16–17
  income tax, 27–29
  insurance, 15–16
  licensing, 11–12, see also Agencies
  payment, 5, 17

  planning for, 60–61
  recruiting clients, 16, 17
  registering, 11
  start-up expenses, 14–16
  welfare, 27
  see also Recordkeeping

Calendar, see Wall calendar
Calories, 266, 274
Carriages, 12, 15
Castor oil, 224
Chemical burns, emergency care for,
  248–249
Chicken pox, treating child with, 229
Child abuse, 79–80, 98
Child care tax credit, 12
Child development, 104–106
  emotional, 109–110
  importance of provider's understanding
    of, 103–104, 105–106
  intellectual, 108–109
  physical, 106–107
  problems in, see Special children
  social, 107–108
Childhood diseases
  immunization, 222
  treating, 232
Child neglect, 98
Child rearing, differences in, 91–93
  see also Problems, in family day care
Children
  accepted into family day care, 33
  daily notes on, 18
  maximum number allowed, 14
  permanent records on, 20–21
  reviewing progress of, 283–286
Cigarettes, as source of burns, 47
Classical music, activities relating to, 67–68
Cleanliness, parental attitudes toward,
  91–92
Climbing stairs, toddlers and, 148–149
Clubs, for school-aged children, 202
Clumsiness, of toddlers, 259
Coatings, for food, 273–274
Cold exposure, emergency care for, 239,
  249–250
Colds
  caring for children with, 221, 227
  in infants, 225–226
Colic, in early infancy, 113–114, 224–225
Collections
  for school-aged children, 202
  as science activity, 192
Comfort, of home of provider, 53–55
Community, children's familiarity with,
  65–66, 168

Competency, physical development
　fostering, 107
Conference with children, to evaluate
　plans, 75
　see also Parent conferences
Contract, for family day care, 33, 34
Convulsions, treating child with, 227–228,
　251
Counting skills, 191
Crafts, see Art
Crawling, in late infancy, 131, 132
Creativity, evaluation of in children, 285
Crib rocking, in infancy, 258
Cribs, 12, 15
　for naps, 48–49, 123
Crisis planning, 58
Crying in infancy, 257–258
　colic and, 113–114, 224–225
　in early infancy, 121
Curse words, 90, 165
Cuts, prevented in home of provider, 46

Daily records, 18
Daily routines, 61–63
Dancing, music introduced through, 68
Danger, differences in attitudes about, 92
Deaf children
　babbling by, 154
　sign language used by, 152
Death, preschoolers' questions about, 177
Dental health of provider
　agency providing benefits for, 13
　dental appointments, 60
Depreciation, on equipment, 28
Development, see Child development;
　Human development
Diaper rash, 226–227
Diarrhea
　caring for children with, 221, 228–229
　in infants, 226
Differences, in mathematics, 191
Digestive upsets, treating child with,
　228–229
Dirty words, 165
Discipline, 209, 214
　control achieved through, 219–220
　evaluation of in children, 287
　fairness and, 220
　first interview discussing, 214–215
　for grabbing, 217–218
　group learning fostering, 217
　for hitting, 217–218
　for infants, 209–210
　late infancy and, 132, 133
　for lying, 218
　planning making unnecessary, 217

　for preschoolers, 213–214
　for pushing, 217–218
　rules of taught to children, 215–216, 220
　for stealing, 219
　for toddlers, 210–213
　see also Behavior problems; Rules
Discovery skills, evaluation of in children,
　284
Dressing
　middle infancy and, 124, 128
　toddlers and, 140–141
Dress-up game, for toddler in beginning of
　family day care, 41
Drug abuse in parents, 79, 80, 109

Early infancy
　babbling in, 119, 154, 257
　Baby Book maintained for, 114
　bathing, 115
　burping, 114
　closeness need of, 112–113, 115, 116, 117
　colic in, 113–114, 224–225
　crying in, 121
　exercise in, 115, 117, 118
　feeding, 88–89, 113–114, 118, 269
　intellectual development in, 119–120
　movement need of, 113, 114
　overstimulation and, 121
　personality development in, 120–121
　sleeping in, 114–115
　social development in, 118–119
　wrapping, 112–113, 115, 116, 117
Eating, see Food; Mealtimes; Menus
Efficiency, of home of provider, 48–50
Electrical wiring, as source of burns, 47
Emergency care
　for accidental poisonings, 238
　agency indicating, 237
　artificial respiration for, 240
　for bleeding, 239, 242–245
　breathing checked for in, 239, 241–242
　for broken bones, 239, 247
　for burns, 239, 248, 249
　for chemical burns, 248–249
　for convulsions, 251
　for fever, 251
　first aid supplies for, 237–238
　form for, 22
　for frostbite and cold exposure, 239,
　　249–250
　for heat exhaustion and sunstroke, 239,
　　251
　planning for, 58
　for poisoning, 239, 245–246
　preparation for, 236–237
　prevention, 233–236

Emergency care—*Continued*
  pulse examined in, 239–241
  records on, 18
  for shock, 239, 242, 246
  for snake bite, 238
  substitute for provider giving, 237
  for sunstroke, 239
  telephone numbers for, 238–239
  tourniquet for, 242–245
  on trip, 237
  see also Safety; Sick child
Emergency medical care forms, 22, 222
Emotional development, 109–110
  in early infancy, 120–121
  evaluation of, 283–284
  in infancy, 258
  in late infancy, 134–135
  in middle infancy, 124–125, 129–130
  problems in, 259–262
Emotional problems
  of school-aged children, 262
  of toddlers, 259
Ending family day care
  child's maladjustment causing, 42–44
  each day, 44
  provider's role in, 42
  reasons for, 42–44
Equipment
  depreciation on, 28
  as expense, 23, 25, 26
Errands, planning for, 60–61
Escalona, Sibylle, 54
Exercise, 64–65
  in late infancy, 131
  in middle infancy, 124, 127–128
  preschoolers and, 174
  see also Physical activity; Physical development
Expenses
  ledger for records of, 21, 22, 23–27
  review of, 282–283
Eyesight, *see* Vision problems

Fabric allergies, treating child with, 230, 232
Falls, prevented in home of provider, 47–48
Family day care, preference for, 2–3
  contract for, 33, 34
  preference for, 2–3
Fears
  in school-aged children, 262–263
  in toddlers, 145–146
Feelings, coping with, 87–88
  see also Emotional development; Problems, in family day care
Fever, treating child with, 227, 251

Field trip, forms for, 21, 22
Fillers, for food, 273–274
Fire department, visits to, 65–66
First aid, *see* Emergency care
First aid supplies, for emergencies, 237–238
First interview
  accepting child in, 33
  discipline discussed in, 214–215
  family day care contract presented in, 33, 34
  family day care explained in, 33–34
  getting to know the parent in, 77–78
  goals of, 31–32
  history of child reviewed in, 33–34, 36
  in home of provider, 32
  initial questions in, 32
  problem prevention through, 93–94
  provider and child making friends in, 34, 36
  responsibilities of parent and provider explained in, 33, 35, 84–85, 93–94
Flexibility, evaluation of in children, 286
Flu, treating child with, 229
Food, 265–266
  agency applying allowance toward, 13
  allergies to, 230, 269, 275–276
  breads and cereals, 267, 268–269
  breakfasts, 275
  calories in, 266, 274
  children participating in preparation of, 51, 270–271, 274
  as expense, 23, 24
  fillers, mixes and coatings for, 273–274
  groups, 267–269
  importance of nutritious, 265–266
  for infants, 88–89, 113–114, 118, 123, 126–127, 131, 269–270
  learning from activities with, 271–272
  lunches, 267–268
  meat, fish, poultry, eggs, dried beans and peas, nuts and seeds, 267, 268, 269
  milk, cheese, and other dairy products, 267, 269
  overweight, 266
  preparation of nutritious, 274–275
  for provider's own family, 276
  sample meal plan, 267–268
  for school-aged children, 196–197, 275
  shopping economically for, 272–274
  shopping lists for, 19, 61, 272
  as socializing experience, 276–277
  store brands for, 272–273
  sufficient supply of, 61
  for toddlers, 139, 269–270
  unit pricing, 273
  vegetables and fruits, 267, 268, 269
  see also Mealtimes; Menus; Snacks

Food stamp program, 27
Fraiberg, Selma, 145
Friends
  leisure time spent with, 196
  school readiness indicated by child playing with, 184
  see also Play
Frostbite, emergency care for, 239, 249–250
Fruits and vegetables, 267, 268, 269
  see also Food

Games
  attention learned through, 185
  in living room, 52–53
  memory encouraged by, 188–189
  middle infancy and, 125, 128, 155–156, 157
  preschoolers and, 162, 168–169, 170–171
  school-aged children and, 187, 188, 201–204
  toddlers and, 159–160, 161, 188
  see also Pretend games; Toys
Gelatin, dessert from, 275
"Goes With" game, for preschoolers, 174
Grabbing, discipline for, 217–218
Group day care, 2–3
Group learning, discipline fostered by, 217

Handicapped, see Special children
Hang up areas, in home of provider, 53
Hay fever, in school-aged children, 262
Head banging, in infancy, 258
Head Start, 183
Health
  discussions about with provider, 97
  evaluation of in children, 287
  of infants and toddlers, 112
  of provider, 8
  see also Emergency care; Sick child
Hearing loss
  in infancy, 255–256
  school readiness and, 182
Heaters, as source of burns, 47
Heat exhaustion, emergency care for, 239, 250
Heat rash, in infants, 226
Help, child's request for
  in late infancy, 132, 133
  by preschoolers, 169
  school readiness indicated by, 183–184
  by toddlers, 142
Hide and seek, for toddlers in beginning of family day care, 41
High chairs, 12, 15
History of the child, 33–34, 36

Hitting, discipline for, 217–218
Holidays, planning for, 60
Home of child, provider visiting, 85
Home problems
  child abuse, 79–80, 98
  child neglect, 98
  drug and alcohol abuse, 79–80, 98
  wife beating, 80, 98
Home of provider, 4, 8–9
  burns prevented in, 46–47
  comfort of, 53–55
  cuts prevented in, 46
  efficiency of, 48–50
  evaluation of space provided in, 281
  expenses for, 25, 26
  falls prevented in, 47–48
  first interview in, 32
  independence provided by, 50–53
  lead-free paint in, 46
  as learning place, 54–55
  poisoning prevented in, 46
  safety of, 14–15, 46–48, 234–235
  sleep space in, 48–49
  storage and hang up areas in, 53
  tour of in beginning of family day care, 37
  see also Bathroom; Bedroom; Kitchen; Living room
Homework, 198, 207
Housekeeping supplies, 19, 20
Human development, 102–103
  provider as student of, 4
  see also Child development
Hurtful language, 165
Hyperactivity, 260
  sensitivity and, 261

Identity, preschoolers and, 178
Illness, see Health; Sick child
Imagination, evaluation of in children, 285
Immunization
  schedule of, 222
  school readiness and, 182
Income, ledger for records of, 22–23, 26–27
Income tax, 27–29
  child care tax credit, 12
  forms for, 22
Independence
  in home of provider, 50–53
  for school readiness, 187
  self-care skills fostering, 73–74, 286
  toddlers and, 90, 139, 141–142
  toilet training and, 146
  wall calendar fostering, 74
Indoor activities, 62, 70–74

Index 295

Infants
  babbling, 257
  bathroom arranged for, 49
  care of during trips, 69
  choking in, 242
  colic, 113–114, 224–225
  crying, 121, 257–258
  daily notes on, 18
  discipline for, 209–210
  effect of early care on, 111–112
  equipment needed for, 15, 16
  food for, 88–89, 113–114, 118, 126–127, 131, 269–270
  friendliness toward provider, 34
  head banging and crib rocking, 258
  illness prevention in, 112
  independence encouraged in, 50
  language development, 153–160
  music introduced to, 68
  physical development of, 107
  positioning in playroom, 49–50
  reading activities with, 71
  safety precautions with, 234
  separation from parent, 38
  sleep space for, 48–49
  social development problems, 257–258
  special problems of, 254–258
  stages of, 111
  teething, 225
  weaning, 89
  see also Baby Book; Early infancy; Late infancy; Middle infancy
Influenza, treating child with, 229
Insects, collecting as scientific activity, 192
Insurance, for provider, 15–16
Intellectual development
  in early infancy, 119–120
  evaluation of, 284–285
  language and, 153
  in late infancy, 133–134
  in middle infancy, 125, 129
  in preschoolers, 172–174
  in toddlers, 142–143
Interior decorator, provider as, 4, 8–9
Inventory, of the supplies on hand, 19–20

Jealousy, of older children toward infants, 122–123

Kitchen
  burns prevented in, 46–47
  cuts prevented in, 46
  equipment needed for, 15
  independence learned in, 51–52
  messy activities done in, 49, 51
  poisons removed from children's reach in, 46
  socializing in, 52
  see also Food

Language, 90–91
  bad uses of, 165–166
  curse words, 90, 165
  dirty words, 165
  good uses of, 166
  hurting people through, 165
  "no" in toddlers, 143–144, 211
  talking back, 90–91
  tattletaling, 165–166
Language development, 151–152
  autism, 152
  babbling and, 119, 125, 154, 257
  deaf people, 152
  evaluation of in children, 287
  infancy and, 153–160
  intellectual development and, 153
  learning, 152–153
  in middle infancy, 125, 155–156
  preschoolers and, 161–162
  problems with, 152, 257, 259, 261
  school-aged children and, 163–164
  toddlers and, 143–145, 158–161
Late infancy, 130–131
  discipline in, 132, 133
  emotional development in, 134–135
  exercise in, 131–132
  food for, 131, 269–270
  help asked for in, 132, 133
  intellectual development in, 133–134
  language development in, 130
  overeating in, 131
  relationship with older children, 134
  social development in, 132–133
  spoiled behavior in, 132–133
  strangers and, 132, 133
  toys and, 133–134
  walking and crawling in, 130, 131
  weaning in, 89, 131
  see also Toddlers
Lead-free paint, in home of provider, 46
Learning disabilities, school-aged children and, 262
Ledger, for income and expenses, 22–27
Leisure time, adult and, 196–197
Library
  art information in, 67
  learning about community in, 65
  music in, 67, 68
  records in, 68
  visits to, 66
Licensing, 11–12

requirements for, 14
   see also Agencies; Business, family day care as a
Life-styles and values
   appreciating different, 85–86
   late infancy influencing, 131
   see also Problems, in family day care
Literature
   activities with, 70–71
   plays, 71, 200–201
   see also Reading
Living room/playroom, 49–50
   block area, 52
   games and projects area, 53
   pretend area, 52–53
   storage area for toys, 52
Lorenz, Konrad, 118
Lunches, 267–268
   see also Food
Lying, discipline for, 218

Make-believe games, see Pretend games
Masturbation, 262
Matches, as source of burns, 47
Matching, preschoolers' ideas on, 174
Mathematics, school readiness helped with, 190–191
Mealtimes
   middle infancy and, 123
   parent/provider conflict over, 81–82
   as social experience, 276–277
   toddler and, 139
   see also Food
Meat, fish, poultry, eggs, dried beans and peas, nuts and seeds, 267, 268, 269
   see also Food
Medical benefits of provider, agency providing, 13
Medical checkups, of provider, 60
Memory, school readiness helped with good, 188–189
Menus, 19, 267–268, 276
   records of, 19, 21
   shopping lists for, 19, 61, 272
   see also Food; Mealtimes
Middle infancy, 122–130
   babbling, 125
   Baby Book for, 123, 124, 127, 128, 129
   baths in, 124, 128
   dressing, 124, 128
   emotional development, 124–125, 129–130
   exercise in, 124, 127–128
   food for, 123, 126–127, 269
   games in, 125, 128–129, 155–156, 157
   intellectual development, 125, 129

   jealousy of other children and, 122–123
   language development in, 125, 155–156
   movement and, 123
   naps in, 123, 124, 127
   rolling over, 124
   sleeping, 123–124
   social development in, 124–125, 128–129
   strangers and, 128, 129
Milk, cheese, and other dairy products, 267, 269
Mixes, for food, 273–274
More and less, in mathematics, 191
Mother Goose rhymes
   for preschoolers, 162
   for very young children, 70
Multigeneration family, family day care in, 8
Museum, trips to, 66–67
Music
   activities relating to, 67–68
   records, 12, 68

Naps
   middle infancy and, 123, 124, 127
   routine for, 50
   space in home of provider for, 48–49
   toddlers and, 141, 159
Neatness, parental attitudes toward, 91–92
Neighborhood, see Community
Newborns, see Early infancy
Nightmares
   school-aged children and, 263
   toddlers and, 145
"No", toddlers' use of, 143–144, 211
Noise, sleeping in early infancy and, 115
Number of children, maximum number allowed, 14
Number skills, school readiness helped with, 190–191
Nurse, family day care provider as, 3, 221
   see also Health; Sick child
Nutrition, see Food
Nutritionist, provider as, 4
   see also Food; Menus

Organization, parental attitudes toward, 91–92
Outdoor activities, 62–70
   toddlers and, 147, 148
Overeating, in late infancy, 131
   see also Food
Overweight, 266
   see also Food

Paramedic, provider as, 4
  see also Emergency care; Sick child
Parent conferences
  planning for, 60
  about problems raised by parents, 94–96
  about problems raised by provider, 96–99
  about problems of school-aged children, 205
  about school problems, 97–98
  about school readiness, 181–182
Parents
  children's reactions to separation from, 38–41
  equipment provided by, 16
  problems with family day care from, 94–96
  provider's role with, 4
  remaining with child in beginning, 37, 39
  responsibilities of, 33, 35, 84–85, 93–94
  special children discussed with, 254
  tour of home of provider for, 37
  see also First interview; Home problems; Provider, relationship of with parents
"Pat a Cake", middle infancy and, 155–156
Payment, for family day care, 5, 17
  agency paying, 13
Pease Porridge Hot, 159–160
"Peekaboo"
  middle infancy and, 125, 155, 156
  for toddler in beginning of family day care, 41
Permanent records, 20–22
Personality, in early infancy, 120–121
  see also Emotional development; Social development
Pets, provider allowing, 192
Physical activity
  in leisure time, 197
  of school-aged children, 198
  see also Exercise
Physical development, 106–107
  in early infancy, 115, 117–118
  exercise for, 64–65
  in late infancy, 131–132
  in middle infancy, 127–128
  preschoolers and, 176
Piaget, Jean, 142
Planning, 57–58
  for business, 60–61
  children participating in, 288–289
  crisis planning, 58
  for daily errands, 60–61
  discipline made unnecessary by, 217
  evaluation of, 74–75, 282
  on large calendar, 59, 60, 74
  in planning book, 60–64

  shopping lists, 19, 61, 272
  see also Activities
Planning book, 60–64
Plants, as scientific activity, 192
Play
  preschoolers and, 168–171
  by rules in school-aged children, 187
  see also Games
Playground, 64, 236
Playroom, see Living room/playroom
Plays, for school-aged children, 200–201
Poetry, reading activities with, 71
Poisoning
  checking for in an emergency, 239, 245–246
  first aid kit for, 238
  preventing in home of provider, 46
Poison ivy, treating child with, 232
Poison oak, treating child with, 232
Poison sumac, treating child with, 232
Potty chair, for toddlers, 50, 146
Pregnancy and birth, preschoolers' questions about, 170–177
Preschoolers, 167
  behavior with adults, 168–169
  behavior with other children, 169–171
  death explained to, 177
  discipline for, 213–214
  exercise for, 176
  games for, 162, 164, 168–169, 170–171, 174
  "Goes With" game for, 174
  help requested by, 169
  identity of, 178
  importance of own bodies to, 175–176
  intellectual development, 172–174
  language development, 161–162
  matching games for, 174
  music introduced to, 68
  neighborhood trips for, 168
  play behavior in, 169–171
  pregnancy and birth explained to, 176–177
  provider making friends with in first interview, 34
  reaction to separation from parent, 41
  reading and, 162
  real versus unreal to, 178–179
  riddles and, 162, 164
  safety precautions for, 235
  same-different understood by, 174
  sassing and answering back in, 90–91, 162–163
  school readiness in, 164
  self-care skills for, 73
  sex roles of, 178
  size understood by, 174

social development in, 167–172
space understood by, 173
special problems of, 260–262
time understood by, 173–174
trips for, 69
word games and, 164
see also School readiness
Pre-teens, self-care skills for, 73
Pretend games
equipment for, 53
living room for, 52–53
preschoolers and, 168–169
school-aged children and, 201–202
toddlers and, 41
Private provider, 11
Problems, in family day care
aggression, 91
child abuse, 79–80
cleanliness, 91–92
feelings and, 87–88
health problems, 97
independence in toddlers, 90
infant feeding, 88–89
language, 90–91
neatness, 91–92
organization, 91–92
parents' raising, 94–96
preventing, 93–94
provider raising, 96–98
school problems, 97–98
solving, 94, 98–99
special needs of children, 97
toilet training, 89–90
see also Behavior problems; Discipline; Home problems; Special children
Problem solving skills, evaluation of children, 285
Professional, provider as, 9, 103
Projects, in living room, 53
Proverbs, preschoolers and, 164
Provider
agency offering training and education programs for, 14
agency providing medical and dental benefits for the, 13
checklist for evaluating job done by, 279–290
definition, 2
family members' attitude toward, 8
insurance for, 15–16
interests of used with school-aged children, 204–206
job of, 3–5
licensed, 11–12, 14, *see also* Agencies
meals for own family, 276
own children's attitude toward, 7–8
own growth and satisfaction, 287–288
payment for, 5, 13, 17
priorities of, 289–290
private, 11
problems raised by, 96–98
as professional, 9, 103
registered, 11, 12
requirements for being, 5–7
responsibilities of, 33, 35, 93
visiting child's home, 85
see also Home of provider
Provider, relationship of with parents, 77
differing values and life-styles and, 85–86
examples used to help parents, 81–82
gaining confidence of parents, 82–83
getting to know parent, 77–78
handling problems raised by parents, 94–96
handling problems raised by provider, 96–98
helping parents through difficulty, 80–85
limits to being helpful, 84–85
listening to parents, 81
paying attention to parents, 82
sharing pleasures with parents, 83–84
showing respect for parents, 83
as social worker, 78–80
visiting child's home, 85
see also First interview; Problems, in family day care
Psychologist, provider as, 4
Public funding, agency paying the fees of children eligible for, 13
Publicity, attitude of provider toward, 7
Pulse, checking for in an emergency, 239–241
Punctuality, different attitudes about, 92
Pushing, discipline for, 217–218

Questioning, school readiness indicated by, 193
Quiet play, 62–63

Radiators, as source of burns, 47
Rashes
allergies causing, 232
in infants, 226–227
Reaching problem, in infancy, 256–257
Readiness, *see* School readiness
Reading
activities with, 70
agency lending books for, 13
attention learned through, 185
preschoolers and, 162
toddlers and, 158
see also Literature

Recordkeeping
  of accidents, 18
  of activities, 21–22
  of agency assistance, 12
  of attendance, 18, 21
  on child development, 110
  daily records, 18
  emergency medical care forms, 22
  equipment needed for, 16
  of expenses, 21, 22, 23–27
  field trip forms, 21, 22
  of income, 22–23, 24, 26–27
  income tax forms, 22
  for infants, see Baby Book
  inventory of supplies, 19–20
  ledger for income and expenses, 22–27
  menus, 19, 21
  notes on children, 18, 20–21
  of parent conferences, 96
  permanent records, 20–22
  of problems with children, 96
  shopping list, 19
  weekly records, 19–20
  see also Baby Book
Records of music, 12, 68
Referral, agencies providing service, 13
Registered provider, 11, 12
Repairs and maintenance, expenses of, 23, 25
Riddles, preschoolers and, 162, 164
Roseola, treating child with, 230
Routines, daily, 61–63
Rules
  acceptance of for school readiness, 186–187
  of discipline taught to children, 215–216
  see also Discipline
Running, toddlers and, 147

Safety, 234
  evaluation of, 286
  of home of provider, 14–15, 46–48, 234–235
  for infants, 234
  outdoors, 235
  in playground, 236
  for preschoolers, 235
  of provider's yard, 235–236
  for toddlers, 234–235, 286
  see also Emergency care
Same-different, preschoolers' ideas on, 174
Sassing and answering back, 90–91, 162–163
Scarlet fever, treating child with, 228
Scheduling, evaluation of, 282
  see also Activities; Planning

School
  parent conference regarding problems in, 97–98
  social skills and success in, 108
School-aged children, 74, 195
  arts and crafts for, 200–201, 203–204
  awareness of surroundings of, 285
  board games for, 202–203
  clubs for, 202
  collections for, 202
  conversations about life with, 204–205
  daily notes on, 18
  food for, 186–187, 275
  friends and, 184
  games for 187, 188–189, 201–204
  language development in, 163–164
  leisure time of, 196–204
  physical activity of, 198–200
  pretend games for, 201–202
  provider making friends with in first interview, 36
  provider's interests used with, 204–206
  school problems of, 97–98
  school viewed by, 196
  self-care skills for, 73
  snacktime for, 196–197
  special problems of, 262–263
  trips for, 69
  see also Homework; School readiness
School readiness, 164, 181, 188
  attention as indication of, 185–186
  behaviors indicating, 183–188
  children having feeling for, 193
  definition, 183
  evaluation of in children, 286
  friends as indication of, 184
  help request as indication of, 183–184
  independence for, 187
  individual styles and interests of children for, 186
  mathematics skills helping, 190–191
  memory helping, 188–189
  parents' role in, 181–182
  provider's role in, 181–182
  questioning indicating, 193
  rule acceptance and, 186–187
  science knowledge for, 191–192
  writing skills helping, 190
Science knowledge, school readiness helped with, 191–192
Scientific experiments, 192
Second meeting, 37
Self-care skills
  children acquiring, 73–74
  evaluation of, 286
  see also Independence
Self-confidence, of provider, 8

Self-control, see Discipline
Self-evaluation, of provider, 279–290
Self-worth, in children, 283–284
Sensitivity, excessive in child, 261
Sex roles, preschoolers and, 178
Shock, emergency care for, 238, 242, 246
Shopping for food, 272–274
  lists for, 19, 61, 272
Sick child, 221–222
  allergies, 230–232
  appendicitis, 224
  avoiding spread to other children, 223
  chicken pox, 229
  colds, 221, 225–226, 227
  colic, 113–114, 224–225
  convulsions, 227–228
  crisis planning and, 58
  diaper rash, 226–227
  diarrhea, 221, 226, 228–229
  digestive upsets, 228–229
  drug allergies, 232
  emergency medical care form and, 22, 222
  fabric allergies, 230, 232
  fever, 227
  flu, 229
  food allergies, 230, 269, 275–276
  general care for, 224
  heat rash, 226
  immunizations, 222
  infants as, 224–227
  parents' permission for provider to treat, 221
  poison ivy, 232
  poison oak, 232
  poison sumac, 232
  quiet place for, 223–224
  rashes, 226–227
  recognizing illness in, 222–223
  roseola, 230
  scarlet fever, 228
  strep throat, 228
  teething, 225
  vomiting, 226, 228–229
  see also Emergency care
Sight, see Vision problems
Signing, deaf people using, 152
"Simon Says", attention learned through, 186
Size
  games concerning, 191
  preschoolers' ideas on, 174
Sleep
  in early infancy, 114–115
  nightmares, 145, 263
  problems with, 82–83, 145, 258, 263
  space for in home of provider, 48–49
  see also Naps
Snacks, 267–268, 272, 274, 275
  as expense, 23, 24
  for school-aged children, 197–198
  see also Food
Snake bite, first aid kit for, 238
"So Big", in middle infancy, 125, 155, 156
Social development, 107–108
  in early infancy, 118–119
  evaluation of, 284
  in infancy, 257–258
  kitchen facilitating, 52
  in late infancy, 132–133
  in middle infancy, 124–125, 128–129
  of preschoolers, 167–172
  taught to children, 72–73
  of toddlers, 258
Social worker, provider as, 4, 78–80
Space, preschoolers' ideas about, 173
  see also Home of provider
Special children, 253–254, 255
  clumsiness, 259
  coping with difficulties, 254
  crying in infancy, 257–258
  emotional development problems, 258, 259, 262
  excessive sensitivity, 261
  head banging and crib rocking, 258
  hearing problems, 255–256, 261–262
  hyperactivity, 260–261
  infants as, 254–258
  language problems, 257, 259, 261
  learning disabilities, 262
  parent conference about, 254
  preschoolers as, 260–262
  reaching problems, 256–257
  school-aged children as, 262–263
  sleep problems, 82–83, 145, 258, 263
  social development problems, 257–258
  toddlers as, 258–260
  vision problems, 256, 257, 261–262
Speech problems, see Language development
Spoiled behavior, late infancy and, 132–133
Stairs, toddlers' climbing, 148–149
Start-up expenses, for business of family day care, 14–16
Stealing, discipline for, 219
Storage
  area for in home of provider, 53
  equipment for, 15
Store brands, for foods, 272–273
Storytelling game, as memory game, 189
Strangers
  late infancy and, 132
  middle infancy and, 128

Strep throat, treating child with, 228
Strollers, 12, 15
Sunstroke, emergency care for, 239, 250
Supplies
  sufficient inventory of, 19–20, 61
  for trips, 69

Talking, see Language; Language development
Tantrums, see Temper tantrums
Tattletaling, 165–166
Tax laws, licensing required by, 14
  see also Income tax
Teacher
  informed of children's interests, 186
  provider as, 4
Teething, 225
"Telephone", attention learned through, 185–186
Temper tantrums
  biting people in, 212–213
  of toddlers, 144–145, 211–213
Thinking, see Intellectual development
Tic, in toddler, 259
Time, preschoolers' ideas about, 173–174
Toddlers, 137–139
  bath fear in, 145–146
  bathroom arranged for, 49
  bottles for, 141
  choking in, 242
  climbing stairs and, 148–149
  clumsiness of, 259
  daily notes on, 18
  diapering, 140
  discipline for, 210–213
  dressing and undressing, 140–141
  emotional problems of, 259
  fears of, 145–146
  food for, 139, 269–270
  games for, 159–160, 161
  help given to, 142
  illness in, 112, 223
  independence in, 50, 90, 138–139, 141–142, 146, 286
  intellectual development, 142–143
  language development, 143–145, 158–161
  mealtimes and, 139
  music introduced to, 68
  naps, 141, 159
  nightmares of, 145
  "no" used by, 143–144, 211
  older children helping with, 148–149
  outdoor play and, 147, 148
  potty chairs for, 50, 146
  provider making friends with in first interview, 34
  reading activities with, 70, 158
  running and, 147
  safety concerns for, 234–235, 286
  self-care skills for, 73, 286
  separation from parent, 38–41
  sleep space for, 48–49
  special problems of, 258–260
  temper tantrums in, 144–145, 211–213
  toilet fear in, 145–146
  toys for, 147–148
  walking and, 147
  see also Toilet training
Toilet training, 89–90, 108, 146–147
  fear of toilet, 145–146
  potty chair for, 50, 146
Tourniquet, for emergency bleeding, 242–245
Toys
  agencies' supplying, 12, 13
  late infancy and, 133–134
  toddlers and, 147–148
  see also Games
Training, agency offering for provider, 14
Tranquilizers, emotional problems handled with, 109
Travel, expenses of provider for, 23–24
  see also Trips
Tricycles, 12
Trip boards, 70
"Trip Game", as memory game, 189
Trips
  emergency occurring during, 237
  planning for, 68–70

Undressing, toddlers and, 140–141
Unit pricing, 273
Utilities, as expenses, 25, 26

Vacations, provider planning for, 60
Values, see Life-styles and values
Vegetables and fruits, 267, 268, 269
  see also Food
Vision problems
  in infancy, 256, 257
  in preschoolers, 261–262
  school readiness and, 182
Vomiting
  in infants, 226
  treating child with, 228–229

Walking, in late infancy, 130, 131, 137
  see also Toddlers

Wall calendar
 independence and self-care in children helped with, 74
 planning with, 59, 60, 74
Water, as source of burns, 47
Weaning, in late infancy, 89, 131
Weekly records, 19–20
Welfare, family day care and, 27
Wife beating, provider's role concerning, 80, 98
Windows, guards needed on, 48, 49

Word games, preschoolers and, 164
Work
 adults' view of, 195–196
 children's view of, 196
Wrapping, in early infancy, 112–113, 115, 116, 117
Writing skills, school readiness helped with, 190

Yard of provider, safety of, 235–236

ABOUT THE AUTHOR

Frances Kemper Alston is the Director of Hofstra University's Child Care Consultants, where she consults with corporations about the child care concerns of their employees. She conducts needs assessments, plans and creates day care programs for working parents, and offers counseling, information, and referral services. She is a graduate of Columbia University and has a masters degree from the Harvard Graduate School of Education. She is most recently the author of *A Survey of Day Care Programs in Teaching Hospitals*, a national study of child care services in medical centers. She has also published articles about children in a national crisis, prenatally addicted children, and about the development of language and reading.